A Dream
Called Home

A Dream Called Home

A MEMOIR

Reyna Grande

ATRIA BOOKS

NEW YORK   LONDON   TORONTO   SYDNEY   NEW DELHI

ATRIA
BOOKS

An Imprint of Simon & Schuster, Inc.
1230 Avenue of the Americas
New York, NY 10020

First Atria Books hardcover edition October 2018

ATRIA BOOKS and colophon are trademarks of Simon & Schuster, Inc.

For information about special discounts for bulk purchases, please contact Simon & Schuster Special Sales at 1-866-506-1949 or business@simonandschuster.com.

The Simon & Schuster Speakers Bureau can bring authors to your live event. For more information, or to book an event, contact the Simon & Schuster Speakers Bureau at 1-866-248-3049 or visit our website at www.simonspeakers.com.

Interior design by Kyoko Watanabe

Manufactured in the United States of America

10 9 8 7 6 5 4 3 2 1

Library of Congress Cataloging-in-Publication Data

Names: Grande, Reyna, author.
Title: A dream called home : a memoir / Reyna Grande.
Description: First Atria Books hardcover edition. | New York : Atria Books, [2018]
Identifiers: LCCN 2017053844 (print) | LCCN 2018021445 (ebook) | ISBN 9781501171444 (eBook) | ISBN 9781501171420 (hardcover)
Subjects: LCSH: Grande, Reyna. | Mexican Americans—California—Biography. | Mexican American women authors--Biography. | University of California, Santa Cruz--Students—Biography. | Teachers—California—Los Angeles—Biography. | Iguala de la Independencia (Mexico)—Biography. | Mexican American—California--Social conditions—20th century. | University of California, Santa Cruz—Student life—20th century. | Mexico—Emigration and immigration—Social aspects. | United States—Emigration and immigration—Social aspects.
Classification: LCC E184.M5 (ebook) | LCC E184.M5 G664 2018 (print) | DDC 305.868/720794--dc23

LC record available at https://lccn.loc.gov/2017053844

ISBN 978-1-5011-7142-0
ISBN 978-1-5011-7144-4 (ebook)

Author's Note

To write *A Dream Called Home*, I relied on my memories and the memories of many of the people who appear in this book. I researched facts when I could, and many of the people I write about read, fact-checked, and approved the content. With the exception of a few events, the story is told in the order it happened. The names of some people in this book have been changed to protect their privacy. There are no composite characters or events, though for the sake of the narrative arc and character development, some people and events were omitted.

To Diana,
for being there when I needed saving.

To Cory,
for being there when I no longer needed to be saved.

All immigrants are artists because they create
a life, a future, from nothing but a dream.

—PATRICIA ENGEL

Book One

TWICE THE GIRL
I USED TO BE

1

EVERY MINUTE THAT went by, another mile separated me from my family. We drove north on I-5, and I felt divided in half, like this highway I was on—one side going north, the other going south. Half of me wanted to turn back, to stay in Los Angeles and fight for my family—my father, my mother, my sisters and brothers—stay by their side even though our relationship was in ruins. The city fell farther and farther behind me, the smog blanketing the buildings as if Los Angeles were already wrapped in the haze of memory.

The other half of me faced north with excitement, optimistic despite my fears. I was transferring to the University of California, Santa Cruz, leaving to pursue the wild dream of becoming the first in my family to earn a university degree. *The key to the American Dream will soon be mine*, I told myself. This was no small feat for a former undocumented immigrant from Mexico. I felt proud to have made it this far.

Then I remembered my father's betrayal, and my optimism disappeared. Though I left of my own accord, I suddenly felt as if I had been exiled from Los Angeles. No longer wanted or needed.

My boyfriend looked at me and said the words I was desperate to hear, "Your father is very proud of you. He told me so." I was grateful that he was doing the driving. If I had been at the wheel, I would have turned back.

Edwin had been accepted at California State University, Monterey Bay, which was about an hour south of Santa Cruz. I had met him at Pasadena City College earlier in the year, right before my father and stepmother decided to end their marriage. Throughout the past months, I had been by my father's side supporting him through the chaotic separation in any way I could. I even considered staying in L.A. to help him get his life back in order once the divorce was final.

My father, a maintenance worker with a third-grade education, spoke little English. Eleven years earlier, when I was nine years old, he had returned to Mexico to bring my older siblings and me back with him to the United States to give us a better life. My older sister, brother, and I took our father's divorce as an opportunity to show him that his sacrifice had paid off. We spoke the language of this country. We had an American education. We could handle ourselves with the police and in court. We knew how to look out for him so he wouldn't end up with nothing.

Then, my father asked my stepmother to reconsider their divorce, and she did, but with one condition—she didn't want us around. So, after months of standing by him and giving him our support, my father banned Mago, Carlos, and me from his life. I had packed up my bags and left his house, and the next day, my stepmother moved back in and gave my bedroom to her son and daughter-in-law. I went to stay with my PCC professor Diana Savas, for the second time since I had met her.

"Try to understand him," Edwin said. "He knew you were leaving at the end of the summer. He didn't want to be alone once you left."

"I could have stayed with him."

"For how long? One day you'll move out and get married. Have your own family. You wouldn't stay with him forever. He knew that. Besides, he didn't want to hold you back."

"He could have stood up for us the way we stood up for him," I said a few minutes later. "It didn't have to be a choice between his wife or his children. Why can't there be room for us in his life, too? Now he's just like my mother."

When I was seven years old, my father left my mother for my stepmother, and she was never the same. She didn't want to be a mother to us anymore. It was as if when my father divorced her, she in turn divorced her children. She left us again and again in her search for another man to love her. When my father took us to live with him, we only saw her if we made the effort to visit her where she lived with her common-law husband. It hadn't mattered to her if we weren't in her life. My departure to Santa Cruz hadn't made a bit of difference to her. "Ahí nos vemos," she had said when I called her the day before. "See you later" instead of "I love you, take care, call me if you need anything"—the words I had hoped to hear from her.

"Parents disappoint us because we set expectations they can never live up to," Edwin said. He had the uncanny ability to know what I was thinking. He squeezed my hand and added, "Reyna, some parents are incapable of love and affection. Don't you think it might be time to lower your expectations?"

I looked out the window and didn't reply. My biggest virtue and my biggest flaw was the tenacity with which I clung to my dreams, no matter how futile they might seem to others. The dream of having a true relationship with my parents was the one I had clung to the most because it was the first dream I'd had, and the farthest from my reach.

As we finally left the city behind us, my body stretched tight like a rubber band, and I felt a hot, searing pain in my heart until finally something inside me snapped. I was released from the bond to the place where I had come of age, the city that had witnessed my desolation and defeats, my joys and victories. Just like my hometown in Mexico, Los Angeles was now a part of my past.

Welcome to campus!

That day in September of 1996, we drove into the main entrance of the campus and were greeted by five words carved into a block of wood that was over twenty feet long: UNIVERSITY OF CALIFORNIA SANTA CRUZ. I jumped out of the car to walk around the entrance sign, trace the huge yellow letters with my fingers, smell the wood into which they were carved, and after each letter had imprinted itself within me, I said to myself the words that needed to be said: "I have arrived."

Higher education is the only way to succeed in this country. My father had drilled that into us the minute we had arrived in Los Angeles after our third attempt at crossing the border. He had been a tyrant about school, and had even threatened to send us back to Mexico if we didn't come home with perfect attendance and straight A's. He believed so strongly in the dream of higher education that he had been completely devastated when Mago and Carlos dropped out of college. Though I had vowed not to do the same, he no longer believed in the dream and had given up on me before I even got my chance. I was determined to prove to him that he had been wrong about me.

We drove deeper into the campus, past fields and meadows, the ocean in the distance, and when we came upon the redwoods, I said a silent thank-you to my professor Diana for insisting that I choose UCSC over UCLA, where I had also been accepted. She said that at UCLA I would be one of tens of thousands, whereas UCSC, with fewer than nine thousand students, was much smaller and better for students who were into the arts. She also believed getting out of my comfort zone would help me grow and mature.

I had never seen trees so majestic, with bark the color of cinnamon and foliage a deep, lush green. The sky wasn't the pale, washed-out blue of the L.A. sky, but the vibrant, pure blue of a Van Gogh oil painting. I poked my head out the window and took deep gulps of the fresh air that smelled of earth, trees, and ocean, and something else I couldn't name. I became light-headed from the scents, sounds, and colors of my new home.

"You made the right choice." Edwin said.

"You and Diana talked me into it," I said, remembering the long conversations with the two of them about which university I should pick. "But I guess I knew I was meant to be here." I didn't tell them that the name of the university held a special meaning for me. *Santa Cruz,* "the holy cross." My father's full name was Natalio Grande Cruz. His last name literally meant "the big cross," a heavy burden for me that at times was too much to bear.

UCSC was divided into small colleges, and since I was majoring in creative writing, I chose to live at Kresge College, where the creative writing program and the Literature Department were located. As a transfer student, I could live in the apartments at Kresge East, which were reserved for juniors, seniors, and graduate students, instead of the dorms in Kresge Proper, where the freshmen and sophomores were housed. I would be sharing a four-bedroom apartment with three other students.

After I checked in, we pulled up at the parking lot of Kresge East. As I got out of the car, I remembered sitting around the kitchen table with Carlos and Mago, listening to our father talk about the future. "Just because we are *ilegales* doesn't mean we cannot dream," he said to us. Thanks to my stepmother's help and my father's determination to legalize our status, our green cards finally arrived in the mail when I was almost fifteen. That day, he had proudly handed each of us those precious cards that, even though they had the words "RESIDENT ALIEN" imprinted on them in accusing blue letters, gave us permission to finally step out of the shadows, to grow and thrive in the light. "I've done my part. The rest is up to you," my father had said.

Here in the parking lot, in the middle of the frenzy of move-in day, at the sight of my peers who had arrived with their parents, grandparents, and siblings, I wished my father were at my side. Though in the end he had lost faith that I would get here, he had set the stage for my arrival. My peers had brought their families to celebrate the beginning of their journey as university students. I thought of the Mexican saying *Sin padre ni madre, ni perro que me ladre.* Without a father, without a mother, without a dog to bark at me.

I turned away from the families and grabbed my suitcase and backpack from the trunk. *Focus on what you're here to do.* If I did things right, I would one day break the cycle my family had been stuck in for generations—a cycle of poverty, hunger, and lack of education. This was the reason why I was here, and that was all that mattered.

Edwin helped me carry my belongings to my apartment—my clothes, some books, and my first computer, purchased on credit from Sears and still in the box.

"Are you going to be okay?" he asked as I walked him back to his car.

"Yeah," I said, doing my best to not let him see how frightened I was. Edwin was handling this new stage of his life much better than I was handling mine. He had left home after high school to join the army and had fought in the Gulf War, witnessing unimaginable horrors. As an army vet, he was independent and knew how to take care of himself. I envied him for that, and as I watched him drive away in his Oldsmobile, heading back to Monterey, I wished he would stay to protect me. Instead, I was now completely alone and about to fight my battles on my own.

I set out to explore the campus. It was late afternoon, and I didn't have much time before the sun went down. I had heard there was real darkness here, and as a city girl, the thought of the dark frightened me. But as I began to walk, I realized that the darkness was the least of my worries. What I was most afraid of was not knowing how to be a university student, that my community college education hadn't prepared me for the work ahead. I was afraid of not being able to let go of my longing for my family, afraid that the distance that separated us would damage our relationship even more than it already had. I was afraid of having come this far only to fail and have to return to Los Angeles with nothing to show for my college education—no diploma, no job, nothing but a mountain of debt and unfulfilled dreams.

I was afraid of not being able to make this new place feel like a real home, a place where I belonged.

The university was nestled in the redwoods at the foot of the Santa Cruz Mountains. I found myself immersed in a grove of the world's tallest trees. As I walked across the footbridge that connected Kresge East and Kresge Proper, high aboveground, with a ravine below me and redwood trees all around me, I let out a long, deep sigh, and the tension inside my body eased.

The wind rustled the trees and caressed my hair. A family of deer foraged for food in the ravine. I couldn't believe there were deer here. I felt as if I had entered a fairy tale. I came to a meadow by Porter College where I could see the ocean shining blue and streaked with orange as the sun set. I was nine years old when I had first seen the ocean, two months after I arrived in Los Angeles to live with my father. I had been scared to go in because I didn't know how to swim, so I had held tight to my father's hand, wanting to feel safe and protected. He had promised he wouldn't let go of me. We stood side by side in the water and, at least that day, he had kept his promise.

As I looked at the ocean in the distance, I told myself there was no need to be afraid. I had come this far, despite everything. My family fell apart when we immigrated. We sacrificed so much for a shot at the American Dream, and I would be damned if I didn't make the dream mine. A broken family was the price for me to be here. Back in Mexico the distance between my parents and me had been two thousand miles. In Santa Cruz, the distance was three hundred, but emotionally, we were light-years apart, and this time, I was the one who had migrated north in search of a better life, leaving them all behind.

Reyna at the Porter Meadow, UCSC

2

WHEN I RETURNED to my apartment to finish settling in, I found a young woman in the kitchen making herself a sandwich. She was a couple of inches taller than me, maybe five-foot-two, and wore a long-sleeved red plaid shirt and blue jeans. She had very short brown hair, and I thought of the times, back in Mexico, when my evil grandmother had cut my hair like a boy's because it was infested with lice. I knew there was no way my new roommate had little critters running around her scalp.

"Hi," she said. "I'm Carolyn."

"Reyna," I replied. I shook her hand, which was soft and warm, and small, like my sister Mago's.

"Where are you from?" she asked.

The question always confused me when asked by a white person. Because I was an immigrant, the question "Where are you from?" made me wonder if I was being asked about the place of my birth, my nationality, my cultural identity, or simply the city where I now lived. It was an innocent question, but it was a question that made me think about my foreignness, a question that made me raise my guard.

"I've come from L.A., but I'm originally from Mexico," I said. It was my way of admitting that I wasn't from here. *Yes, I'm a foreigner, and everything from my brown skin to my accent to my Mexican birth certificate prevents me from laying claim to the U.S. even though I have a green card that gives me permission to be here.* I couldn't simply say I was from Los Angeles, which might imply I was American born. I wasn't. I was an outsider, and I had to claim that part of me so that no one could make me feel ashamed about being an immigrant. So that later I could say, *I never pretended to be something I was not.*

"Cool, cool," Carolyn said. "Well, welcome to Santa Cruz." She offered me half of her sandwich.

"No, thanks," I said, even though I hadn't thought of going grocery shopping before I arrived and had no food to eat. I was embarrassed and suddenly ravenous, but I had just met this white girl and didn't feel comfortable taking food from her. "Well, nice to meet you," I said, eager to get to my room, to be alone, as I had been in the three years since Mago moved out of our father's house and I no longer had her as a roommate, best friend, and protector.

But Carolyn wasn't done with me.

"There's a welcome party tonight next door. It's hosted by the residential preceptor so the new students can start getting to know people. You should come."

I didn't know what a residential preceptor was, and I was too embarrassed to ask. Besides, I didn't want to go to a party. I wasn't ready to be social, and the thought of going to a party where I knew no one was too much to deal with on my first day in a strange place. I wanted to lock myself within the safety of my room's four walls.

"I need to unpack," I said.

"Doesn't everybody?" Carolyn asked, taking a bite out of her sandwich. I could see a piece of avocado peeking through. My stomach growled, and I wondered if she heard it because she added, "There'll be food there."

I wanted this place to feel like home, and if it was ever going to, I had to learn to live with these strangers.

"Okay," I said. "Let me know when it's time to go."

My room was eight feet by ten feet. It had bare white walls and dark blue office carpet. It came with a twin-sized bed, a dresser, and a desk, all made of oak that matched the furniture in the living room and dining room. The mattress had no sheets, no comforter, no pillow, and I realized now that I had neglected to bring these with me.

The window faced a path that led to the parking lot, and I could see students and their parents carrying their belongings to their apartments. "Do you need anything else?" I heard parents ask their sons and daughters, and I wished I'd had someone to ask me that question. Did those students realize how lucky they were? I imagined myself in their place—at a farewell party showered by relatives with their congratulations and best wishes and I'm-so-proud-of-you's; at the store with my parents shopping for towels, bedding, and new clothes; at the local supermarket walking down the aisles side by side with my parents, pushing a shopping cart loaded with my favorite foods. My stomach growled at the thought.

I closed the curtain and began unpacking. I looked at the room, the small, empty closet. *You're alone, yes, but you're here. That's what matters.*

I put away my clothes and unpacked my computer. My first big purchase had put me $2,000 in debt, but for a new university student it was a necessary expense. At PCC, I had used the computer lab, but I knew the workload would be much heavier here. I took out the monitor, the hard drive, and the keyboard, and stared at the cables, wondering where they went, how to make it work.

"Ready?" Carolyn said, knocking on my door.

I dropped the cables back on the desk, leaving it for the next day.

Dizzy with hunger, I followed Carolyn to the next apartment. She said she was starting her senior year and knew the campus like the back of her hand. I hoped one day I could say the same about my new home. When we approached the door, and I heard the laughter and chatter inside, I felt like running back to my room, but Carolyn was already pushing me into the apartment. She was so different from me. She went around saying hi to everyone, smiling, cracking jokes, giving people high fives, acting as if she knew them all, even though many were new arrivals like me. She disappeared deeper into the apartment and left me on my own to hide in a corner.

Except for two or three brown faces, and some Asians, every person in the apartment was white. I felt hyper-aware of my foreignness, my brownness. In Los Angeles, I hadn't felt like a minority. PCC had a large Latino population, and I had never once felt out of place. I had known that UCSC wasn't as culturally diverse as my old school, but now that I was here, confronted by its whiteness, I wanted to flee. I retreated deeper into the corner.

No one in this room had any idea how far I had come to get here. I had never told anyone—except Diana—that twenty-one years before, I had been born in a little shack of sticks and cardboard in my hometown of Iguala, Guerrero, a city only three hours from glittery Acapulco and from the bustling metropolis of Mexico City, but a world away from there. Iguala was a place of shacks and dirt roads, where most homes didn't have running water and electricity was unreliable.

Because of the national debt crisis and the devastating peso devaluations, in 1977 my father became part of the biggest wave of emigration ever from Mexico when he left Iguala to look for work in the U.S. My mother followed him two years later. By the time I was five, I no longer had a father or a mother, and the border stood between us, keeping us apart. My siblings and I had been left behind on the wrong side of the border, under the care of my paternal grandmother, Abuela Evila, who more than lived up to her name.

My grandmother had never liked my mother, and she transferred her dislike to us, often telling us we might not even be her grandchildren. "Who knows what your mother was doing when no one was looking?" she would often say. Living with her had made the separation from our parents even more unbearable. My grandmother spent most of the money our parents sent for us on other things. So, for the most part, my siblings and I were dressed in rags, wore cheap plastic sandals, had lice and tapeworm, and ate nothing but beans and tortillas every day. "What's the point of having parents in El Otro Lado if we are treated like beggars?" we often asked ourselves.

My childhood was defined by the fear that my parents might forget me, or worse, replace me with children born in the U.S. Worst of all was the fear that I might never have a home and a real family again. The only thing that sustained me through the dark times was my dream of one day having my parents back in my life.

Then my father left my mother for my stepmother. Finding herself all alone in the U.S., my mother returned to Mexico with no husband, no money, nothing to show for her time in El Otro Lado except for the American baby girl in her arms, my sister Betty. She took us out of my evil grandmother's house and we went to live with my sweet maternal grandmother. My siblings and I were elated and relieved to have our mother back, but it wasn't long before we realized that she had changed. All she cared about was finding herself a new husband, and once she did, the family we'd once had was gone.

Eight years after he had left, my father returned for us and hired a smuggler to sneak Carlos, Mago, and me across the border. I was almost ten when I arrived in Los Angeles to live with my father and his new wife. A year later, my mother returned to the U.S. and lived in downtown Los Angeles with her husband, Betty, and her new baby, my half brother Leo.

Both Betty and Leo were American born, and for many years I felt inferior to my younger siblings. Just like I felt inferior to all the students at the party, especially the blond, blue-eyed girls who flipped their hair back and laughed with a confidence I had never had. Too many of them were gathered around the food table, and though I was desperate to get some of the chicken wings and vegetables on the trays, I was too afraid to leave my corner.

One of the Latino students spotted me and came over. He walked with a limp and held his right arm at an angle. "Hi. I'm Alfredo," he said. His speech was slurred, and I wondered if he was drunk. But he couldn't be! We were on campus. Alcohol wasn't allowed. Had he already, on his first day, broken the rules?

"Where are you from?" he asked.

Coming from a Latino, the question didn't shake me up the way it had with Carolyn. "L.A.," I said, this time without any hesitation.

"No kidding? Me, too. I'm from East Los, and you?"

"Highland Park."

"And that there is Jaime," Alfredo said, pointing to the other Latino student in the room. "He's also from L.A. Huntington Park, I think." Jaime waved at me but didn't come over. He was busy chatting with a girl.

How crazy that all three of us new Latino students were from L.A. It made me feel better to know that at least Jaime and Alfredo might understand how I was feeling, what I was going through.

Alfredo was much older than me. I had turned twenty-one less than two weeks earlier, and he was in his thirties. He told me that when he was eighteen he had gotten beat up by an older man. His attacker was wearing steel-toed boots and had kicked Alfredo in the head several times. "I almost died," he said. Instead, he had sustained a brain injury that affected the right side of his body, which was why he limped and held his right arm at an angle, and why his speech was slurred. I felt embarrassed that I had thought he was drunk.

"I had to learn how to do everything again," Alfredo said. "How to walk, talk, read, and write." That beating had set him back many years, but he hadn't given up. Finally, at thirty-three, he was here at UCSC, trying to make his dream come true. Just like me.

Before he could ask questions about me, I excused myself to grab some food from the table while it wasn't so crowded. I didn't feel alone in the room anymore, and I felt that I should share something about myself with Alfredo, just like he had. Maybe another day I might be ready to open up to him. I could tell he had come to terms with his past and had managed to move beyond it. I hadn't yet. I was constantly picking at the wounds of my memories and bleeding again, and again. I hadn't yet learned how to allow the scars to form and fade with time.

Besides, what would I say to Alfredo? He wouldn't believe me even if I did tell him. My life until now had been a Mexican telenovela. I didn't get kicked in the head with steel-toed boots, but like him, I'd also had to learn how to read and write and speak all over again—in a language that wasn't my own.

When the party was over and I walked back to my apartment, I was glad I had gone with Carolyn. If I hadn't, I wouldn't have had a full belly, and I wouldn't have made a new friend and heard his story. Alfredo was a survivor, and his resilience inspired me.

Reyna in her student apartment, UCSC, 1996

3

THE NEXT MORNING, with my stomach growling again, I walked to the Kresge Food Co-op, a little store where Carolyn said I could buy a few things to eat. I tossed the name around in my head as I walked there, wondering what a co-op was.

I asked a few people for directions until I found it tucked into the rear side of some dorms near the Maintenance Department. The co-op was just a small room with shelves and containers of things I didn't recognize. Plastic bins labeled for granola and oats, barley, couscous, quinoa, wheat germ, and wild rice. In the fridge, I saw something called tofu, soy milk, and deli meat that claimed to be meatless, things I had never eaten in my life or even known existed.

The girl at the cash register sat on a stool staring at me. She had the strangest hair I had ever seen. When I first saw her, I thought she had snakes for hair, like Medusa. But as I made my way closer to the counter, pretending to be interested in a bag of peas with something called wasabi, I studied her from the corner of my eye and wondered if she had ever brushed her hair, because the strands had twisted and formed into what looked like dirty brown ropes. The girl had piercings in her nose, left eyelid, and lower lip; she wore a tattered multicolored dress, and yet she looked at me as if *I* were the weird one in this place.

"Are you a member?" she asked.

"A member of what?"

"Of the co-op, obviously."

I didn't know if I had to be a member to make a purchase. All I knew was that whatever they had in here, except for the bananas and apples, looked like something from another planet. I wanted corn tortillas and rice and pinto beans. I wanted some pan dulce and bolillos, a can of jalapeños and chipotle, a bag of fideo, and frozen tamales if freshly steamed ones weren't available. I wanted a container of Chocolate Abuelita, a package of pineapple barritas, a bag of chicharrones, and a bottle of hot sauce to go with it. I wanted green mangos and jicama and a shaker of chili powder to sprinkle on them. I wanted comfort food. I wanted something I would know how to cook or eat.

"I'm sorry," I said. "I shouldn't have come."

After eating some chocolate chip cookies from the vending machine, I walked across the campus to the bookstore. I was taken aback by the hundreds of books on the shelves. I had my required reading list, and I hoped the money I had from my financial aid package would be enough. As much as I tried not to pay attention to the parents, I watched them help their children find their books. "I read that when I was in college, too," I heard a mother tell her daughter as they leafed through a book together.

I would never hear such a thing from my own parents. With my father's third-grade education, and my mother barely managing to finish sixth grade at seventeen years old, the day I started junior high school I had surpassed my parents in terms of education. I never had a parent help me with homework, tell me about the books they had read in school, or go book shopping with me. The few times my father went to my school for teacher-parent conferences, my siblings and I had to translate what the teachers said. My school experiences hadn't been something I could share with either of my parents.

I had had enough of the textbook section, so I moved on to school apparel. Hanging on racks and displayed on shelves were T-shirts, sweaters, sweatpants, jackets, socks, hats—all imprinted with the school mascot: the banana slug. The slug had round eyeglasses on and was reading Plato. In the background were the words FIAT SLUG—"Let There Be Slug." Of all things, I thought as I ran my fingers over a T-shirt, a slug as a mascot, a slimy, spineless yellow creature that crawls on the ground and can be easily stepped on. Reading the history of UCSC, I had learned that the original mascot had been a sea lion, but the students had protested and fought for the mascot to become a banana slug to honor the spirit of Santa Cruz as a place that embraces peace, loves the environment, and celebrates its counterculture ideology.

I held the school T-shirt in my hand. Even though I wanted it, I put it back on the rack. I couldn't afford it. I had enough money for only the most essential textbooks. The rest I would have to borrow from the library.

As I was about to make my way back to the textbook section, I caught sight of a few parents admiring the garments hanging in the corner. The T-shirts were imprinted with the words UCSC DAD, UCSC MOM, UCSC GRANDMA, etc. I tried to imagine my parents wearing one of those shirts, announcing to the world that their daughter was a university student—the first in the family—and their faces beaming with pride.

I stood before the shirts, wondering if I could buy one for each of my parents. I took them off the rack and held them against my chest. I could put them in the mail first thing tomorrow. Maybe I could sacrifice the purchase of a textbook for these two shirts. But would they wear them? How would a silly T-shirt make my father and mother feel proud of me, anyway?

I put the shirts back on the rack. I would just be wasting my money on something they might never wear, on pride they might never feel.

I hopped on the bus and went downtown to shop at the big grocery store on Pacific Avenue. The New Leaf was just a bigger version of the food co-op, full of strange stuff I had never eaten. There was a large selection of bread, and I didn't know the difference between whole grain and sprouted grain and multigrain and sourdough. I grew up eating Bimbo, a Mexican white bread. The tortilla section was just as overwhelming in its selection. The store even carried red and green flour tortillas, which I'd never seen before. Who knew you could put tomato or spinach in the dough? I bought corn tortillas at twice the cost I was used to. Too many food choices at too high a price. I would have to find a cheaper place to shop. I wished there were a Mexican market nearby.

I stopped at the thrift store and bought gently used sheets, a towel, and a blanket. My last stop of the day would be the laundry room at Kresge, and I hoped to get a good night's sleep with my new used bedding. The night before I'd had to cover myself with my jacket.

I was shocked to find that downtown Santa Cruz had homeless people everywhere. I would have never expected to see homelessness in such an idyllic place. In L.A. I had seen panhandlers when my siblings and I visited our mother, who lived in the worst part of downtown. The street from the bus stop to my mother's apartment was lined with the homeless, most of them African-American. I was shocked that in Santa Cruz every man I saw sitting on the sidewalk asking for handouts was white. Many of them had weird hair like the girl at the co-op.

"Got a buck to spare?" they asked as I made my way back to the bus station. The sight of these men begging bothered me immensely. I wanted to tell them they had no right to be asking *me* for money. They were white, male, and American born. Those three facts alone put them at an advantage over so many of us—

especially immigrants and women of color. In L.A., I'd seen Latino men selling bags of oranges or flower bouquets off freeway exits, and selling tamales, corn on the cob, or chicharrones from shopping carts that they pushed up and down the streets. I'd seen them congregate in the Home Depot parking lot waiting to be picked up for construction jobs, and pushing lawn mowers or carrying leaf blowers, covered in sweat and grass as they maintained other people's properties. On the drive to Santa Cruz, I'd seen them bent over fields, picking strawberries and onions. But I had never seen Latino men beg.

From the moment my siblings and I arrived in the U.S., my father drilled into us the expectation that we were to grow up into hardworking adults who could take care of our own needs. "Never, ever, do I want you asking anyone for anything," he often said to us. My father had many flaws, but he was the hardest-working man I'd ever known. He looked down on beggars. He had even criticized my mother for getting food stamps to feed my U.S.-born siblings. I wondered what he would say about all these men lining the sidewalks of Pacific Avenue, grinning at me, asking me to give them the precious few dollars I had in my purse.

And then I spotted a young woman sitting by the bus station, her hand stretched out to passersby. She was my age. She could have been a university student, but instead she was here, sitting on the sidewalk, dressed in rags and hungry. I looked into her green eyes and saw an emptiness in their depths found only in a person who is truly broken—or high on drugs, as I would later discover was common around here—but at this moment, all I wanted to know was who had broken this girl's spirit?

I thought of my father, and the words he had said to me three years earlier came back to haunt me again, as if he were standing beside me. *You're going to be a failure.* His words had hurt me more than the beatings.

Had her father said that to her, too, and she'd believed it?

"Got any change?" she asked.

I handed her a couple of dollars. I wanted to tell her, *You aren't a failure*. But I said nothing. She had already looked away from me, stretching her hand out to someone else.

On the way back to campus, on a bus full of strangers, it took every ounce of effort I had to stop the tears from coming. I had tried so hard not to let anything break my spirit, but the sight of the homeless girl reminded me of how close I had come to that.

When I had set foot in this country, it didn't take me long to realize there were two sides to my father. First and foremost, there was the man who was my hero. I would always be grateful to my father for the one gesture that completely changed the course of my life— he brought me to live in the U.S. At first, he hadn't wanted to bring me, only Carlos and Mago, because they were older. He worried that at nine years old I was too young to attempt the dangerous border crossing. I begged him to take me with him. He could have left without me, but he didn't. He took me out of the misery in Iguala and brought me to the place he knew I could flourish.

He didn't leave me, I would tell myself over and over again every time my hero turned into my tormentor. Since he was an alcoholic, living with him had been like living with Dr. Jekyll and Mr. Hyde. One day my father would tell us to reach for the stars and to dream big. Then the next day when he had drunk too much and his other side emerged, he was literally beating us to the ground, calling us a bunch of pendejos, ignorant fools.

Carlos was the first to leave. At twenty years old, he dropped out of college to get married. He wanted to show our father that he could do a better job at being a husband and father. His marriage didn't last, but the damage did. The next one to leave was Mago, who had turned to shopping and clubbing to deal with our traumatic upbringing. But soon the material things and the dancing weren't enough. She dropped out of college to get a full-time job to pay off her credit card debt and her brand-new car. Though she had promised to take me with her, she left my father's house to start her own family without me.

I understood that my siblings had done these things out of desperation. My father's alcoholism and abuse had forced them to leave in pursuit of their own home.

In my senior year of high school, I was accepted into the University of California, Irvine. When my sister left our father's house and got pregnant soon after, my father was so disappointed with my siblings that he assumed I would disappoint him, too, even though I was still there with him, still in school, still the dutiful daughter. I was seventeen, and I needed him to sign the paperwork to secure my spot at UCI, but he refused. Mago was his favorite daughter. He had believed that she would reach the dream of higher education first. But her priorities had changed, and now I had to pay the price for my father's disillusionment.

"You can forget about going to that university. You're going to be a failure, too, just like them, so don't even bother going," he said, and with those words, he had crushed my dream the way he crushed a can of Budweiser when he was done with it.

Now, on the bus, I realized that if I had let my father's words break me, I could have ended up like that homeless girl. And the thought that I still might made the tears come.

Just as I was about to unravel on that bus, a miracle happened. I caught sight of a Mexican market through the window; its name, painted in bright red letters, made the tears go away: LA ESPERANZA MARKET. The bus sped up Mission Street, and I could no longer see the building, but I knew I hadn't imagined it. I had found the one place I could come back to again and again to taste the flavors and smell the aromas of the homes I once had! What a beautiful name for a grocery store, I thought. Esperanza—hope, expectation, possibility. Esperanza was also the name of the heroine in my favorite book, *The House on Mango Street* by Sandra Cisneros. Like me, Esperanza had left her family and her community to go in search of her dreams, but she had promised she would come back one day and help those who couldn't escape. Like I hoped one day to return for those I had left behind.

When I got off the bus at Kresge, I took a deep, deep breath, filling my lungs with the Santa Cruz air until I felt as if I could soar across the sky. If the word esperanza had a scent, I thought this was how it would smell—like a redwood forest.

Reyna looking toward the future

4

Reyna and Diana at PCC, 1996

Aᴛ FEW DAYS LATER, school officially began. I walked to my literature class—Theory and Interpretation—anxious about my
very first university lecture. The crispy air nipped at my grogginess
as I crossed the footbridge. Golden sunbeams radiated through the
morning fog, making the redwoods appear dreamy and magical. It
was a sign, I told myself. It was the forest telling me things would
be okay.

Despite my father's prophecy, hadn't I avoided failure so far?
After he refused to let me attend UCI, I fell into a gloomy place.
But just like sunbeams on foggy mornings, my determination had
cut through the gloom. I defied my father and enrolled myself at the
community college, where I had graduated with not just excellent
grades, but the knowledge that I was responsible for my own learn-

ing. I had learned how to adapt, how to use my creativity. There was nothing to be afraid of.

I hurried to class, and the fog had completely dissipated by the time I got to the lecture hall. Students rushed by me—some still wearing their pajamas—and I froze at the door. Over a hundred people were jammed into the lecture hall. *What have I gotten myself into?* At PCC, the only class I had been in that had a hundred students was marching band. For literature, thirty people max. Not this.

"Take a seat," the teacher said, and I forced myself into the room. All the seats in the back were taken, and I had no choice but to sit near the front. The teacher, a bearded man in his fifties, went over the course outline and expectations, telling us about the books and authors we would be reading—Voltaire, Marx, Engels, Stendhal. I had never heard of any of them.

As I sat there looking at the overwhelming syllabus, I reminded myself I was good at English and literature—they were my strengths. At least that was what Diana had said.

Diana was the first person to give me my very own book, one that I could keep, *The Moths and Other Stories* by Helena Maria Viramontes. That book was followed by *The House on Mango Street*. She was the first person who told me I had writing talent, that my stories mattered. It was because of her that I was now majoring in creative writing.

But the best thing that Diana had done for me was to take me into her home two years earlier when my father was arrested for spousal abuse. I lived with her for four months, and then again after my father got back with my stepmother, Mila. The time that I spent at her house was a time that I will cherish for the rest of my life. She helped me finish my studies at PCC and kept me from dropping out because of my family problems. I was at UCSC because of her, but as I sat there surrounded by all these students, and as I read the list of assignments and tests we would be doing, I couldn't help but wonder if she had been wrong. What if I didn't have what it took to succeed in this place?

At the end of class, the teacher took attendance. I listened to the names, looking at the sea of students around me, most of them white. I dreaded whenever teachers took roll. Having the name Reyna Grande, "the big queen," when you are only five feet tall sets you up for a lifetime of ridicule. I braced myself for the laughter that would follow as soon as the teacher said my name. But there was no laughter. My name wasn't even called. Instead, the teacher said, "Renée Grand?" No one raised her hand to claim that name, and I suspected he was trying to say my name but mispronouncing it. It had happened to me before. When we first arrived in the U.S., Mago's teachers had changed her real name—Magloria—to Maggie because they claimed it was unpronounceable. At home, she was always Mago, but outside in the world she was Maggie. At times, I got called Renée and sometimes my last name—Grande—was pronounced like the river in Texas, a river I hadn't crossed, though I had on numerous occasions been called a wetback.

"Renée Grand," the teacher said again, and this time I knew he meant me. I looked at the students around me. The ones wearing their pajamas, the ones who hadn't brushed their hair and had what I later learned were called dreadlocks, the ones who had stayed up too late drinking and partying, who walked around campus so sure of themselves. I wanted to be like them. I wanted to be Renée Grand because I knew she would blend in with them in a way Reyna Grande might not.

"Renée Grand," the teacher said a third time. I didn't raise my hand to claim that name as my own, though there was a part of me that wanted to. I was in a new city, starting a new life, and I could reinvent myself into Renée, the girl who belonged.

But if I did, what would happen to the Big Queen, the grandiose name my mother had given me and which I knew one day I would have to live up to?

After class, I gathered up the courage to approach my teacher. "My name wasn't called."

"These are the students enrolled in my class." He let me look at the list and sure enough, there I was.

He checked the roster where I was pointing and said, "I did call you. I called you three times."

"My name is R-r-reyna Gran-*de*."

He shrugged and marked me present. If he mispronounced my name again, I knew I wouldn't be afraid to correct him, just like I wouldn't be afraid to tackle the works of those white European men we would be reading.

Luckily, literature was my only big class. My other classes were more manageable. As a transfer student, to my great relief, I realized that the study skills and academic confidence I had acquired at Pasadena City College had prepared me for university work. It turned out I knew how to hold myself accountable for my own progress. Some of the students at Kresge didn't know how to manage their independence. They just wanted to party, drink, and do drugs, instead of focusing on their studies. When it rained, they would go out into the redwoods and dance naked in circles, pretending to be fairies or wood nymphs. They didn't care about getting in trouble with the school administration. Without their parents keeping them in check, they were doing everything they hadn't been allowed to do at home. Others missed home too much and walked around wallowing in their homesickness. The couple of times I ran into Jaime, the other Latino student at Kresge East, he reminded me of the protagonist in Voltaire's novel. Seeing Jaime's tragically sad face—like the face of someone who had been ejected from an "earthly paradise"—made me think of Candide.

Jaime mentioned that he might return home by the end of the quarter. "I feel lonely up here," he said. "I miss my family. My girlfriend."

Don't you understand that this is an opportunity of a lifetime? I wanted to say to him. *To be at a university, working hard toward your future, and you would throw it all away simply because you miss your family and some girl and now you want to go home?* But the truth was I envied Jaime. I wished I had a home that I could return to. Candide had been kicked out by the baron and was never allowed to return to the "most beautiful of all castles," and though the home where my father reigned had never been beautiful, I wasn't allowed back, either.

"School just started," I said to Jaime, trying to be kinder, more understanding of his añoranza, that deep longing I knew well. "Give it time. It'll get easier. This place could be home, too."

Also like Candide, I had come to learn that not all is for the best, but if there was anything that life had taught me so far, it was to try my hardest to make the best of things, no matter how difficult they might be. I focused on this until it became routine, until I no longer felt lost and disoriented.

My roommate Kim, who was a foreign student from China, helped me set up my computer and even gave me a pet. He installed a program on my computer that was a screen saver unlike any I had ever seen. When my computer wasn't in use, a little dog ran around the screen, and I could feed him, give him water, and throw balls for him to catch. He even barked! That old Mexican saying didn't apply to me anymore. I still didn't have a father or a mother, but I finally did have a dog to bark at me.

5

Edwin came to visit me on the weekends, but soon the demands of our schoolwork, the distance, and our jobs became too much and we went our separate ways, though we remained friends. I had taken a tutoring job at the writing center, which kept me busier than I would have liked. My financial aid package—loans, grants, and work-study—wasn't enough to cover my expenses. In my last semester at PCC, Diana had helped me apply for scholarships, and though I had gotten several small ones, without parental support I had no one to turn to when money was tight, which was often. This California beach town was an expensive place to live. It was full of wealthy retirees, people with trust funds, and high-tech workers from Silicon Valley, but the jobs, on and off campus, were low-paying compared to the crushingly high cost of living.

My work as a tutor was to help students with their writing assignments, and one of my students was Alfredo. Because of his brain injury, writing didn't come easily. I helped him with the essays he had to write. The other students I tutored were struggling with their writing as well. I taught them how to put together a good sentence, a good paragraph, how to take ideas, thoughts, and opinions and make them come to life on the page. It amazed me that I was mostly teaching students whose native language was English but who had worse grammar than ESL students and couldn't write a decent paragraph in their native tongue.

"Where did you learn to write like this?" Alfredo asked me one day.

We were sitting at the dining table in my apartment. The dining room had a big window where I could see the redwoods.

"I don't know." I shrugged. "I've been writing in English since I was thirteen."

I told Alfredo about the very first story I wrote. It was for a writing competition at my school when I was in fifth grade. I wrote it in Spanish because I had only been in the U.S. for a few months and my English was limited. My teacher didn't read Spanish, and when it was time to select the stories to be entered into the competition, she put mine in the reject pile without another glance. "I swore I would never write again," I told Alfredo. "To me, my teacher hadn't just rejected my story, she had also rejected me, and I felt ashamed to be an immigrant, a Spanish speaker, a person of color."

"I'm sorry she did that," he said.

When I was in eighth grade, I told Alfredo, my junior high had a writing competition as well. By then, I had graduated from the ESL program at my school and was enrolled in regular English classes. My accent was still pretty thick, but my writing and reading skills were solid. I made myself enter the competition because I wanted to be judged on the same terms as everyone else. My story was inspired by my relationship with my little sister. Whenever Betty and I saw each other, things were awkward between us. Having grown up in two separate households, she with my mother and I with my father, made us feel disconnected, distant. I had been reading books like *Sweet Valley High*, and so the story I wrote was about twin sisters who get separated when the parents divorce, each parent taking a daughter, and when the sisters are reunited years later, they're complete strangers to each other.

"And I got first place!"

"That's awesome!" Alfredo had put his essay aside and was listening to my story with interest. "I'm glad you overcame that first rejection."

I was glad, too. If I hadn't, my writing career would have ended before it had even begun.

I didn't know that at thirteen years old I had turned to writing as a way to deal with my traumatic experiences before, during, and after migration. Because I was a child immigrant, my identity was split; I often felt like an outcast for not being completely Mexican but not fully American either. The border was still inside of me. Physically I had crossed it, but psychologically I was still running across that no-man's-land. I was still caught back there, and so were my parents because the truth was that we were never the same after we crossed the border. We all changed. Perhaps it was because we had left something of ourselves behind, the way migrants leave a shoe, an empty can of tuna, a plastic water bottle, a shirt. What we each left on the border was a piece of our soul, our heart, our spirit—clinging to the branches of a bush, flapping in the wind.

Depression, anxiety, post-traumatic stress disorder—these words were not part of my vocabulary, so I never used them to describe how I felt. I expressed my feelings through stories while my father drowned his in a can of beer.

I turned to writing to save myself, to record and remember, to give meaning to my experiences. Writing was an act of survival. It wasn't until PCC that I discovered it could be a possible career option. Having grown up never reading any Latina writers, I thought Latinas didn't write and publish books, so I had assumed I couldn't either. I hadn't thought I could pursue a career in writing until I met Diana. "If Sandra Cisneros can do it, you can do it. If Isabel Allende can do it, you can do it," she would say to me while handing me a copy of their latest books.

After Alfredo left, I went to my room to work on a story that wasn't part of any class assignment. Talking to him about my writing had given me inspiration to sit and write, which I hadn't done the whole month I had been at UCSC. My creative writing classes wouldn't start until winter quarter. For now, I was stuck writing academic essays about *Candide* and *The Red and the Black*.

Usually my stories were about Mexico. I had now lived in the U.S. longer. Only through my writing could I hold on to my native country and keep it from floating into the mists of my memory. By writing about it, I could claim Mexico in a way I couldn't in real life. Despite everything I had gained by emigrating, I had also lost things: my relationship with my sweet maternal grandmother, my aunts and uncles, my friends, and my native country itself. The Mexican way of life felt different now; my Spanish was broken, my Catholic religion almost nonexistent. I knew little about Mexico, just pieces of its history, its customs, its geography. It was, in many ways, a mystery to me. Like my parents, my native country was full of flaws, and it had mistreated and abused me, and yet I still loved and clung to Mexico with childish hope and optimism, dreaming of the day it would change for the better, in the same way I hoped my parents would change.

On my first return visit to Mexico three years earlier, everyone treated me like a foreigner because I had been "corrupted" by being Americanized. To the people who had seen me grow up, I was no longer Mexican enough. But in the U.S. I wasn't American enough either. For years, I had struggled to fit in, to learn the language and culture, to find my way. But no matter how hard I tried, I still felt like a foreigner, especially here in Santa Cruz where I was struggling with feelings of isolation, loneliness, otherness. UCSC wasn't yet the Hispanic-Serving Institution it would one day become, so I hardly saw anyone who looked like me. I took refuge in my writing. The words I put on the page created a bridge that connected both countries, both languages, both cultures. I hoped someday to write my way into a place where I finally belonged, where I finally felt I was "enough."

Kresge footbridge

One day in November, as I was walking across the footbridge to my Latin class, I ran into my roommate Carolyn.

"Are you going to the protest?" she asked as she walked alongside me with her usual briskness.

"What protest? I'm going to class."

"You have to go to the protest, Reyna. You have to support your people."

I had no idea what she was talking about, and I wasn't going to miss my class just because of some protest. I had never been to a demonstration, and I didn't want to get into any kind of trouble that might jeopardize my studies. So far I had kept a low profile, stayed focused on my classes, and done very little besides studying and working.

"Maybe another time," I said.

"There might not be another time. You have to come with me. You have to stand with your people." She grabbed me by my elbow, and by the look she was giving me, I knew she would drag me over there whether I wanted to go or not.

"Okay, fine, I'll go," I said. She let go of my elbow, and I followed her, getting angrier and angrier just thinking about my class and what I would be missing, the work I would have to make up to get an A.

I followed Carolyn to Hahn Hall, the building where the administration and student services were located, and as we neared the building, I heard them. The chants of the students rose up into the sky, and I couldn't believe what I was hearing. Spanish. "¡El pueblo unido, jamás será vencido! ¡El pueblo unido, jamás será vencido!"

Once we cleared the redwood trees, I could see the building and the hundreds of students who were marching around it, holding signs. Carolyn's words suddenly made sense. There they were—all the brown faces I had been looking for. Students who looked just like me. Hundreds of them mixed in with black, white, and Asian students. Where in the world had they been all this time?

"What are they protesting?" I asked Carolyn.

"Prop 209." At seeing the blank look on my face, she added, "It's a proposition that was voted on yesterday and passed. It does away with affirmative action in California." When I didn't say anything, she got angry at me. "Don't you get it? It affects you as a Latina. It affects me as a woman. We have to make ourselves heard!"

I liked to believe that my good grades and my dedication had earned me a spot at the university, but the reality was that as a Latina I was up against not only gender inequality but also racial inequality, and in some way affirmative action had given me a boost. I suddenly realized that if Prop 209 no longer required schools to consider race, ethnicity, and the gender of their students, minority students—and females of all backgrounds—would have a harder time being admitted to four-year universities.

"I get it," I said. "Come on." I hurried down to Hahn, my backpack swinging from my shoulder, and I made my way to the students who were forming a human chain, preventing anyone from entering or leaving the building. They broke the chain to let me in, and I took the hands of the students on either side of me and began to shout.

"What do we want?"

"Diversity!"

"When do we want it?"

"Now!"

My voice rose to join theirs until we all became one. For the first time since I had arrived at the school, I felt connected. We began to walk around the building, still holding hands and singing, "This little light of mine, I'm gonna let it shine. Let it shine, let it shine, let it shine."

I had never heard this song before, but as I sang it, I felt my chest expand, the pressure making me hurt. There was a little light inside of me that life's challenges had tried to extinguish on more than one occasion. But it was still there, shining bright, and I knew I had to protect that light no matter what. For me, for my family, for my community. For both my countries.

"Let it shine, let it shine, let it shine."

Our protest didn't have much of an effect. Prop 209 had passed, abolishing affirmative action so that people like me wouldn't get "preferential treatment," and there was nothing I or anyone could do to reverse its passage. The defeat was felt across campus, and though demonstrations at other universities were also held, nothing came of our student protests. Yet it was the first time I realized I had a voice and that it was my responsibility to use it.

It was also when I finally discovered that most of the Latino students were at two of the other colleges at UCSC—Oakes and

Merrill, which hosted the Latin American Studies and the Languages Departments. I would later find out that 15 percent of the student body at UCSC was Latino, but I wouldn't have known that being at Kresge College, where the majority were white and Asian. To my delight, Oakes and Merrill also housed the two taquerías on campus, and I soon started going over there after class to grab a carne asada taco or shrimp burrito, and to surround myself with other Latinos who, like me, were struggling to figure things out as the first in their families to attend a university. Most were majoring in education, Latin American and Latino/a studies, math, Spanish, or history. They encouraged me to take Chicano literature the following quarter.

It was then that I realized that the protest did have a profound effect—on me, that is. It led me to a place of belonging and brought me closer to making Santa Cruz and the university my home.

6

Mago, Reyna, and Betty

I HAD BEEN SO wrapped up in surviving my first quarter at UCSC, I hadn't yearned for my family as much as I had when I first arrived two months earlier. I had talked to Mago and Carlos a few times, and my father and mother not at all. Once, in a moment of weakness, I had walked over to the pay phone and picked up the receiver to call my father. I was desperate to hear his voice. To hear him call me "Chata," my special nickname. But I didn't dial. Clutching the coins in my fist, I listened to the dial tone until the phone started screeching like a dying rooster and then I hung up.

I knew I should call my mother. Right before I left for Santa

Cruz, she had sent my fifteen-year-old sister to Mexico as punishment for her behavior. For a few years now, Betty had been going down the wrong path: getting into gangs, having unprotected sex, stealing the rent money, ditching class, and the last straw—dropping out of high school.

My mother said that she sent Betty to Mexico because if she no longer wanted a high school education, then she would get a different kind of education—she would learn how to be a woman. My aunt would teach my little sister how to cook, clean, and obey the men in her life, especially her future husband, whoever he might be—just the kind of upbringing my grandmother, mother, and aunts had had in our hometown.

I hadn't known what my mother was planning until it was too late. My sister was already on a plane to Mexico by the time I found out what was happening. "I can't deal with her anymore," my mother said when I told her it was the most irresponsible thing she had ever done. Her decision reinforced my idea that my mother had been born without a maternal gene. Or at least when it came to her four oldest children, because she indulged my little half brother and gave him everything.

It shamed me to realize that I hadn't given Betty much thought since I arrived in Santa Cruz, and I should have. Just as my father had banned me from his life, so had Betty been banned from my mother's, though for opposite reasons. I had done nothing but try to make my father proud and help him during his hour of need. Betty had done nothing but make life difficult for herself and my mother, but she had her reasons. She was reacting to my mother's physical and emotional abuse in the only way she knew how—by rebelling. But by hurting my mother, she was also hurting herself in the process.

I picked up the phone and called my mother to see how Betty was doing in exile. My family in Mexico didn't have a phone, which meant I would have to go through my grandmother's neighbor to reach my sister. Besides, I didn't have money for international phone calls.

"She's driving your aunt crazy" was the first thing my mother said. "She's running wild, and your aunt can't control her anymore."

"Well, you shouldn't have sent her down there in the first place," I said. "She's your responsibility, not my aunt's. Why are you always making other people raise your children?" It was a low blow and I knew it, but every time I spoke to my mother, it brought out the pain of the many times she left me, and I retaliated.

As usual, she ignored my comment and said, "Your sister is having an affair with a married man. ¿Me escuchas? She's fifteen years old and already her reputation is ruined!"

I didn't have anything to say to my mother then. The year before, Betty had asked me to take her to the clinic for a pregnancy test. She was fourteen, and as we sat there waiting for the results, I had prayed so hard for it to be negative, which to our relief it was. A pregnancy would have ruined her life. And now here she was again, jeopardizing her future. I couldn't let that happen.

"I'll go check on her," I said. "I'll go to Iguala."

As I walked back to my apartment, I realized there was a big problem with what I had just committed to—I didn't have money for a trip to Mexico. But something told me I needed to make it happen. I was worried about my little sister, so I wracked my brain wondering how I could come up with the cash. I paused halfway across the footbridge, looked up at the redwoods, and said a silent prayer, though I was no longer religious. When my siblings and I arrived in the U.S., it didn't take long for us to lose our religion and forget the teachings of our sweet maternal grandmother, Abuelita Chinta. When we asked our father to take us to church, he refused, raising his can of Budweiser and proclaiming, "This is my God." That quickly put an end to our Catholic faith.

Now I was an atheist, yet when surrounded by such natural splendor here in Santa Cruz, by trees that seemed to nearly reach the heavens, I couldn't help but want to believe in a higher being. God? Goddess? Mother Earth? Tonantzin, Aztec mother goddess?

One of them heard my prayer. The next day, when I stopped at the main office after picking up my mail, I spotted a flyer announcing a $500 research grant Kresge was offering to students. That was the perfect solution! I hurried back to my apartment and filled out the application and letter of intent, explaining that I needed to go to Mexico for a short-story collection I was working on. It wasn't true. I wasn't working on a collection, and I felt ashamed about lying, but it was the only thing I could think of. On the application, I stated that I needed the funds to do research on the town and the people I was writing about.

A few weeks later, I knew that I was meant to go see my sister when I received a letter from Kresge informing me I had received the grant.

This trip would be my second time visiting the country of my birth since I had left at nine. The first visit had been three years before, when I was in high school and I had gone with Mago and my mother. It was on that visit that I realized I was no longer Mexican enough. Everyone treated me like an outsider, as if I was no longer one of them, as if I had lost my right to call Mexico my home.

As soon as winter break arrived, I headed south. My plane landed in Mexico City at 7:00 a.m. and I began the three-hour journey to my hometown. As I rode in the taxi from the airport to the bus station, I lowered the window and breathed in the smell of the city, a mix of diesel fumes, urine, and corn tortillas.

"You aren't from here, are you?" the cabdriver asked me. I held my breath, feeling the floor sinking under me as I imagined the worst. He thought I was American. I was going to get kidnapped!

"*Chale, claro que sí,*" I said, trying to speak Spanish like a real Mexican. But the man shook his head.

"I can hear America in your voice," he said.

Thankfully, I arrived at the bus station safely, where I waited until it was time to board. As my bus traveled south, I thought about my mother. Every time I talked to her, I couldn't control the anger that raged inside me.

Even after all these years, I still felt the devastating blow of her abandonment.

The first time my mother left, I was four years old. She walked away from me, Mago, and Carlos to join my father in El Otro Lado. For many years, I hadn't been able to understand why she had made the choice to leave her children behind to go to my father's side simply because he wanted her to join him. Why did she have to obey him? Why couldn't she have said no and stayed with her children? Later I understood that my mother hadn't wanted to be an abandoned woman. In Iguala, there were women whose husbands had gone north long ago and had completely forgotten about them. How happy and proud my mother had been when my father telephoned and said, "I need you. I want you to come."

And just like that, she packed her bags and, complying with my father's request, dropped off her children at his mother's house. We had to watch her walk away from us, wondering if we would ever see her again. Then we went inside Abuela Evila's house to endure two-and-a-half years of hell.

The irony was that even though my mother left for the U.S. to save her marriage, my father still left her for another woman. Mila was a nurse's assistant, a naturalized U.S. citizen, and a fluent English speaker—a woman who was everything my mother wasn't. When my mother returned to Mexico with my little sister, Betty, it was one of the happiest days of my life. But soon after, she ran off to Acapulco with a wrestler and abandoned us once again. My maternal grandmother did her best to make up for the pain of my mother's absence. But no matter how much Abuelita Chinta loved us—it wasn't enough.

When my father returned to Mexico to get us, my mother refused to let Betty come with us, so we left without her to reunite with our father and find something better in El Otro Lado. I had never gotten over the guilt of leaving Betty behind.

Though my mother, and then Betty, moved to Los Angeles a few years later, and we were then all on the same side of the border, my family had completely disintegrated by then.

I slept during the three-hour bus ride and woke up when the bus was making its way around the mountains cradling my hometown like cupped hands. I looked out the window, holding my breath in anticipation of the first glimpse of my city in the valley below.

Iguala de la Independencia is a city of about 110,000 people. The first Mexican flag was made in Iguala in 1824. The treaty that ended the Mexican War of Independence was written in Iguala, and the Mexican national anthem was sung for the first time there. Despite its richness in history, Iguala is a poor city, with 70 percent of the population living in poverty. Through the years to come, things would get much worse—the mountain on which my bus was traveling would one day be covered in poppy fields to supply the heroin trade with the U.S. Iguala would become a distribution center where buses would leave the station loaded with drugs destined for cities like Chicago and Los Angeles. It would become a place of infamy when, in 2014, forty-three college students were attacked and forcibly disappeared by the police working with the cartel. During the search for the missing students, numerous mass graves would be found not far from where I grew up.

But those things hadn't happened yet, and when I arrived in Iguala in December of 1996, all I saw were the shacks, the dirt roads, the crumbling houses, the trash—the grinding poverty my father had rescued me from. When I was a child, I had been able to see past the imperfections and find the beauty of my hometown, but now, after all my years of living in the U.S., I no longer could.

I hailed a cab at the bus station. Immediately, the driver said, "You aren't from here, are you?" And I wanted to say that I hadn't even opened my mouth to speak yet, so why the hell would he be asking me that already?

"You put on your seat belt," he said with a smile, anticipating my question.

And I laughed.

The road where my grandmother lived wasn't paved, so taxicabs and buses didn't venture there. I got off at the main road and walked to my grandmother's house, dragging my suitcase behind me. I inhaled the smoke from the burning trash heaps along the nearby railroad tracks. City sanitation services didn't exist in Iguala, so people had to burn their trash every day. I passed the canal in which my siblings and I swam when we were kids, and was shocked at seeing the canal full of trash—old car tires covered in mud, broken pieces of furniture, the skeletal remains of an old mattress. The stagnant water smelled worse than a dead animal, and I held my breath as I hurried past it. Abuelita Chinta lived in a shack made of sticks and cardboard. When I lived here, it had been the only shack on the street, but now there were two of them. My aunt, Tía Güera, had built her own shack next to my grandmother's.

I stood there in front of my grandmother's home, scanning the dirt road, the abandoned freight car left to rust on the train tracks, the piles of burned trash, the children walking barefoot, their feet and legs covered in dust.

I was a long way from Santa Cruz, California.

7

Abuelita Chinta

MY GRANDMOTHER'S DOOR was open, so I poked my head in and saw her sitting at the dining table with a cutting board on her lap, on which she was slicing a tomato, an onion, and a green jalapeño pepper. I hadn't seen her in three years, but she looked the same to me. As usual, she wore her gray, curly hair tied back, a flowery dress that reached below her knee, and black sandals.

"Abuelita, ya llegué," I said as I came in.

When she smiled at me, I could see that another tooth had fallen out since I had last seen her. I hugged my tiny grandmother and inhaled her scent of almond oil and herbs.

"Gracias a Dios que llegaste bien," she said, squeezing me tight. She looked at her altar, where a candle was burning next to the statue of La Virgen de Guadalupe, and she crossed herself to thank God I had arrived safely. "The journey can be dangerous for a young girl traveling alone."

"Sí, Abuelita. But I was careful." I sat at the small table with her and watched her finish cutting her vegetables. "What are you making, Abuelita?"

"A taco. Would you like one?" She got up to heat the tortillas on her stove, and I looked around to see where the meat was. There was no pot on the stove, and I could see no food except for the vegetables she had cut up. There were no beans or rice either.

The shack looked exactly as it had when I lived here with my grandmother and my siblings. It was one big room, with no interior walls. My grandmother's bed, the stove, and her altar were near the front door; in the middle was the dining table and in the back a hammock where my uncle slept. The bed that had belonged to my parents was still there, tucked into a corner. Hanging from the rafter on the ceiling was a cage with two sleeping white doves in it. Shafts of sunlight filtered through the bamboo outer walls. The heat of the sun radiating from the corrugated tin metal roof made me sleepy, and I yawned.

My grandmother put the hot tortillas on two plates and filled them up with the tomato, onion, and jalapeño slices. She handed me a plate and apologized for the modest meal.

"Your uncle hasn't been working much lately," she said. "And the little money your mother sent me is gone now."

I took the plate from my grandmother and looked at the taco. In Santa Cruz, I had met my first vegetarians and vegans, and I had been shocked that such things even existed. What would my grandmother say if I told her that in the U.S., people *chose* to eat the way she was eating now, especially the rich kids who thought being vegan was cool and who shopped at the thrift store, like I did, because they wanted to and not because they had to? Over there, I wanted to tell her, eating a tomato taco was a personal preference and not an act of survival forced on you by poverty and a system of corruption and oppression.

As if reading my thoughts, she said, "Let us be grateful for what God has provided, m'ija."

God wasn't providing all that much, I wanted to say. Or maybe He was a vegan and was trying to get my grandmother to be one, too. Yes, I was being cynical, and I knew full well what my grandmother was saying to me—sometimes even vegetables are hard to come by and you should be grateful when you have them. When I lived here with my grandmother, there were times when we would have nothing to eat except tortillas sprinkled with salt. As a university student, I was struggling to get by, and I wasn't in a position yet to help support my grandmother. But I made a promise to myself that one day, when I was making the kind of dollars that would come from my college degree, I would take care of her, just like she had once taken care of me.

She took a bite of her taco, and I did the same, the tomato juice spilling down my hand, and I licked it because there were no napkins.

"How's it going in El Otro Lado?" my grandmother asked, licking her own fingers. "Your mom tells me you are at a university now."

I nodded and excitedly told my grandmother about Santa Cruz, about the redwood trees, the deer, the bay, the boardwalk, the way the air smelled—a mixture of leaves, soil, salty ocean breeze, and esperanza. What I wouldn't give to be able to take her there! I pictured myself walking around that gorgeous place with my tiny grandmother, pointing out a banana slug crawling on the cinnamon-colored bark of a redwood, plucking a needle from a branch so that she could smell its scent. I reached out to hold her hands, as if by magic I could transport her there with me. I wished I had thought to buy a UCSC Grandma T-shirt for her.

"There are trees near the library that bloom with flowers so white they look as if they are covered in snow," I said, and then, remembering that she had never seen snow, I added, "Or as if a thousand white palomas have landed on them." Doves, she knew well.

Abuelita Chinta smiled and had a faraway look in her eyes, as if she were trying hard to imagine this magical city. When you live in a place like Iguala, it's hard to believe that the world can look any different. My guilt brought me back to reality, and I could feel the calluses in her wrinkled hands, see the layer of dust on her feet, feel the heat radiating from her tin metal roof. Why did I get to enjoy such a beautiful place, but not my grandmother who from a young age had had to work to feed her family? My grandmother never went to school, lived only three hours from Acapulco and yet had never seen the ocean with her own eyes.

"I'm glad you're living in a beautiful place, m'ija," she said, smiling her gap-toothed smile. "After everything you kids went through, you deserve it."

You do, too, Abuelita, I wanted to say.

Just then, Tía Güera came home, trailed by my little cousins, Diana and Ángel. "You're here," she said. "Good."

"Where's Betty?" I asked, standing up to give her a hug. "Is she with Lupe?" I had arrived in the afternoon, and had been surprised no one was home except for my grandmother. My cousin Lupe was fourteen, a year younger than Betty. In Mexico, the schools had two shifts—morning and afternoon. Usually, especially in junior and high school, the poor kids got stuck in the afternoon shift and would have to travel through the dark city at night to get home. It was a dangerous journey, especially for the girls.

"Lupe is in school," my aunt said. "But not your sister. She didn't want to enroll, and I didn't want to force her."

"So where is she now?"

"I don't know," Tía Güera said. "She goes to see her friends, sometimes without telling me." She took a seat on the opposite side of the table and said, "Look, Reyna, I love your sister, and I don't want anything bad to happen to her, but the whole neighborhood is gossiping about her improper relationships with the boys here. I don't want the responsibility anymore. If she ends up pregnant, or worse, I don't want it to be on my watch. Maybe she'll listen to you."

I sighed. I didn't tell my aunt that I might not be able to help much. If the adults around her couldn't get through to my sister, what made them think I could? Betty and I had a good relationship, but not the kind I had once had with Mago.

Finally, my cousin Lupe came, but there was still no sign of Betty. "She's probably over there, by the train station. That's where Chon lives."

"Who?"

"He's the guy Betty has been hanging out with," Lupe said. "But he's already married."

I gave Lupe money and sent her to the nearest food stand to buy us quesadillas. While we sat there and continued waiting, I wondered why both Betty and I had an unhealthy need to be loved and wanted by men. Since our parents rarely showed any tenderness toward us, we had to look outside of home to find it. No matter what anyone said about Betty, I wasn't going to judge her.

When Lupe returned, she wasn't alone.

"Look who I found," Lupe said.

Betty came over to hug me, and everything anyone had said about my little sister faded away as I held her in my arms. This was my Betty. When I first heard that my mother was going to have a baby in the U.S., I hated that baby. I was jealous of the little girl who had come to take my place as the youngest in the family. But when I met her, I thought she was the cutest little girl I had ever seen, with thick, curly black hair and the longest eyelashes. When my mother ran away with a wrestler, leaving us behind—including her American baby—I realized that Betty was like me, nothing special to our mother and just as easy to abandon. I had tried to protect her like Mago had protected me.

But once Mago, Carlos, and I had taken off to the U.S. with our father, and we were forced to leave Betty behind, we drifted apart once again. Through the years, even when Betty ended up in L.A. with our mother, we hardly saw her. We tried to bring her to our father's house on some weekends, but the visits were brief and infrequent. Mago and I had a wonderful bond that did not include Betty. The distance had kept her on the periphery of our sisterhood.

It wasn't until Mago left me to start her own life and make a home for herself that I understood what it was like to have no one, just the way Betty had felt for many years.

This was why I had come to Mexico. It wasn't because I thought I could help her, but because I knew what it was like to be alone.

"I'm here," I said holding her even tighter. "I'm here."

Later that night, Betty and I shared the bed that had once belonged to our parents. My uncle, Tío Crece, slept on a hammock hanging from the rafters and my grandmother slept on her bed near the front door. Between the snoring of my uncle and grandmother, the barking of the dogs outside, and the chirping of crickets, it was hard to fall asleep. Not that I was trying very hard. Betty and I had too much to share.

"I didn't want to be in L.A. anyway," Betty said to me after I told her how sorry I was that my mother had sent her away. "Here, at least, I can get away from her. From *them*."

She meant our stepfather, of course. Even though we had lived apart, in a way our lives hadn't been much different. Living with my father, Mago, Carlos, and I had suffered from my stepmother's indifference. Mila had kept us at arm's length and didn't want much to do with us. She never yelled at us or hit us, but that didn't mean we didn't suffer because of her. Whatever complaints she had, she would give them to our father, who would barge out of the bedroom with belt in hand to give us a whipping. Most of the time we didn't even know what we were being punished for, since Mila never told us directly how we had displeased her.

Rey, our stepfather, was the opposite of Mila. He was quick to beat Betty and yell at her, and he didn't have to go through my mother to show or act on his disapproval. Though we had both grown up in households where beatings and verbal insults were the norm, I had received them only from our father, whereas Betty got them from both our mother and stepfather.

"I'm sorry, Betty," I said. And I meant I was sorry about everything, how immigration and separation had taken a toll on all of us, how even though our parents had emigrated from this very city to go to the U.S. to build us a house, they ended up destroying our home.

As if reading my thoughts, Betty turned to me and said, "Do you think things would have been different if they had never left? Do you think we would all be together as a family?"

The silver moonlight streamed through the gaps in the wall made of bamboo sticks tied together with rope and wire. Her moonlit eyes looked at me with so much hope and innocence, I knew she wanted me to paint a different picture—a different reality—than the one we were living. But there was no point in what-ifs. There was no point in wishing our family's past away.

"There's nothing we can do to change it, Betty. But you know what I want? I want to one day look back and say that it was worth it. All the pain, all the heartache."

"That's why you're going to college?"

"Yes," I said. "We've already paid a high price for the opportunity. We might as well take advantage of it. We have it in our power to make our future better than our past, Betty, even though at times it doesn't feel like we can ever escape it."

Betty didn't say anything. She turned her back to me and faced the wall. "I don't want to go back there," she said before she fell asleep. "I hope you aren't here to take me back to her."

8

Reyna and Betty washing clothes

I N MEXICO, the Christmas season had been my favorite time of the year because of the celebrations leading up to Christmas Day known as Las Posadas. All the kids received a goodie bag each night at the posada, one filled with candy, a tangerine, a jicama, sugarcane, and freshly roasted peanuts. It was one of those rare times in my childhood when I went to bed with a full belly for nine days straight. This year, I had arrived in Mexico in the middle of Las Posadas, so every night I went to the posada hosted by the church in my neighborhood. With candles in hand, my cousins and Betty would follow the procession making its way from house to house, reenacting the journey that Mary and Joseph had taken as they sought shelter. I walked through the streets of my old colonia and

remembered myself as a child, burning my hands with the candle wax or singeing the hair of the person in front of me.

I felt like a child again as we ran back to the house that night, emptied our goodie bags on the table, and swapped candy and fruit. Then Las Posadas were over, Christmas was over, and it was almost time for me to return to Santa Cruz. I still didn't know what to do about Betty. All I knew was that she didn't want to go back to my mother's, and I wasn't going to force her. She would only return to more physical and emotional abuse. But she couldn't stay in Iguala either. This place had nothing to offer her.

I wished I could do more for her beyond our daily chats and our walks around the neighborhood and our trips to the pool at La Quinta Castrejón, the fancy local country club. To Betty and me, going to the pool was a triumph of sorts—as little girls we had only been able to dream of swimming there since our family would never have been able to afford it. Now I could afford to go with my sister every day, or twice a day if we so desired. The admission price per person was two U.S. dollars. But in a city where people made less than five dollars a day, that was a fortune. The bitter irony was that absolutely no one from the neighborhood could afford a day of fun at the local swimming pool.

I wanted to help my sister as much as I wanted to help the people who lived here, but I didn't know how. I was ready to return to Santa Cruz, the place I longed for more and more. The poverty in Iguala was a burden I was tired of carrying. The guilt, the helplessness, the anger that bubbled up at seeing my family living in these circumstances became too much, and I was desperate to leave—to go back to my little paradise and not have to think about this misery anymore. I wanted to go back to UCSC and bury my head in my literature books and read about exotic lands that had nothing to do with my family's reality. I wanted to read about someone else's struggles and misery. Not my own. Not my people's. But how could I forget? By forgetting Iguala, I would be abandoning those I left behind.

⬭

I had been putting off visiting my father's mother, Abuela Evila, but two days before my departure, I knew the time had come for me to go. Abuelita Chinta asked me about Abuela Evila, and I knew she disapproved that I didn't want to go see my own grandmother.

"You might never see her again," she said. "I heard her health is not very good."

Abuelita Chinta was so kind and loving, I couldn't tell her how for all these years I had held on to my resentment toward my paternal grandmother with fierce stubbornness, often revisiting my memories of living at her house and feeling anew the pain and sorrow of my miserable childhood. To Abuelita Chinta—to my Mexican culture—it was unacceptable to question your elders, to criticize them for their faults. We had to honor and respect them no matter their shortcomings, abuses, or failures.

But now that I was here, I told myself, I might as well try to get answers from her, or at the very least, an apology.

I took a combi—a public minibus—to Abuela Evila's neighborhood, La Guadalupe, which was close to the mountains. When I got to her house, I looked over the rock wall encircling the property and scanned the backyard, my eyes taking in the plum, guava, and guamúchil trees my siblings and I had once loved to climb. Here in my grandmother's backyard, Mago, Carlos, and I had learned how to survive. My grandmother had fed us as little as she could, enough to keep us alive but never enough for us to feel satisfied. After a meager lunch, our stomachs would still be rumbling from hunger, and we would come to the backyard to scavenge for food. Beans and tortillas don't fill you up if that's what you eat day after day after day. Soon, we discovered that the leaves of the plum tree were tasty if we sprinkled them with salt. They were really sour though and made our eyes squint while we chewed. Another day we discovered that the plum saplings had thick bulbous roots that were crunchy and starchy, like jicama. So we dug up the saplings clinging to the soil and ate them.

When fruits were in season, it was easier to find treasures. We climbed up the guava tree and then munched on the pink flesh of its guayabas, or we plucked ripe red plums and ate them while licking the juice that ran down our hands. When there was nothing else to be had, there were always the lemons, which we could sprinkle with salt and chili powder, or we would eat the mint leaves growing wild around the water tank. We would then have minty breath as well as a full belly.

Abuela Evila didn't know we had learned to feed ourselves from her yard. Whenever we got in trouble, she would send us off to the back for punishment and tell us to stay out of her way or so help her God, she was going to beat the hell out of us. And we would run to the backyard, laughing all the way.

One day, as we were finishing our chores, we heard someone calling our names from the front gate. It was our uncle, Tío Mario, my mother's youngest brother.

"What are you doing here, Tío?" we said as we rushed to the gate. He said he had come to spend a few days with Abuelita Chinta and decided to come see us.

Abuela Evila came out of the kitchen and told him to leave. "I don't want Juana's no-good family at my house," she said. It hurt me to hear her insult my mother's family.

"Can I at least give them the ice cream I brought for them?" he asked, but my grandmother refused to let him near us and threatened to send for my grandfather and his friends if he didn't go. We were sad to see Tío Mario walk away and sadder still to see him take away the ice cream he'd brought us. I couldn't remember the last time I'd had any.

"Get out of my sight before I grab a belt and spank all of you for inviting him over," Abuela Evila said.

We didn't waste our breath telling her we had done no such

thing. We rushed to the backyard to pretend we were explorers and dig up roots, climb trees, trying to forget my uncle and his present. But no matter how hard we tried, we couldn't be explorers. We were simply three hungry kids, and all we could think of was that bucket of ice cream that had come within our reach.

"Pssst. Mago. Carlos. Pssst. Over here." Tío Mario was standing on the other side of the corral. We jumped off the branches and rushed to where he was hiding.

"Hurry and eat this before it melts," he said, handing us the ice cream. "Go on. I'll come back again another day to see you. Keep an eye out for me when you're up there climbing trees."

He ruffled our hair and left us to eat our ice cream, but just as we were about to eat it, Abuela Evila snuck up from behind us. She picked up a branch off the ground and beat us with it. "This is for disobeying me," she said. "Give that to me." Mago reluctantly gave her the bucket. "Now you will sit on the ground and learn never to disobey me again."

Because we didn't want another beating, we did as we were told. Abuela Evila put the ice cream a few feet away from us and forbade us to touch it. We sat there for a long time, watching the ice cream melt under the hot sun. When it was completely melted, my grandmother finally left and went back to her chores. We looked at one another, not knowing what to do.

Then Mago said, "Forget her, I'm still going to eat it anyway."

We plunged our hands into the golden goo and started scooping it up with our cupped hands, and soon there was nothing left of our magic feast but our sticky hands and our bellies full of vanilla warmth.

With the taste of vanilla in my mouth, I stood before my father's dream house, which was built twenty-five feet from my grandmother's adobe house.

It was this little three-room house that had started it all.

My father had gone to the U.S. to pursue his dream of building us a real house made of brick and concrete, a far cry from the shack in which I was born. That dream somewhat came true—it took him eight years, but he managed to have this house built. Then, my siblings and I left for the U.S. to live with him and never lived in the house. Not long after, my father's sister, Tía Emperatriz, had the deed of my grandmother's property transferred to her name and stole the house from him.

I stood in the shadow of my father's house and thought of how much this house had cost us—spending our childhood without our parents so that they could earn the money to build it. And all for what? So that my aunt, her husband, and daughter could now enjoy it? This house was built on the foundation of my family's pain and loss. I hated it. My aunt could keep it for all I cared.

I knocked on my grandmother's door, and Tía Emperatriz opened it. When I was a child, she had seemed so tall. Now I was at eye level with her, and I realized that my days of looking up to her were over. Before, her thin figure had looked elegant in pencil skirts with a slit in the back. Now she was fat, and the stylish skirt had been replaced with a shapeless flowery dress. When we had lived here, my aunt had been the only nice person in this household, but when she stole my father's house, our relationship with her was ruined. Seeing her now I felt joy and anger all at once. I loved her and hated her at the same time.

"How's life in El Otro Lado?" she asked as she ushered me in.

"Fine," I said.

She waited for me to say more. In her eyes I could see the desire often seen in the people around here—they want to know everything about the mysterious land across the border. They want to know if it's truly as close to paradise as you can possibly get. But I wasn't about to satisfy her curiosity, so I said nothing. Instead, I turned around and headed to the living room.

Abuela Evila was eighty-six years old, but she was the size of an eight-year-old child. Osteoporosis had shrunk her. She was a wisp of a woman, completely unrecognizable from the grandmother in my nightmares. The grandmother that I had feared as a child, the one who bullied us and beat us, the one who made us feel unwanted and unloved, had been turned into a helpless old woman who was shriveling before my very eyes.

"Abuela, it's Reyna," I said as I approached her. But she sat there in the living room, sinking into the couch, looking at me as if she couldn't see me, as if I weren't there. She looked past me, at something behind me that only she could see.

"Abuela, don't you know me?" I asked. Her eyes fell on me and she smiled in a way she had never done before. Was she really this happy to see me?

"Vámonos," she said in a weak, raspy voice, so different from the sharp, loud voice I remembered. "It's late. Apá is waiting for his lunch. Come on, where's the donkey?"

"What donkey?" I asked.

"She thinks you're her sister," my aunt said from behind me.

"What do you mean?"

"She's become a child again, tu abuela. She thinks everyone around her is her sister, or mother, or father. We don't exist to her anymore." My aunt sighed and left the room.

"Vámonos," my grandmother said again. "Apá is waiting."

I sat there, swimming in my anger and disappointment. All these years longing for an apology from this woman and this is all I would get? She didn't deserve to end life like this—free from all the hurt and pain she had caused. Memory loss for her was a blessing, one that she didn't deserve.

"Come now," she said. "Let's go."

But I allowed my imagination to take me to my grandmother's childhood, and I could see her and her sister getting on the donkey, making their way to the sugarcane fields with lunch for their father. What would they have brought him? Handmade tortillas with beans, maybe chicharrón or a chunk of cheese. Or maybe, if money had been good, a chicken thigh or a pork chop. Meat here was a luxury.

I shook my head and tried to erase the image of my grandmother as a young girl. I wanted to hold on to my anger. I wanted her to come back to the present so I could ask her why she'd been so cruel to me and my siblings. I wanted her to be here and to *see* me so I could tell her about Santa Cruz, not the way I had told Abuelita Chinta but in a different way—to punish her. *I have found my paradise. I am finally happy, despite what you did. I have found a beautiful home that you will never see, even when you die. Because those kinds of places are not for the wicked, even in the afterlife.*

Then my grandmother started plucking at her left arm. Slowly, the fingers of her right hand would come down and pinch the wrinkled skin of her left arm as if removing a piece of lint.

"Abuela, what are you doing?" I asked. I turned to see if Tía Emperatriz was back, but she wasn't. No one was in the room except me and this skeleton of a woman.

"The maggots," she said, pinching her arm. "The maggots are eating me."

"What maggots?" I asked. I looked at her arm, where she kept pinching, but there was nothing there but wrinkled, saggy skin. Did she think she was already dead and buried, decomposing and returning to the soil?

"The maggots are eating me," she said again.

I jumped to my feet and ran out of the room, my heart pounding in my chest. I looked for my aunt and found her in the patio.

"I'm leaving," I said. And then, because I couldn't hold it inside of me I said, "She thinks maggots are eating her already. She thinks she's dead!"

My aunt laughed. "She doesn't think she's dead. I told you, she thinks she's a child again."

Seeing my perplexed look, she told me the story of a little girl who was born during the Mexican Revolution, who struggled to survive even though everyone around her was dying. Over a million people died, but she had lived. "When she was a little girl, your grandmother got measles," my aunt said. "The sores festered and her parents didn't have money for the doctor. Your grandmother had to pull maggots out of the open sores."

I said goodbye to my aunt and left. I didn't say goodbye to my grandmother because there was no point. She was already gone. I decided to think instead about that little girl who had to pull maggots out of her own flesh and, despite all odds, had found the will to live.

I didn't know that would be the last time I'd see my grandmother alive. In three months she would leave this world and join the father she had so longed for. The legacy that she would leave me was the realization that there *was* something I had inherited from her. For years now, I had been plucking at the invisible sores in my heart. The wounds of my childhood had festered and would not heal.

But, just like my grandmother, I had found the strength to survive.

Abuela Evila and Reyna

9

Abuelita Chinta and Reyna

THE NEXT DAY, my last in Iguala, as Abuelita Chinta and I were shopping by el zócalo, we passed by the beautiful Parroquia de San Francisco de Asís, which was built in 1850. Every year, the church put on a nine-day pilgrimage around Iguala, with stops in small towns like Pueblo Viejo, Huixtac, Paintla, Taxco el Viejo, El Naranjo. Now that she was seventy-five, my grandmother no longer participated in the pilgrimage, but she still went to church almost every day.

"We should go in and pray for your safe trip back," Abuelita Chinta said. So I followed my grandmother inside the church, but I didn't have the courage to tell her I wasn't much of a Catholic anymore. Abuelita Chinta didn't know I had lost my religion, that La Virgen de Guadalupe and the saints hadn't crossed the border with me to El Otro Lado.

What would she say if I told her that I rejected any religion that made me feel devalued as a woman, or which pressed upon me the belief that being poor was a good thing, or that all the misery in my life was God's will and I should shut up and not complain?

Yet being in my grandmother's presence reminded me that I had once wanted to believe there was a God watching over me, protecting me, even though for most of my life I hadn't felt protected at all.

As we knelt at one of the pews, I thought about the first time I went on a pilgrimage with my grandmother. At eight years old, I was the youngest in a group of a hundred. Most of the pilgrims were old ladies like my grandmother, but there were also some men, a handful of teenagers, and the three of us: me at eight; Carlos, ten; and Mago, twelve. In the early hours of the morning, we gathered in the courtyard of the church just as the sky was turning pink and yellow, like the flowers of a plumeria. Everyone here had come for one of two reasons—to have their prayers answered or to atone for a sin. Abuelita Chinta went on the pilgrimage every year to ask God to take away Tío Crece's illness. My uncle suffered from what I now suspect was schizophrenia. In my psychology class at PCC, I gained a different understanding of my uncle's erratic and violent behavior, but according to my family in Mexico, my uncle suffered from witchcraft. When he turned eighteen, a woman had given him a love potion made from menstrual blood and jimson weed, but instead of falling in love with her, he went crazy.

Regardless of what he had, my grandmother had prayed to God to make my uncle well again. But after many pilgrimages, her prayers had still not been answered. Would God answer my prayer to have my mother back?

We lined up in the courtyard of the church, and at sunrise, the procession exited the black metal gates. We were handed an orange, and Abuelita Chinta told us to put it in our bag for later. We carried a water gourd on a strap over our shoulders, and a straw hat hung from each of our necks. This land was known for its heat, and we would be walking for nine days straight under the scorching Guerrero sun. The women—including Mago and me—wore long skirts down to our ankles. She and I wore leather sandals, but Carlos had a pair of old tennis shoes given to him by the people who brought donations to our neighborhood after the floods. He was spared the blisters Mago and I got from our huaraches.

We walked in a double line toward the highway, then past the sugarcane fields, the mango groves, and the cemetery. By the time we got to the outskirts and were making our way to Pueblo Viejo, I was already out of breath and my feet hurt. Once we crossed the last neighborhood, we veered left by a dairy farm and walked along the canal into the fields, leaving the city behind. I didn't know how I would last for nine days walking from town to town. But if I wanted my mother back, I knew I had to endure.

The church leaders led us in prayer and songs.

Desde el cielo una hermosa mañana,
La Guadalupana, La Guadalupana, La Guadalupana
Bajó al Tepeyac.

Flocks of birds flew above us. Wildflowers grew along the trail on which we walked. I wanted to pick flowers, sit under the shade of a guamúchil tree and take a nap, but we were hours from our destination, and Abuelita Chinta said we wouldn't be taking a break yet.

"Focus on your prayers, mi niña," Abuelita Chinta said as she held my hand. So I thought about Mami and the wrestler she had run off with to Acapulco, and I prayed for her to realize she should love her children more than any man that came into her life, that it wasn't our fault Papi left her for another woman, and she shouldn't punish us for his betrayal. I knew I should also pray for Papi to return, but I thought that if I prayed for too many things, God might not listen. Mago said she was coming to the pilgrimage for Papi. She said she didn't care whether or not Mami returned, but she still hadn't given up on our father. Carlos said he didn't care which one of our parents came back as long as one of them did, so that we could finally have a home. I wanted him to pray for Mami. I wanted both of them to pray for Mami because I was afraid my little prayer wouldn't be enough.

When my stomach started rumbling, and we still had another hour to walk before we rested, Abuelita Chinta told us to eat our oranges. Mago, Carlos, and I devoured ours in a minute, and we were still hungry. The old lady in front of us turned around and handed me her orange.

"Toma, tortolita," she said.

I reached for it and said thank you to the old lady.

"She called me sparrow," I said to Abuelita Chinta.

My grandmother smiled. "That's because you're the youngest here, a little sparrow among us old crows."

The old lady laughed with my grandmother. She looked at me and said, "And why is the tortolita coming along on this journey?"

"Because I want my mami back," I said.

The old lady sighed. "Then I will dedicate my prayers to you. Little sparrows need their mothers, at least until they learn to fly."

When we arrived at the first town, the procession headed straight to the church. By this point I was too exhausted to continue walking, and Abuelita Chinta practically had to drag me along. My prayer, for the past hour, had been for the day to be over.

At the gate, all the pilgrims knelt on the ground and prepared to make the thirty-foot journey from the gate to the church on their knees. Abuelita Chinta said that children didn't have to go down on their knees, that we could walk on our feet.

"Let's not take any chances. What if God thinks we're cheating?" Mago said to us.

"But it hurts," I said, wincing in pain as the pebbles on the dirt path dug into my knees.

"Do you or do you not want our parents back?" Mago said. Of the three of us, Mago had always been better at overcoming her pain. So Carlos and I followed her lead and remained on our knees. With one knee in front of the other, with each pebble digging into my flesh, I thought of my mother, of the home I wanted to have, and I pushed away the pain. *Please God, bring her back to me.*

Now, thirteen years later, as I sat in the Parroquia de San Francisco de Asís with my grandmother and bowed my head before Jesus, I realized that my prayers had never been answered. My mother hadn't returned to me, at least not in the way I had prayed for all those years ago. Emotionally, she was still so far from me, from us all. She had become the kind of mother I would no longer pray for. She was a mother whose own child was terrified of living with her.

I didn't blame Betty for not wanting to go back. After all the abuse she had endured at my mother's house, how could I make her? But how could I let her stay here? Iguala was a place where dreams died.

Betty needed a home as much as I did. What if I could provide that home for her? For us? *Little sparrows need their mothers, at least until they learn to fly*, the old lady had said. I could be the mother Betty needed, and I wouldn't be so lonely anymore if I had her with me.

As my grandmother and I walked out of the church, back into the blinding light of that December day, I finally knew what I had to do.

10

Reyna and Betty, December 1996

I USED PART OF my tuition money to buy Betty a plane ticket to California. She needed Santa Cruz as much as I did, and she willingly followed me north to live in the place I told her could help her heal, allow her to dream, and be the kind of home we'd always wanted to have. "One day," I said to her, "we can both be college graduates, accomplished career women capable of taking care of our own needs and fulfilling our own desires."

"I could start over again," she said. "I could stop being Betty, the troublemaker, and become Elizabeth—someone different from the girl I used to be."

"You'll always be my Betty," I said. "But using your full name does make you sound sophisticated. Elizabeth sounds elegant and mature."

She giggled at that. My mother had named her Elizabeth to make sure everyone knew that her youngest daughter had been born in the U.S., with all the rights and privileges of an American citizen. Perhaps by becoming Elizabeth, my little sister could finally honor the good fortune she had had by being born on the "right" side of the border.

I smuggled her into my apartment without permission from the Campus Housing Office. I gave my roommates no warning, but no one said she couldn't stay. I was afraid of getting kicked off campus for having my little sister with me, but it was a risk I was willing to take.

I enrolled her at Santa Cruz High School as a tenth grader and took full responsibility for her. When her old school faxed over her transcripts, and I saw the row of fails scrolling down the sheet of paper, I wondered what I was getting myself into. I was a twenty-one-year-old university student, struggling to figure things out in my own life, and now I was taking in this teenage girl who took no pride in her grades and was rebellious to the core. But Diana had taken me in when I had most needed her, so what kind of person would I be if I didn't take in my own sister and help her reinvent herself?

When the new year arrived, Betty started high school, and I started my second quarter at UCSC. I dropped her off at the bus stop on campus and then headed to my advanced fiction class.

To my disappointment, I was the only Latina in the class.

My visit to Mexico, though painful, had once again reinforced my need to write about the place of my birth. It was by writing about the people I knew, describing their plight, that I could honor their difficult experiences and keep them in my heart and mind. I had to remember each of them, write their stories, share their pain, so that they knew they weren't alone. The ten days I spent in Iguala had inspired me to write that story collection I claimed I was writing to get the grant from Kresge. I had gotten the funding, gone on my trip, and though the money was given to me with no strings attached, I felt an obligation to follow through on what I had said I would do.

The stories were all set in my hometown, so every assignment I turned in to my fiction teacher was about a world—an experience—neither she nor my classmates knew anything about.

"You have a wild imagination," my teacher said of my story about a flood that devastated the whole neighborhood, forcing the people to spend a week on their roofs, navigating makeshift canoes to retrieve the floating bodies of their dogs, cats, and chickens.

"Your work is over-the-top and overwritten," my teacher said of my story about a young girl who was forced to go to school barefoot because her family was too poor to buy her shoes. And just like I had been, she was physically abused by her teacher for being left-handed.

"Your work is too flowery and full of clichés," my teacher said of my story about a young mother who falls into the community well where she was getting water for the wash, leaving her two children to be raised by their abusive, alcoholic father.

But when it came to the work of white students—who wrote stories about drinking, doing drugs, going to parties, and having sex—the teacher praised them as if they had just written a masterpiece worthy of a Pulitzer.

There were times when I wanted to run out of my classroom and never come back. *What am I doing here?* I thought. *Who do I think I am to even consider that my stories are worth telling?*

I thought of my fifth grade teacher who had rejected my story because it was in Spanish, and by doing so had also rejected who I was. Now I was experiencing the same disapproval. The experiences I put on the page were so foreign to everyone in my class, I might as well have written them in another language.

I could choose to leave. I could choose to drop out of the creative writing program, to be silenced. I could choose to believe that my stories didn't matter.

Or I could fight.

Hadn't my own grandmother survived the Mexican Revolution?

If I allowed rejection to defeat me, my dreams would fester. I would be eaten by maggots. How could I allow that to happen?

When I first met Edwin, he had given me a copy of Ayn Rand's *The Fountainhead*. Regardless of the author's controversial political views, I loved her book and appreciated the lesson *The Fountainhead* had taught me. The story was about a young architect, Howard Roark, who constantly had to fight for his vision of the buildings that he wanted to design; not replicas of what had come before, but his own original work. He had to fight for his designs because almost no one around him understood them. People were always telling him what he should build, how he should create—by copying the old masters and doing the same thing as everyone else. He went up against society and clung to his unique vision, his art, his voice.

In *The Fountainhead* I came upon a word I had never heard before—"impervious." When I looked it up in the dictionary I knew that it was a word I wanted to be defined by. I wanted to be unaffected by the scarcity of love around me, unaffected by the lack of support I encountered with my family, and now at UCSC, unaffected by the ignorant remarks of people who had no clue whatsoever about my reality, my truth, or my world. I had to fight for the right to create the kinds of stories I wanted to write.

So when my teacher handed me back my latest story, looking as if it were bleeding from the red ink of her criticism, I put it in my backpack and said, "I'll see you next week, then." I rushed into the grove of redwood trees to heal, to be renewed by the scent of hope.

Fortunately, that quarter I also enrolled in Chicano literature, and my teacher, a Chicana named Marta Navarro, reminded me of Diana—she was kind and generous and seemed to care genuinely what happened to her students inside and outside of class. Once, I mentioned to Marta the experiences I was having in my creative writing class. "I feel that no one gets my stories."

Reyna and Marta

"Why don't you let me take a look?" she said. The next time I visited her in her office, I brought her one of my stories. When she finished reading it, she said, "Reyna, your writing reminds me of Juan Rulfo."

"Who?" I asked.

Juan Rulfo, as it turned out, was one of the finest Mexican writers of his generation. Marta gave me a Spanish copy of *The Burning Plain and Other Stories* and *Pedro Páramo*. "Rulfo writes about nature as something beautiful and powerful, but also as a menace, something that destroys," Marta said. "The towns he writes about are poor and forsaken, populated by people who are lonely and destitute. He writes about men who leave and don't return, floods that devastate neighborhoods. These are things you write about, too, Reyna. It isn't melodrama. It's your truth."

I went home that day and read the books, and when I finished, I felt deeply honored that Marta had compared my work to that of this great writer who had captured, so eloquently, the harsh reality of being poor in Mexico.

"You write like Tomás Rivera," Marta said to me another time. She handed me a copy of *And the Earth Did Not Devour Him* and I went home to read the book about migrant workers in the U.S. living an oppressive life of poverty and limited opportunities. With even more conviction, I continued writing, because one day I hoped to write like those incredible authors that Marta so admired, and who were now influencing my own writing with their simple and elegant prose.

Thanks to Marta, I remained confident in my work and managed to become impervious to the criticism of my creative writing teacher and peers.

As the weeks passed, Betty and I fell into a daily routine. We went to our classes, then in the afternoon we were back in our apartment, cooking dinner, going for afternoon walks on campus and planning our future, taking the bus to explore downtown Santa Cruz. We would spend the evenings doing homework.

When I called my mother, I would say with pride, "She's doing great. We're both happy."

"Nothing to worry about," I proudly reported to Mago. "I'm looking out for her."

When I got her first report card, the worry that had been sitting in my stomach like a rock finally disappeared.

"I'm so proud of you," I said. Compared to all the previous fails, this report card was an enormous accomplishment. I would say to her the very words I had longed to hear from my father: "You're doing great!"

For the first time, things were going smoothly for me, too. I was getting the hang of being a university student, I had my tutoring job on campus that gave me enough extra cash to meet our basic needs, and I was making progress on my collection of stories. We both had a safe and stable home where there were no abusive parents, no one to yell at us or demean us, no one to make us feel like failures. I felt proud of being able to provide that kind of home for my little sister and myself. The best thing I had ever done, I thought, was to come to Santa Cruz and bring Betty along as well.

One day, as we were walking to our classes, Carolyn asked me about my summer plans. I had just learned that by the end of the spring quarter all students had to vacate their rooms. Most would be going home for the summer. That wasn't an option for Betty and me. I didn't know what I was going to do, where we were going to end up. I would need to find a place to sublet. I told Carolyn I didn't understand why we had to move off campus during the summer.

"What about those of us who have nowhere to go?"

"They do it every year," she said. "That's the time when the dorms get repaired. You wouldn't believe how destructive college students can be!"

I thought about my room at Kresge East. It was a room that I loved, that Betty and I kept clean and tidy. I didn't understand why Carolyn said college students were destructive.

"And speaking of," she said, "the Kresge Maintenance Department is hiring students for the summer, if you're interested."

"To do what?"

"For the paint crew. I've worked there every summer. We clean and paint the dorms. Get them ready for the new school year. Do you want me to help you get a job?"

If I had a job, that meant I would be able to support myself and Betty through the summer. "Yes!" I said. "That would be amazing. Thank you."

Later that day, when I picked up my mail, there was a letter from Santa Cruz High waiting for me in my box. I didn't know why—maybe it was intuition—but my stomach started hurting as I picked it up and opened it. Standing there in the mailroom, I felt as if I had just been thrown into the icy waters of Monterey Bay.

Betty was back to her old habits again. She was ditching her classes.

"All I want is for you to do well in school, don't you understand?" I said to Betty when she came home. "That's all I ask of you. To do your best. Your future depends on it, don't you see?" I sounded just like my father when he was sober; for one second, I wished he was here with me. But whenever he had said those words to me, I had listened attentively, hung on his every word. Betty, on the other hand, was completely tuning me out. Who knew what she had done to Elizabeth, because the girl staring back at me was the same rebellious, insolent teenager my mother had sent to Mexico.

"What else do you want?" I asked when she didn't say anything but just glared at me. "I'm giving you the home our mother never gave you. And all I ask of you is to be responsible and focus on your studies."

"Fine, fine, I'll try harder," she said. "Lay off me, okay? Do you think it's easy for me, being here in this new place, trying to make new friends, to fit in with all those white kids at my school who always know the right answer?"

"No, I don't think it's easy, but don't make it harder than it needs to be, Betty. For both our sakes."

The letters continued to arrive. Letters telling me that Betty had missed a class or two. "What do you do? Where do you go?"

"Nowhere," she said, and shrugged.

Then another letter arrived, but this one was from the Campus Housing Office. I was being asked to move out of my apartment or give my sister up. Someone had told on me. I eyed my three roommates with suspicion—including Carolyn, though so far she had been nothing but kind—and wondered who had betrayed me.

"Mándamela," my mother said to me when I told her the news of my impending eviction. I knew I had to move out for the summer. I had already made plans for the temporary move off campus, and, thanks to Carolyn, had secured a summer job. Now I would have to move out by the end of the month if I wanted to keep Betty. And for as long as I kept her, that meant I couldn't return to live on campus, my little paradise.

"Send her to me," my mother repeated.

When I gave Betty the news, her eyes filled with fear. "Don't send me back to her," she said. "I don't want to go back there." She held on to me and cried, and I cried, too. "Don't send me away! I'll stop ditching. I'll do what you say, Reyna."

For days, I struggled with my decision. I couldn't concentrate in class, and for once I didn't care that my teacher and the students ripped apart my stories. My heart was being ripped apart as it was. On one hand, there was a part of me that understood I had taken on more than I could handle. But how could I give up on Betty now? If I kept her, though, I would have to give up my campus apartment. I would be a commuter. No more evening walks in the forest. I wouldn't be able to participate in as many school activities or think of the campus as a true home. I would be a visitor.

"What are you going to do?" Betty asked when she got back from school one afternoon. Her eyes were red and swollen. She looked so scared of being sent back to our mother. It pained me to see her fear. How much abuse had this little girl dealt with from our mother and stepfather?

Now she was biting the hand that fed her, unable to distinguish the difference between the one who loved her and the one who had mistreated her. I felt an overwhelming desire for her to trust me. I wanted her to know that she mattered to me, that she wasn't alone. And the truth was, I didn't want to be alone either.

She sat on the bed next to me and said, "It's hard, Reyna."

"What's hard? Help me understand."

Betty looked down at the floor. "It isn't that easy to start somewhere new with the old you still inside you."

I sighed and looked out the window. It was my favorite view—a grove of redwood trees was the first thing I had seen every morning in the five months I had been here.

"We're moving out," I said, hugging her close to me. "I'll find us a room to rent in town."

11

Reyna at Monterey Bay

WE MOVED INTO the Westcliff Apartments, a block away from Monterey Bay, though we couldn't see it from the apartment unless we stretched far enough over the balcony to catch a sliver of blue. Our new roommate was named Robert and he was a very nice man, though it was incredibly awkward to share an apartment with a man. I didn't have much of a choice. March was not a good month to try to find off-campus housing since everything had been taken in the fall. Even though Robert gave us a good deal on the room, the location and the amenities, such as a pool, made the rent a challenge.

Since I didn't have a car, Betty and I had to walk the fifteen minutes to the nearest bus stop, on Bay Street, and from there she continued on foot because now the high school was closer to her. For me, it was a new experience to have to take the bus to campus. When the bus passed by Kresge East, I felt a stab of pain at the loss of my former apartment. I hoped that my sacrifice would be worth something.

But another letter from the high school arrived and, finally, Betty confessed the truth. "I have a boyfriend."

My instinct was to tell her no, absolutely no boyfriends allowed. But I remembered my father, and what a tyrant he had been about boyfriends. Mago and I had to sneak around to have them, and I knew that if I forbade Betty a love life, she would find a way to have one anyway. But I remembered that the last time she'd had a boyfriend in L.A., we had ended up at the prenatal clinic.

"I'll let you have a boyfriend if you promise to do better in school. And no more ditching to be alone with him. Bring him here when I'm home. He can visit you here where I can see you. Promise me you'll be responsible."

"I will," she said.

Soon, Omar started showing up at our apartment after school and on the weekends. He seemed nice enough. What I especially liked about him was that he always showed up with his little sister and brother in tow. He took care of them after school while his mom picked mushrooms at a farm in Pescadero. I liked that he was responsible and was helping his mother. Like me, he was looking out for his younger siblings. I felt relieved that Betty had found a boyfriend who was a good son and brother.

I finally felt that I could relax and focus on my studies and my writing. Thanks to Marta, I had discovered a writer's group of Latina students at UCSC, who published a literary journal twice a year called *Las Girlfriends*. "You should submit your work, join this group," Marta had said. I was shocked to hear there were aspiring Latina writers on campus though I hadn't seen them in my writing classes. Perhaps they'd decided to stay away from the program. I submitted a few stories, and it was through *Las Girlfriends* that I had the opportunity to publish my work and present it in public readings. Best of all, it was wonderfully empowering to be onstage with other Latina artists.

Things were looking up for me at school, and Betty seemed to be more focused on hers. Though we couldn't walk around campus anymore like we used to, we walked on Westcliff Drive, right along the bay. We looked at the cypress and pine trees which were leaning against the wind, beautiful in their struggle for survival, clinging to the soil with fierce determination. A few of them had been uprooted and lay on the ground, their intricate root system exposed for all to see. Even in their death, they were still beautiful to me. Standing under the lighthouse, Betty and I would watch the surfers and wish we had the courage to try. Betty didn't know how to swim. I had learned to swim two years before, when I took a class at PCC, and I was an okay swimmer but not strong enough to do battle with unpredictable ocean currents. In Mexico, I had almost drowned in the canal when I was three. My mother found me just in time and pulled me out of the water. My cousin Catalina didn't have the same luck. She drowned when she was five, during the rainy season, when she had slipped into the raging river. When her body was found, my uncle hung her up by her feet so that the river water would drain out of her. I had never been able to get that image out of my head—the bloated body of my cousin, water seeping out of her mouth and nostrils. I had been afraid of drowning ever since.

As much as I loved Monterey Bay, I rarely went in.

During our walks, Betty and I would wander around the Boardwalk even though it was off-season and the roller-coaster rides were still and silent, or we would meander through the streets during dinnertime. The magnificent houses on Westcliff Drive with their giant glass walls facing a sparkling Monterey Bay fascinated us.

"What kind of jobs do you think people have to be able to afford these awesome houses?" Betty asked. "Do you think we could ever have a house like these?"

"If we worked hard enough, maybe one day we could," I said, and I wondered, *How many words would I have to write to build my dream house?*

Through the large glass windows, we could see families sitting at the dining table sharing a meal, perhaps talking about their day or planning family vacations. Or they would be sitting together in the living room watching TV. Parents would be tucking their children in to sleep, reading them a book.

We wondered what it would be like to be part of those families and fantasized about walking into one of those big houses and being adopted by the family living there, being welcomed with open arms. We both wanted to have a beautiful place to come home to.

For now, we had our little apartment and each other, and at least for me, that was enough.

Then another letter arrived, and then another, and Betty confessed that she was ditching with Omar to go to his house while no one was home, and they were having unprotected sex. I was devastated. I remembered my aunt's words in Mexico. She had said she didn't want Betty to end up pregnant on her watch, and neither did I. What the hell would I do with a baby?

"Mándamela," my mother said again when I called her. "At least you've tried."

And failed, I wanted to say. I was so ashamed to realize that when I brought Betty to Santa Cruz, I had been both extremely arrogant and ignorant. I had wanted to prove to my mother that I could do a better job than her. In a way, I was beginning to understand why my mother had sent Betty away. If you can't keep someone from being self-destructive, maybe it's easier to send them where they can destroy themselves without you having to watch it happen.

I had thought I could save myself and my sister and give us both a home. Now I felt as if the two of us were drowning in a deep, vast ocean, and the truth was I no longer had the strength to save us both. So I had to let her go.

When Betty came home from school, I gave her the news. "I'm sending you back to her," I said, unable to look her in the eye. "I can't do this anymore."

I sank into the couch and didn't hear anything she said to me. She cried. She begged. But my mind was made up. I knew it was hard to let go of bad habits, but there had to come a point when enough was enough. For the first time, I understood that what I wanted for her—to do well in school, to go to college one day—wasn't what she wanted for herself. I could not give my dreams to her. She would have to find her own. She would have to find the ganas, the fierce desire that my father often said would drive us to become the people we knew we could be.

She didn't need to go to school the next day since I was putting her on the Greyhound bus to L.A. the day after, but she begged me to let her say goodbye to Omar.

"And come straight home," I said. "You need to pack."

I went to my own classes, only half listening to anything my teachers said, wallowing in the bitter realization that I had failed to save my sister from herself.

I came home to help her get her things ready, but Betty wasn't back yet. The hours went by and there was no sign of her. I called Mago to get her advice.

"You have to focus on what you need to do for yourself, Nena. Don't let her screw it up for you. When she shows up, just tell her to leave. Don't even let her into the apartment. Let her figure it out. She obviously wants to do what she wants to do. Let her see what it's like to be on her own."

Mago was always so drastic in her decisions. I hung up feeling more confused than ever. I sat in the living room and heard a helicopter above, then an ambulance rushed by. I went outside and saw people gathering on Westcliff Drive, near the rocks that plunged into the water. I ran over to see what was happening.

"Someone jumped," I heard people say. "They think it's suicide."

What if it was Betty? What if I had pushed her to kill herself? I stood there with the crowd, watching as the rescue team dove into the bay with their gear, trying to find the person. The helicopter circled above us; the lights of the siren atop the ambulance made everything red. As the sun set, I stood there watching the whole scene feeling as if I had stepped into a horror movie. I held on to the railing and felt my knees go weak.

I bent over the railing, my eyes scanning the water. The waves crashed against the rocks, and my eyes blurred with tears. I wanted to jump in and search for her, tell her I would keep her. Tell her that no matter what, I would never let her go and give up. *I made a mistake. Come back, to me! Please don't be dead.*

When it was too dark to see anything, the crowd dispersed and I pried my hands from the railing. They were calling off the search and would resume the next day. I walked back to my apartment, forcing my feet to take one step and then another. I returned to an empty apartment and sat in the living room, imagining my sister in the depths of the ocean, dead because of me. I cried myself to sleep, and when the door finally opened and Betty stood there, I was relieved. *She's alive!* And then, I was furious.

"Where the hell have you been?" I yelled, though what I wanted to say was that I was glad she was okay. But the fact that she was okay and had deliberately made me suffer like this angered me more than anything. It was well past 10:00 p.m.

"Hanging out with Omar and my friends," she said.

"While I've been sitting here all day, worrying about you? You're so damn ungrateful!" I said. An argument broke out, and she yelled

at me and I yelled at her. "I am not getting on that stupid bus, and you can't make me," Betty said. "I'm not going back to L.A.!"

The next thing I knew I was doing the very thing Mago had suggested. "Well, you can't stay here. No way. I've had enough of this. Go back to Omar and your friends if that's what matters more to you."

"Fine," she said. "I'm outta here."

And just like that, Betty walked out the apartment door and disappeared down the hallway. As I stood there in the empty hallway, I felt more alone than ever. Like Betty, all my life I had been on the receiving end of punishment, and it was the hardest thing I'd ever done to be the executioner, but in my rage, that was what I had become. I was no better than my parents.

Betty said she would never again return to our mother, and she kept her word. She moved in with Omar, and a few months later, at sixteen, she was pregnant. Though we lived in the same city, I hardly saw her. Her belly grew, and the guilt ate at me thinking that it was all my fault. I worried that she would drop out of school again. I felt lonely in Santa Cruz, just like I had when I first moved here, and I couldn't even take refuge in the campus as I once had. The redwoods had lost their power to heal me. They no longer smelled of hope, but failure. I began to doubt myself, wondering if there was a point anymore to what I was doing. Not only was Betty pregnant, but so was Mago and so was Carlos's second wife. There was a pregnancy epidemic happening in my family! I saw all those babies as obstacles to higher education because if my older siblings had dropped out of college—even when they were single and childless—pursuing higher education while supporting a family would prove a challenge too difficult to overcome.

Santa Cruz was small, and for that reason, I felt the distance between Betty and me even more strongly. Unlike L.A., where it's

so easy to disappear, here in Santa Cruz we were only a mile apart, but as the months went by without seeing each other, I felt our separation becoming insurmountable, and that realization tore me up inside.

What am I doing here? I wondered. I would go to my classes, half listen to what was said, and ask myself that question again and again.

12

ONE DAY WHILE walking to the market, I passed by a little shop that offered palm readings for ten dollars. It was a bit pricey, and I needed to shop for groceries, but my spirit was hungrier than my stomach so I went in and handed those precious ten dollars to the woman sitting behind a small round table, her eyes like Cleopatra's, smoky and mysterious.

"What would you like to know?" she said, as I sat on the chair across from her and gave her my hand. The room was decorated with cheap products from foreign lands to make it look exotic, the smell of the incense was overwhelming, and the purple cloth wrapped around her head made her look ridiculous, but I was desperate to believe.

"Is it worth it?" I asked.

She ran her fingers along my palm, her Cleopatra eyes studying its surface. My palm lines reminded me of the uprooted cypress trees lying on the ground along Westcliff Drive. I once read that 80 percent of what happens with a tree takes place beneath the soil. What if that were true for humans? What if by looking at the lines of our palms we could see what we keep hidden, even from ourselves? I shook my head. This woman couldn't predict the future any better than I could, and yet her words were all I had to cling to that day.

"What do you see? Is there a point to all this?"

She closed my fingers to form a fist, and I could no longer see my palm. She looked at me and said, "You will break the cycle. So yes, it is worth it."

She's a charlatan. Everything that came out of her mouth was pure speculation, I told myself, but when I stepped through the beaded curtain and back out into the light, I felt the gloom begin to lift.

I returned to my studies with determination, and under Marta's supervision, I finished the short-story collection I had been working on.

"Reyna, why don't you publish your collection?" Marta said as she handed me her edits for the last of my stories.

"How?" I had never heard that you could publish your own work.

"There are student grants you can apply for that are specifically for special projects," she said. "Check to see if the Literature Department, or Kresge College, can help."

I did as she suggested and applied for a grant to self-publish my collection of short stories, and was awarded $1,000 to pay for printing costs. For the cover of my book, I used a painting on parchment paper I had bought in Mexico from an indigenous artist selling his work on the street. I titled my collection, *Under the Guamúchil Tree.*

Guamúchil trees were common in my hometown. They lined the dirt road that led to my grandmother's house. When I was little, my siblings and I would grab a fifteen-foot bamboo stick, tie a metal hook to it, and walk around the neighborhood cutting down the reddish green pods of the guamúchil tree. We would fill a bucket or two with the fruit if we got there early and beat the competition, and would keep some to eat, but the rest Mago would take to the train station to sell.

I picked up the box of books from the printer, and the next day Marta threw a publication party for me. She promoted the event with the Latino Studies and Languages Departments, and encouraged all her students to come. Thanks to her, my very first book signing was a success.

"You should look into making a stage production of your work," Marta said to me another time after I finished reading a play she had given me—*Los Vendidos* by Luis Valdez of the Teatro Campesino. "I think your stories would be great onstage."

"Is that possible?"

"Books get adapted for the stage or film all the time," Marta said. "Though rarely the works of Latino authors, which is a shame. Pero tú puedes, Reyna."

So, I applied for another grant from Kresge to turn my short stories into skits, and I recruited the few friends I had, some of my peers, and even some of the students I tutored, like Alfredo, to perform my work onstage. The provost allowed me to use the Kresge Town Hall for the performance, and I had a good, supportive audience who bought copies of my self-published book. Once again, Marta was there, encouraging me as best she could.

The three grants I had received made me feel confident and excited about the creative work I was doing and my progress as an artist. Once again, I had turned to my creativity to help me deal with my pain and sorrow, and it carried me through the difficult months during my trials with Betty, but especially after we had our falling out.

Reyna at her first book signing, 1997

Marta was also a Spanish teacher, and I enrolled in her Spanish for Spanish Speakers class, where I learned to speak my native tongue in a way I hadn't before; that is, "properly." I had known that the language I had inherited from my parents wasn't perfect—their grammar and vocabulary reflected their poverty and lack of education—but I hadn't truly known until then how riddled with "mistakes" our Spanish was. We spoke words that were mispronounced, words that didn't exist, verbs that were conjugated completely wrong. It was in Marta's class that I finally learned about accent marks and their correct placement, the right conjugations of regular and irregular verbs. I also discovered that I spoke a third language that described who I was—a mixture of two cultures, two languages, born from the collision of two identities—Spanglish. Not only did I speak incorrect Spanish because of my family's poverty, but growing up in America had added yet another layer to my native tongue.

Though Marta repeatedly said that there was nothing to be ashamed of—there was no right or wrong way to speak Spanish—I did feel ashamed not speaking it with fluency and mastery. How could I claim it as my mother tongue if the words came out twisted and distorted as if my mouth were a hand-cranked clothes wringer?

"When it comes to Spanish, we all have different ways of expressing ourselves," Marta said. "There are colloquialisms unique to our upbringing and the places where we've lived. To be ashamed of how you speak is to be ashamed of where you're from, Reyna, and that is not how I want my students to feel."

I told Marta about Don Oscar and his family. When we lived in Mexico, my mother had a job at a record shop. Her bosses, Don Oscar and his wife, were wealthy Mexicans who looked at us with pity whenever they saw us. They had three children who were always clean and well dressed, who attended private schools, and who were treated with the utmost respect by my mother and other adults. Never mind that they were just kids, the same age as my siblings and me, they were rich and therefore were treated like royalty. I remembered my shock the first time I heard my mother address Oscar Jr.—who was twelve—as "usted" instead of the informal "tú." I had never heard a child being addressed as usted until that day.

When I was in Mexico over Christmas, I had been invited to Don Oscar's for lunch with the family. Sitting there in the living room of their two-story brick house, located in Iguala's only gated community, with its own security guard, I struggled to feel comfortable around Don Oscar and his wife, but even more so with their children. I kept telling myself that things were different for me now. I was no longer the little girl walking around with lice and tapeworm, barefoot and dressed in rags. I was now a university student, just like the couple's oldest son, Oscar Jr., who was attending UNAM, Mexico's largest public university.

But it was my Spanish that remained a barrier. When they spoke, I could hear their wealthy upbringing in the fancy words they used. The words rolled out of their mouths perfectly formed and polished, like shiny marbles. When I spoke, I could see them glance at each other. Ever since I was little, I had sensed that my Spanish was different from theirs, but now I was more aware of it than ever before. Who cared if I was a university student like their son if I continued to talk like the Mexican actress and comedian María Elana Velasco, who rose to fame by playing La India María, a caricature of an indigenous woman who spoke the most awful Spanish?

Things turned around for me later that day when Oscar Jr. and his sisters put on their favorite English music and asked me to translate the lyrics for them. Drinking a Bailey's on the rocks for the first time, I listened to the familiar lyrics of George Michael's "Careless Whispers," and the music and the alcohol made me feel confident once again. Oscar Jr.'s and his sisters' Spanish was perfect, unlike mine, but now I could speak a language they struggled with but were desperate to speak, which suddenly put me at their level.

When I translated the lyrics for them, my painful struggle to learn English suddenly seemed worth it just so that I could have this moment—seeing the profound admiration in the eyes of these rich young people who, up until then, had seen me as the poor little girl who deserved their pity and required their charity.

In Marta's Spanish class that memory of Don Oscar's children made me work extra hard to learn my mother tongue. "So that next time I see them," I told Marta as I walked her to her office after class, "I can speak with confidence."

She listened attentively as I told her about the feelings of inadequacy that came over me when I visited my native country. "Over there, everyone treats me differently, as if I'm not Mexican enough."

Marta stopped walking and turned to look at me. "Reyna, let me tell you something. It isn't that you aren't enough. In fact, the opposite is true."

I waited for her to explain. What did she mean that I was the opposite of not enough?

"If they treat you differently in Mexico it is because you *are* different," Marta said in that soft, tender voice of hers I had grown to love. "You are now bilingual, bicultural, and binational. You are not less. You are more."

After our talk, as I sat on the bus heading back to my apartment, I thought of what she had said. From the moment I stepped foot in this country, I had felt cut in half. But now I wondered if Marta was right.

Could it be true that without me knowing I had transformed into twice the girl I used to be?

In Marta's Chicano literature and Spanish classes, I made a lot of Latino friends—not just the students in her class, but also the authors Marta assigned us to read. Diana had introduced me to the works of Helena María Viramontes, Sandra Cisneros, and Isabel

Allende. In Marta's class, I was exposed to even more Latina writers, and I fell in love with hard-core feminist writers who inspired me to keep fighting for my stories: Ana Castillo, Alicia Gaspar de Alba, Cherríe Moraga, and many more. Through their words, I would hear them tell me, *Yes, your stories matter!*

Marta introduced me to the work of Sor Juana Inés de la Cruz, a feminist nun who lived in seventeenth-century Mexico—or New Spain, as it used to be called—who wrote some of the most powerful poetry and prose I had read. I felt connected to Sor Juana's struggle to write and thrive as an artist in a patriarchal society that subjugated and censored her and, on many occasions, had tried to silence her.

> *Hombres necios que acusáis*
> *a la mujer sin razón,*
> *sin ver que sois la ocasión*
> *de lo mismo que culpáis.*

> *Stupid men, quick to condemn*
> *women wrongly for their flaws,*
> *Never seeing you're the cause*
> *of all that you blame on them.*

I memorized her poem and repeated it to myself as a mantra.

Another time, Marta gave us an excerpt of *Borderlands/La Frontera*, by Gloria Anzaldúa. At the time Anzaldúa lived in Santa Cruz, and although I never had the opportunity to meet her, her words resonated with me.

"The U.S.-Mexico border *es una herida abierta* where the third world grates against the first and bleeds, and before a scab forms it hemorrhages again, the lifeblood of two worlds merging to form a third country—a border culture," wrote Anzaldúa.

Because I was an immigrant, the border was something that had always been part of my life. That fateful day in 1977 when my father decided to emigrate was the day the border changed my life. I was two years old.

A third country. Not Mexico, not the U.S., but the hyphen between Mexican and American. Not my father, not my mother, but the sum of their genes that was greater than their parts. Not English, not Spanish, but the language formed of their commingled blood— Spanglish. The third country was inside me. I was a product of the merging of those two worlds, two people, two languages. My heart was the open wound, la herida abierta.

Anzaldúa wrote: "I am a turtle. Wherever I go, I carry my home on my back."

It was then that I understood what I needed to do. If I could become a turtle and build a home that I could carry on my back, I would never feel homeless again.

13

Reyna on the paint crew, 1997

WHEN SUMMER ARRIVED, my maintenance job at Kresge College began. Since my apartment was far from the nearest bus stop, I bought a used bicycle for transportation. UCSC is located on a hill. A very steep hill. As I made my way at 7:00 a.m. to my first day of work, I didn't even last a quarter of the way. I was soon panting and gasping for air. I had to get off my bike and walk up Bay Street, praying for the bus to come so I could throw my bike on the rack and hitch a ride to campus.

My boss, Robin McDuff, knew everything there was to know about working with your hands. I had never seen a woman use drills and hammers and saws, but Robin handled tools with the same expertise as a man, and I was in awe of her. I wanted to learn everything she had to teach me, and I threw myself into my job completely. The first thing Robin had the paint crew do was to enter each dorm and take out everything the students had left behind. Carolyn hadn't been kidding when she said that college students were destructive—the holes in the walls were proof of that. She forgot to mention that they're also dirty. There was trash everywhere. We hauled away all the abandoned furniture (most of it broken and useless), unwanted or damaged clothes, tattered books, and other discarded belongings. We took the leftover nonperishable food to our rec room to eat during our breaks. After the cleaning was done, we set out to repair the many holes and to prepare the rooms for painting, things my father had done at his own job.

The irony was that in Santa Cruz I had hoped to forget my father, and yet my work on the paint crew brought me closer to him. My father had been a maintenance worker for many years. When we came to live with him, he was working at Kingsley Manor, a retirement home in L.A., making $300 a week. He wore a blue uniform with his last name, GRANDE, embroidered over the left pocket of his shirt. Every day he would come home from work with streaks of white paint in his hair and white splotches on his hands and arms. The paint Kingsley Manor used was the same color we used on student housing at UCSC.

As I painted walls for the first time in my life, I thought of my father. Standing there in the dorms, inhaling the dizzying fumes, dipping my paintbrush into the white paint to carefully coat the walls or cut their edges, running the roller up and down, side to side, I began to get a glimpse into my father's daily life. This is what it had been like for him. The endless rolling and cutting, dipping and stroking. I got white paint on my hands, my arms, my hair. If I had had a blue-collared shirt with the word GRANDE embroidered over my pocket, I would have looked just like him.

At PCC, when I was nineteen, I'd been infatuated with one of the maintenance workers because he wore a blue uniform that looked exactly like my father's. Just like my father's uniform shirt, Alberto's last name was embroidered over the left pocket. He had skin darkened from too much work in the sun and his hands had bulging veins, like my father's. Whenever I walked to my classes and caught a flash of blue, my heart would skip a beat, imagining I was seeing my father, that he had come to see me at school, but it was Alberto. I would go over and talk to him. Sometimes he would be wading in the mirror pools removing debris. Other times he would be using the leaf blower. Or he might be painting. Always, it was the blue uniform that drew me to him. He was in his late twenties, the age my father had been when he'd headed north. I thought I was in love with him, and yet, whenever I saw him after work without his blue uniform, his presence diminished before my eyes.

"You're so tiny, I could fit you in my pocket," Alberto would say to me, and I'd look at his blue uniform, his name embroidered over his left pocket, and I would want to be in there, safe and protected.

After I finished painting a room, I would sit quietly during my break smelling the fresh paint, getting drunk on the smell of my father, and for a second the hole in my heart would fill with his presence. I would take deep gulps of air, getting dizzy with the paint fumes, imagining conversations I would have with him the next time I saw him. I could talk about brush and roller techniques, how to repair holes, texture walls. Now we had something in common.

When the painting was done, I moved on to other things: cleaning rugs; stripping, staining, and refinishing the oak dining tables and end tables; snaking drains and removing hair balls the size of mice; cleaning moldy refrigerators.

When the days were long and grueling, and summer seemed eternal, I yearned for school to start, so I could finally go back to my classes, my books—and it hit me that this was only a temporary job, a job that was going to help pay for my college degree. For my father, being a maintenance worker was all he had. It was the job that had helped him support his kids. He made $15,000 a year; I was paying almost $15,000 a year to be at UCSC. Some students were in college thanks to their parents' occupations. I was there in spite of mine.

I had never had a full-time job, and it took half the summer to get used to it. Even though it was grueling to make the ride up the hill to campus every morning, and I would curse the founders of the university for building the place on a damn hill, in the evening I was grateful for the downhill ride all the way to my apartment. I would get on my bike and fly across campus, down Bay Street, my hair flapping wildly around me, my blood pumping from my heart with sheer joy. I would make a right turn to my apartment, where I could see that sliver of Monterey Bay from the balcony.

As I took a shower and scrubbed the white paint and dirt off with lavender soap that dissipated the memory of paint fumes, I began to get an insight into my father in a way I never had.

Now I knew why he had been such a tyrant about school—he didn't want any of us to be a blue-collar worker like he was. He wanted us to succeed in a way he had never been able to. I had never understood why, when my father would come home, he just wanted to sit in front of the TV and watch the basketball game or the news. He didn't want to go anywhere once he was home, so he rarely took us out. On the weekends, instead of resting and doing something fun, he would get up early and work around the house— cut the grass, repair a leaky faucet, paint over graffiti on the fence. He worked endlessly. Whenever we complained that school was too hard and demanding, he would scoff and say, "You don't know what it's like to work hard."

After my shower, I sat in front of the TV and rested my tired, aching body, massaged my feet, saying to myself, "You were right, Papá. I didn't know."

As I rode my bike to work, finally making it all the way up the hill to Kresge without stopping, the pain I had felt when my father banned me from his life gave way to something else—understanding.

I met Gabe during the last three weeks of my summer job. Now that the painting was mostly done, I was sent to clean the moldy refrigerators in the apartments and get them ready for move-in day. A professional builder, Gabe was in his mid-thirties and was part of an outside crew the university had hired to remodel some of the buildings. The first time I saw him, he was operating a drill. The shrill sound reminded me of my father, and I stopped outside the door just to listen to it. He saw me watching him work in the living room and turned off the drill.

"I'm here to clean the refrigerator," I said.

He was dressed in a sweaty T-shirt and jeans that were stained and torn. He had yellow knee guards and steel-toed boots, like the kind my father wore to work. His face was sunburned and wrinkled from spending too much time working outdoors. He was covered in a film of white powder, and he was too old for me, and yet I was immediately attracted to him.

He seemed uncomfortable with me there. "I'm not done putting up this drywall," he said, taking off his safety glasses. "It's going to be noisy in here."

"I don't mind," I said.

He had brown hair and light brown eyes, and his last name meant "cherry" in Italian, he said. After we introduced ourselves and shook hands, he turned the drill back on and resumed his work. The sound distracted me from the task at hand. The refrigerator was covered with so much mold it looked as if it were being eaten by a shapeless green monster.

"I don't envy your job," Gabe said a few minutes later as he stood behind me.

"I suppose you wouldn't want to trade?" I said, handing him the bucket of soapy water and my latex gloves the color of a banana slug.

"You'll hurt yourself with this," he said, holding his drill close to him, as if protecting it from me, not the other way around.

"Maybe," I said. "It all depends on how you hold it, right? And the trick is to not be afraid of it." I remembered my father telling my brother that once. I knew I had no business flirting with a man in his thirties, but I couldn't help it. "I can tell you're an expert with the drill."

"I sure do know how to use it," he said, and grinned.

He returned to his task, and I did the same. When he was ready for a break, he came over to watch me work on the refrigerator. I felt embarrassed to have him watch me do that nasty job. I would rather he had seen me paint.

"Damn if that fridge don't look brand-new," he said. I tried not to let him see how his words pleased me, but I couldn't hide my smile.

He asked me what I was studying, where I had come from, how old I was. "And how do you like Santa Cruz?"

"I love it," I said. "These trees are amazing."

He said he lived in Boulder Creek, which was a few towns over, and if I liked the trees so much, then I would surely love his house. "It's in the middle of a forest. I built it myself."

"Really?" I was genuinely surprised. I had never met anyone who had built his own house. In Mexico, my father had been a bricklayer, and he had dreamed of being able to build his dream house himself but he couldn't afford the building materials, so the only way to build the house was by coming to the U.S. to work and hiring someone else to do it. With Mexico's weak economy, he would never have earned the money he needed, but if he had been able to stay and build his house brick by brick, he would have been like Gabe. He would have been a man who lived in a house built with his own hands, sweat, and labor.

Two weeks later, after spending more time with Gabe on campus and going out to lunch with him a few times, after telling him about my complicated relationship with my father, I agreed to go to Boulder Creek with him. So, on a Saturday, he picked me up at my apartment, and off I went to see the house that Gabe built. I had expected a crude cabin, a cute rustic cottage at best, but it was a real house and just as beautiful as he had claimed. Not only was it surrounded by a forest of redwood trees, but the house itself seemed to be made of the same wood. The house had what he called an open floor plan, so there were no walls to divide the kitchen, dining room, and living room. It was the most spacious, brightest house I had ever been in. He had put floor-to-ceiling windows in the living room, so even though we were indoors, it felt as if we weren't. You never forgot you were in a forest. Even the ceiling had windows, and I could see the deep, blue sky through them.

"I've never been in a house with windows on the ceiling," I told him, shocked at the sight. By now, I thought the man was a genius.

"They're called skylights."

"Skylights," I repeated. The word sounded like poetry.

The house had a bedroom where his daughters slept when they stayed with him. He and his ex-wife had joint custody, he said, and the girls came every week.

"I sleep upstairs in the loft. Come, I'll show you."

I hadn't planned to sleep with Gabe, and before I came here I'd told myself I wouldn't let things go that far. We hadn't even kissed, because deep down I knew this relationship was all wrong for me. But now I found myself not wanting to leave. I wanted to spend at least one night—not with Gabe, but with his beautiful house. So when he drew me into his arms and lowered me onto his bed, I let it happen. And that night, while we had sex in the loft, I could see the moon and the stars peeking through the skylights.

Afterward, he said to me, "What are you going to do when your summer job is over?"

"Look for another one," I said. The money I made this summer was going toward paying off my debt at Sears for my computer. I had no money left over, and finding a job was my top priority.

"You know," he said, "I've been looking for help with my daughters. I could pay you to babysit them when they come over and I'm still at work. You can live here in the house. I'll build you a bedroom, not charge you rent. Then you can just focus on school and not worry about money."

"I'll think about it."

"No strings attached," he said. "I'm serious."

But I wondered if that was true. I was suddenly filled with dread. His was a dangerous proposal. To live in his dream house, to become part of the fabric of his life, to take care of his daughters, to be his lover—because surely, now that we had done it once, how could it not happen again? This wasn't like the time I had gone to live with Diana. She had never asked me for anything in return, only that I honor my dreams.

Gabe knew what he was asking of me, and I was tempted. Here was a man who had done what my father hadn't been able to do. To build his dream house with his own hands—and actually *live* in it. And have his children live in it, too, though part-time.

In the morning, as we got ready to go back to Santa Cruz, I took a long look at his house. Bathed in the golden light streaming through the skylights, I knew I would never go back there again. So as we drove away, I said goodbye to Gabe's house. *This isn't my dream house*, I told myself as it got swallowed up by the trees. *It's someone else's.*

I didn't know if I would ever have the money to buy or build my own house, but even if I never did, I would build my home out of the only things I had—words and dreams.

14

I MOVED INTO A new place because, without Betty, the apartment by the bay didn't feel the same anymore. I couldn't afford to move back to campus, so when the lease ended, I rented a small room in an apartment I shared with three roommates. It was $100 less per month than my old place and was located directly across from Santa Cruz High School, close to the bus stop and five minutes from La Esperanza Market. The place was small and dark, and I had nothing in common with my roommates, two white men who were not students and drank too much and a Chinese guy who was a student and studied too much. I hated spending time there with no one to talk to. I would usually go to the coffee shop downtown to do my work. I would walk by the high school, my heart racing, wondering if I would run into Betty. Weeks later, on my way to the coffee shop, I finally did. Betty came out through the front doors of the school with a group of friends. She looked like a regular teenager, young and carefree.

My eyes went straight to her big belly, and I realized that her life wouldn't be carefree for long. I didn't want to judge, yet all I could think of was that my sister had turned seventeen two months before and would be a mother in ten weeks. I stopped walking and stood there, wondering what to do. She came down the steps and saw me watching her. For a second I thought she was going to pretend I wasn't there, that she would look away and keep walking with her friends. Instead, we found ourselves face-to-face on the sidewalk, and her friends continued on their way, leaving us alone.

"How are you?" I said. It was a stupid thing to say, but I didn't know how to start the conversation.

"Fine."

"How's school?"

"Fine."

"How's the pregnancy going?"

"Fine."

"Okay," I said. "Well, take care," I started to walk away, disappointed about not saying what I had wanted to say—that I was so damn happy to see her! I wished she would at least meet me halfway. Didn't she miss me at all?

"I'm having a boy," she said. I turned around and retraced my steps, the tightness in my chest loosening.

"Cool," I said. "Have you picked a name?"

"We aren't sure yet," she said. "We're still thinking about it."

She told me about the program for pregnant teens that SCHS had and how grateful she was for the support she was getting from her teachers. She loved Omar's mother, she said. The woman treated her like a daughter. "I finally found the mom I always wanted to have." I could tell in her voice that she really meant it. That was the first time it ever occurred to me that something positive had come from this situation. "I'm learning from her what it means to be a real mother. The kind of mother I want to be."

She seemed so grown-up when she said that, and I leaned in to hug her. I wasn't happy that she was pregnant at this age, but at the same time I could see the effect this little human being growing in her womb was having on her. She seemed confident and mature.

"Come visit me whenever you want," I told her as I said goodbye.

Little by little, Betty and I found our way back to each other. We never talked about that night when I kicked her out, and even though I wanted to apologize, I didn't have the courage to bring it up. Whenever I saw her belly, I felt it was my fault, though I suspected it would have happened whether or not I had forced her to go live with Omar. She never acted as if being pregnant was the end of her life. She didn't resent it the way I did.

I still couldn't let go of the dreams I once had for her.

My nephew was born in August 1998, during my second summer in Santa Cruz. I went to see Betty at the hospital and to meet the new addition to the Grande family. Mago had already given birth to her second baby in May. Carlos and his new wife had had a baby girl in July. And now Betty had had her baby on this first day of August. Three Grande babies in a period of four months!

"What's his name?" I asked as I took the baby from her.

"Randy Alexander."

He was a cute baby, tiny and fragile. I felt his warmth against my

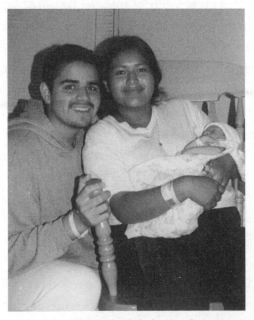

Betty and Omar with baby Randy, 1998

chest, and I rocked him so that he would fall asleep. It was awkward in the hospital room, and I didn't know what to say as I took in the beeping machines, the uncomfortable cot, my sister in her blue hospital gown looking exhausted and older than seventeen, as if motherhood had already aged her.

I knew that on this occasion I was supposed to say, *Congratulations! I'm so happy for you,* or something like that. But I just couldn't say it. I couldn't stop thinking that my little sister's life was over because she had become a mother so young. Somehow, along the way, I had grown to believe that being a teenage mother was the worst thing one could be, especially for Latina girls, who already had too many obstacles to overcome because of race, gender, and class inequality. The statistics weren't good for Latina teens and their rate of success. Whether I wanted to admit it or not, I cared too much about not being a statistic. Betty, on the other hand, didn't give a damn what society thought of her.

When he fell asleep, I handed my sister the baby and stood to go. "I know you'll be a great mom," I told her because I believed that she would be. I knew Betty needed to be a great mom, because that was the only way to heal the little girl inside of her. Giving her child the kind of mother she, herself, had never had was how she would make things right and ease the pain.

As I was about to go out the door, she said, "Reyna, I have nothing to forgive you for, and you have nothing to regret. I know what you were trying to do for me, and I thank you. But I'm not going to regret anything either, especially my baby."

"I'm glad to hear that," I said. "No regrets then."

Two years later, at Betty's high school graduation, I would realize that she was right—there was nothing to regret for either of us. I was extremely proud of her as I watched her go up onstage to receive her diploma. I had been afraid that she would drop out of school again,

Betty at school with baby Randy

but instead, Omar and her baby had grounded her. Santa Cruz be-longed to Betty in a way it didn't belong to me. Her child had been born here. She had her own family now. Once she had been a leaf in the wind; now she had roots and had landed in a place where she would flourish and be happy.

15

I WAS SITTING ON the bus on the way to my apartment after a long day at school, looking out the window at the darkness, when a laugh—loud and unapologetic—pulled me back to the light. I looked across the aisle to see a young Latina sitting with a guy, laughing about something he had said. I couldn't hear their conversation, but I could see his flamboyant gestures, his whole body animated and deeply focused on the story he was telling her, pausing once in a while for her laughter to settle, only to make her laugh again. The sound erupted from her mouth like butterflies taking off into the air. She had long black hair that was braided and crisscrossed behind the nape of her neck. She wore a white Mexican dress and, instead of a jacket, a black rebozo with little white polka dots was wrapped around her slender shoulders. It was the kind of Mexican shawl my own grandmother wore every time she went out, one I didn't expect to see on anyone my age here in this country, much less in Santa Cruz.

I wanted to know why she was dressed that way—the braids, the rebozo, the dress. It shocked me to see a university student looking as if she had been plucked from a remote rural village in Mexico and transported to this surfer town. She held herself with total confidence, perfectly comfortable in her own body, dressed as if she were going to a Cinco de Mayo party even though it was February, and laughing unapologetically on a bus full of gringos who couldn't hide their curiosity.

She was flaunting her Mexicanness for all to see, and I was in total awe of her.

"Why are you dressed like that?" I asked her before I knew what I was doing.

Her friend stopped talking and they both stared at me, perhaps in disbelief that I had leaned across the aisle to ask such a thing. Then she smiled at me and said, "Nomás porque quiero." Just because I want to.

That was how I met Erica in my second year at UCSC. She was my first hard-core Chicana feminist friend. She reminded me of the writers I had read in Marta's class. Unlike me, she handled her Mexican-American identity without the conflict and turmoil I had about my own split identity. She would teach me that it was possible to rotate in and out of both cultures instead of feeling like an outsider in both. On that first day on the bus, I thought her confidence came from the fact that she was a Chicana, a U.S.-born Mexican, not an immigrant and border crosser like me. She had that precious U.S. birth certificate to whip out whenever someone asked, "Where are you from?" Whereas I had a green card that literally labeled me an alien. But I would come to learn the source of Erica's pride in her Mexican roots, the reason why her closet was filled with embroidered peasant blouses and rebozos, and why her apartment was decorated with Mexican artesanías: folklórico. She was co-director of Grupo Folklórico Los Mejicas, a dance group on campus which was composed of students and some community members. Never in a million years would I have guessed there was Mexican folk dancing happening at UCSC.

"You should join Los Mejicas," she and her friend Benigno told me on the bus. "The group is open to all students, and you get credit for it."

"I've never danced folklórico in my life," I said. "And my older sister once said I dance like a horse."

I saw Erica a few more times on the bus, and I learned that she was also from Los Angeles and a transfer student, like me. She had gone to Glendale Community College, which was the other local college I'd thought about attending before deciding on PCC. She told me how lonely she had felt in Santa Cruz when she first arrived, and how she and her mother talked on the phone every day. What saved her from the loneliness, she said, was discovering Los Mejicas.

She told me she was majoring in Latin American and Latino/a studies. "How about you?" she asked.

"Creative writing and film and video," I said. The previous quarter, I had added film as a second major so I could stay an extra year at UCSC to explore a different kind of storytelling through images, and I was loving my film classes. I was running around town shooting films and would spend my nights in the editing room putting the story together. I loved figuring out how to string the scenes together to create a whole, the way a novel is written. I told Erica that my film classes were making my writing better. When I wrote, I felt I was watching a movie in my head.

"Folklórico tells stories, too," she said. "It tells the story of Mexico from before the Spaniards arrived all the way to the Mexican Revolution."

I had never thought of dance as a form of storytelling.

When she invited me to her apartment, the first things I saw, prominently displayed on her living room wall, were prints of two paintings, one of a woman with a unibrow and parrots, and the other of the same woman wearing what looked like a bunch of lace around her head, but which I would later learn was actually a Tehuana dress.

"Who's that?" I asked Erica.

She looked at me in disbelief. "¿Qué, qué? ¿Cómo que no sabes? Girl, let me tell you. That's Frida Kahlo, the best Mexican painter of all time. She's my hero."

And that was when I discovered this female artist who had done what I was trying to do—turn her pain into art. Crippled by polio as a child and then severely injured in a bus accident in her teens,

Frida Kahlo had spent much of her life in a wheelchair, painting self-portraits and conquering her suffering with every stroke of a brush.

From that day forward, Frida Kahlo became my hero, too. Especially when I discovered her famous double self-portrait, *Las Dos Fridas*. I saw myself in that painting. The Two Reynas holding hands, the two versions of me—the Mexican and the American—holding tightly to each other. It was by looking at this painting that I finally understood what Marta had meant. I was twice the girl I used to be.

In her kitchen, Erica tried to teach me a step called "el huachapeado," which she said the dance group was currently practicing. It was a step from the state of Veracruz, which had one of the most beautiful dances. After I tried the six-part step a few times, she said, "Don't worry, we have all levels in the group."

On Sunday afternoon, Erica took me to practice with her, and everything changed for me that day. I stood in a corner of the studio and watched the dancers do the complex combinations of steps. The girls wore long skirts down to their ankles and black shoes with heels. The guys wore black leather boots. Later I learned that the heels and toe tips of their shoes were covered with tiny nails to increase the sound. I watched their sweating bodies turning and turning, their feet tapping and stomping, their skirts twirling like butterfly wings. And I found my own feet wanting to stomp, my heart beating to the strumming of the mariachi music, and I wanted to burst out onto the floor and dance with the butterflies.

Once I joined the group, I learned that folklórico was not merely to entertain. It was a source of pride, a rich cultural tradition that celebrates the unique history of my native country through dance. In addition to honoring our indigenous roots, folklórico also celebrates el mestizaje—the cultural intermixing—that took place in Mexico. The dances reflect the influences of Spanish, African, French, and native cultures. I was surprised to learn that the northern states, such as Sonora, Nuevo León, and Chihuahua, had inherited the polkas brought by German and Polish immigrants to the area. Who knew

Mexicans danced polkas! I knew little of my own country's history, but I began to learn about it through its dances. Instead of focusing on what was lost in the collision of cultures, folklórico tells the unique story of Mexico and the beauty that resulted from the chaos.

Just as it had with Erica, Los Mejicas took away my loneliness. I made friends who were like me, either immigrants or children of immigrants, and first-generation university students. It was my first time standing before floor-to-ceiling mirrors and being fully aware of my body, of what it could do. It took some effort to see past the imperfections of my too-short legs, my too-wide shoulders, my big belly, but thankfully, unlike other types of dance, folklórico is more forgiving when it comes to body shape. Hardly any of us Latinas were tall and skinny, and the good news was that we didn't need to be tall and skinny to dance folklórico. What mattered was the joy and pride the dance gave us.

Through the weeks of practice, I learned how to coax my body to move, spin, twirl, stomp, and sway to the rhythm of accordions, guitars, harps, marimbas, and violins. I wasn't a natural dancer, not gifted the way other girls in the group, like Erica, were. I knew I would have to work hard, push my body in a way I had never done before. As a beginning dancer, I was only able to do the polkas from northern Mexico, though in a simplified version. Polkas didn't require intricate skirt work, which I hadn't learned yet.

It was wonderful to perform with the group at cultural celebrations happening around Santa Cruz County, which turned out to have more Mexicans than I had previously thought.

Two months after I joined, we all drove up to San Jose in a caravan to attend Danzantes Unidos, a three-day festival of hundreds of folkloristas who came together to celebrate our Mexican culture and dance traditions. It was my first time being at a conference where everyone looked like me, hundreds of Latinos joined together by our love of folklórico and pride in our heritage.

At the end of spring quarter, as I wrapped up my second year at the university, Los Mejicas put on a recital to showcase the dances we had learned throughout the year. It was my first big performance, and though I only danced for ten minutes onstage, I got a taste of what it was like to be under the bright stage lights, bathed in reds, blues, and yellows. Onstage, I had no past and no future—only the present moment mattered. There were no alcoholic fathers, no absent mothers, no wild dreams to pursue, nothing to make me feel ashamed, unwanted, unloved, or afraid. There was only the dancing, the music flowing through my body, my mind focused on making the right movements, my muscles contracting and releasing, my lungs expanding with each breath I took.

When the show was over, the audience erupted in applause, and I stood under the bright lights with my peers as I let the adulation envelop me and carry me off the stage, back into a world which, in that moment of euphoria, I was no longer afraid of.

Reyna in Jalisco dress

16

Reyna and Claudia

Thanks to my friend Claudia, whom I met in Los Mejicas, I got a job at the Capitola Mall working as an assistant to the optometrist she worked for. Two other friends worked at the optometrist, too: Paola, who was also from Highland Park, the neighborhood in L.A. where I grew up, and Leticia, whom I met in the paint crew at Kresge my second summer.

One day, when I returned from my lunch break, Claudia handed me a chart and pointed at the guy sitting in the waiting area. She took her lunch break and left me in charge of the patient, who sat with his legs stretched out before him, completely exhausted, as if he had had a late night of studying. Even sitting down, I could tell he was tall. He had hair like brown sugar, and it curled around his ears and the nape of his neck. His eyes were lighter than his hair, like raw honey. His fair skin was red from too much time in the sun, and I wondered if he was a surfer, or perhaps a volleyball player; I pictured him playing at the beach, barefoot and bare-chested, his skin glistening with sweat.

I wondered what year he was, what his major was, and if he lived on campus or off. I wanted to know where I could find him again. When he saw that I was coming for him, he smiled at me and stood up, but when I said, "Hello, I'm Reyna, nice to meet you," his smile disappeared and was replaced by a deep, red blush. He looked away from me and lowered his gaze to the floor.

I had been too busy drooling over him to look at his chart and find out his name. The information on the chart didn't match my image of this boy surfing in Monterey Bay, or walking around campus with textbooks in hand drinking a latte to stay awake in class.

His name was Arturo and he lived in Watsonville, the town half an hour from Santa Cruz with a large Mexican population. It was an agricultural town, known mostly for its strawberries. I had passed through there on my way to UCSC and performed there once with Los Mejicas.

"No hablo inglés," he said in a soft voice. He towered over me, at least by a foot. He extended his hand and I shook it. The calluses on his hand and his sunburned skin gave me a new vision of him, bending over fields picking strawberries under the hot sun.

"No hay problema," I said. I took him into the room to do the pretests before he saw the doctor.

"Do you see the hot air balloon?" I said in Spanish as he scooted up to the chin rest of the auto-refractor. "Keep looking at it and don't move." I looked at his eyes, as bright as yellow amber from the light of the auto-refractor, and felt a pang of sadness to know I had been wrong. He could have been a university student but wasn't, because, as someone once said, talent is evenly distributed around the world, but opportunity is not. Such was the case for most people in Mexico.

"What state are you from?" I asked him as I transferred him to the NCT machine to do the eye-puff test.

"Jalisco," he said. That explained the light skin, the amber eyes, the hair like a shiny penny. There were a lot of light-skinned Mexicans who came from Jalisco. European ancestry still had a strong presence in that state. The dances of Jalisco, accompanied by mariachi, were exquisite, but only the most advanced dancers in our group got to perform them.

I warned him about the puff of air, and he laughed when, despite my warning, it still startled him and made him jump. I laughed with him.

"¿Y tú, de dónde eres?" he asked.

"De Guerrero," I said. Guerrero, my warrior state. We didn't have many light-skinned people like him there. Our indigenous heritage was strong. My father's skin was the color of rain-soaked earth, though mine was more yellow in tone. I shopped for makeup at Asian stores to find a good foundation and powder that went with my skin tone.

Arturo asked me if I would go into the exam room with him to translate for him what the doctor said, and I willingly did, happy to spend more time with him. He left that day with a prescription for new glasses and my phone number, both tucked into his shirt pocket. When he asked me out a few days later, he also asked me if I had any friends that might want to come along. "I have two cousins," he said.

Leticia had a boyfriend, so Claudia and Paola went with me to Watsonville to hang out with these three cousins. We were curious about their lives, so different from ours at the university.

I was fascinated by Arturo, the surfer-looking Mexican farmworker with hands rough and calloused and skin sun-blistered from field work. Though he was six feet tall, he stooped a little, as if ashamed of daring to be taller than the average Mexican and taking up too much space, or from bending over the fields for so long. I

told Arturo that my father had once been a field-worker. When he had arrived in the U.S., he had worked in the Central Valley harvesting crops. He once told me that he had lived in an abandoned car to save money for the dream house. I pictured my father living in that car, with no tires and broken windows, all alone in an empty field, of how many sacrifices he had made for a house he would never live in and in the end not even own.

Arturo's house was in the middle of lettuce fields, and the only way to get there was by a bumpy dirt road. Dirt and lettuce as far as the eye could see. He shared the place with several men, including his two cousins. It was a dilapidated house, as filthy inside as it was on the outside. His landlord took no pride in it, and the house had deteriorated to the point where only desperate immigrant men would live in it. I couldn't wrap my head around seeing him in this place. In my mind, I saw him walking down the aisles of the McHenry Library on campus, checking out some books for his research paper. I wanted that for him so badly that, not long after I met him, I gave him a tour of the university so that I could see him there for real, not just in my fantasies.

But Arturo wasn't comfortable in Santa Cruz. The campus intimidated him. He clung to me as we walked hand in hand from building to building. Though he towered over me and many of the other students on campus, he seemed small. "Ya vámonos," he said to me not long after the tour had begun. And we returned to Watsonville, back to the fields and the bar he loved, where we drank Coronas and listened to the jukebox play rancheras—the melancholy music from Jalisco, the place he longed for. He fed the jukebox more quarters, and with Vicente Fernández singing in the background, he told me about his home, his family, everything and everyone he had left behind. We sang along to "Canción Mixteca," which he played on the jukebox again and again: "México lindo y querido, si muero lejos de ti, que digan que estoy dormido y que me traigan a ti."

I joined him in his añoranza, and didn't have the heart to caution

him on the perils of indulging in nostalgia, of how easy it is to fall victim to your fantasies of a place that might no longer exist.

We went out to clubs, and Paola and Claudia and his cousins would be on the dance floor having a great time. My friends went out with the cousins to have fun and nothing else, and I wished that was all I wanted, too.

"Maybe I can marry him and get him his papers," I told Mago one day. "I could teach him English. He could go to school, get a better job."

"Ay Nena, why are you always trying to rescue people? Focus on your dreams. Olvida ese lechugero. Don't let him distract you from your goals."

Lettuce picker? I wanted to say. *How dare you call him that?* I wanted to do for him what I wished someone had done for our father when he had slept in that abandoned car and had been far from home. Mago hadn't seen where Arturo lived. She hadn't seen him so tired and drained from the field work that for a minute in that club, despite the dim lights, he hadn't looked twenty-two, but fifty. If she met him, maybe she would feel differently.

"You can't save him," Mago said, reading into my silence. "You can't wish him into being something he is not, like you do our father."

The next time I visited Arturo at his house, I lay on his dirty mattress that had no sheets, only a threadbare blanket to cover himself with, and I still wanted to help him.

"The adult school in Watsonville offers English classes," I told him. "You could go after work, start learning English."

He smiled and shook his head. "I know I look like a gringo, but I'm not. And I'll never be one. Mexico is my home. One day, I will go back."

"You can't spend your life looking backward. You have to look at what's ahead, too. Besides, learning English doesn't make you a gringo. It'll give you job opportunities. You can make a better life for yourself. Don't you want to learn to communicate with Americans in their own language?"

"I have *you* for that," he said, and held me tight with fierce ownership. I thought of my stepmother, of how for all the years she was with my father, he depended on her for everything because he was afraid to interact with the outside world and overcome his fear of speaking English and navigating the choppy waters of American culture. Even when he was dying of cancer many years later, Mila was the bridge between him and his doctors. His life had literally depended on her.

Arturo was using his nostalgia for Mexico as a barrier between him and American culture, the same thing my own parents had done, the same thing I had done on occasion. I had spent too many years mourning for what I lost, wandering the borderlands trying to find my way, pretending, adapting, and reinventing myself, trying not to buckle under the strain of assimilation and the pressure to hold on to my roots. I had spent too many years torn between wishing to forget and needing to remember, between wanting to fit in and resisting being a sell-out, between dreaming of the future and longing for what used to be but was no longer.

I was trying to be Arturo's cultural coyote and translator, but perhaps it was time to let him find his way. How could I save him from his torment when I could barely save myself from mine?

17

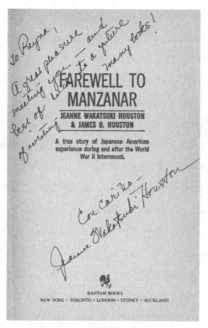

Farewell to Manzanar *autographed*
by Jeanne Wakatsuki Houston

I N MY THIRD—and final—year at UCSC, I met my first professional writer. The creative writing program hosted a reading
by Jeanne Wakatsuki Houston. She spoke about her work to an
auditorium full of literature majors and aspiring writers. Seeing
her onstage made my dream of being a writer feel more real. There
she was, a flesh-and-blood author standing under the bright stage
lights. She was tiny, just as small as I was, but she held herself with
such confidence and spoke with such conviction that a minute into

her talk, I stopped seeing her as small. She was larger than life, and I clung to her every word as she spoke about her memoir, *Farewell to Manzanar*.

I had read the book in preparation for her visit. Though it was about the effects of the bombing of Pearl Harbor on Japanese-Americans, I related to her story. As a woman of color and an immigrant, I knew what it was like to be marginalized, to have to prove constantly how American I was, always to have to fight for my right to remain. I was filled with anguish and rage at reading about the way Japanese people were abused and mistreated, torn away from their homes and families and sent to internment camps. Similarly, during the Great Depression, Mexicans were scapegoated and blamed for the economic woes of the country. Calling it a "repatriation," the U.S. government rounded up Mexicans, 60 percent of whom were American citizens, and dumped them into Mexico by the busload, to be trapped again by the poverty they had escaped. Hundreds of thousands of families had been torn apart by those heartless decisions.

When Jeanne Wakatsuki Houston spoke that night at the Kresge Town Hall, something changed for me. I recognized my struggle in her story as she shared her difficulties of trying to navigate American culture while trying to hold on to her Japanese heritage. She couldn't find books that she could relate to, books that spoke about the difficult experiences her family had endured in the internment camp. She wrote the book that she couldn't find. Through *Farewell to Manzanar*, she had become a voice for her people and others, like me.

When I learned to read in English in the eighth grade, I remembered feeling that same desperation that she spoke about—the need to find books I could relate to. As a child immigrant from Mexico struggling to adapt to the American way of life, I had had a hard time finding my experiences reflected in the books given to me by my teachers at school or the librarian at the public library. Instead, I grew up reading stories mostly about white, middle-class kids whose only worry was what kind of pet to get or what to wear to the prom. Books like the *Sweet Valley High* series gave me access to an America that wasn't mine, and I felt a yearning inside of me to feel connected, to see my story as part of American literature. I would often ask myself, *If I am not in literature, does that mean I don't exist?*

Later, I found books about adult immigrants that touched on the struggles that first-generation immigrants—like my parents, like Arturo—experienced when they arrived in the United States: low-paying jobs, abuse and discrimination in the workplace, fear of deportation, struggles to assimilate and learn English, and the hardships of navigating and understanding the nuances of American culture and society. But I would ask myself, Weren't child immigrants as much a part of the immigration narrative? Weren't the stories of our pain and heartbreak, struggles and triumphs, also worth telling?

While in Santa Cruz, I had read novels and memoirs assigned to me in class or that I found at the library, yet I still felt a void, a yearning, a missing piece that I desperately wanted to find. What I wanted most of all was to not feel invisible. Where was the book that spoke about the effects of separation and how immigration can turn parents and children into strangers?

I had complained about this to my new writing teacher, Micah Perks. The year before, UCSC had finally hired a tenure-track professor in the Creative Writing Department, and I was happy to know Micah was there to stay, unlike the adjuncts who had come and gone when the quarter was over, never to be seen again. She was the first teacher in the creative writing program who understood me and my culture, who didn't think I had "a wild imagination" and instead accepted my writing for what it was—my reality, my truth. In addition to the classes I took with her, I had signed up to take an independent course to work one-on-one with her. She had told me, "Reyna, sometimes you have to write the book that you want to read."

In other words, I would have to write my way into existence.

I tried to visualize that book I wanted to read and needed to write. I knew in my heart what it was, yet I was frightened. What if I wasn't up to the task?

Now here was Jeanne Wakatsuki Houston saying what Micah had said to me before: *Write the book that you want to read.*

I had never met a professional writer before, so being a real writer had seemed abstract. Sometimes I felt I was clutching at a dream made of smoke. When I was younger, I imagined that books just magically appeared on the bookshelves of libraries and bookstores. But seeing Jeanne Wakatsuki Houston on stage, answering our questions, and later, sitting at a table so that we could meet her, shake her hand, and have our books signed, I couldn't believe that she was there. That she was real. When I had read her book, I had felt connected to her, but not the way I did at that moment when she was only three feet away from me and we were in the same room breathing the same air. I realized then that a writer shouldn't just write all day, removed from the world. The books a writer produced were important to be sure, but a writer's physical presence could be just as powerful to readers. Jeanne Wakatsuki Houston's presence and the words she spoke that night empowered me as a woman and as a writer of color.

Many of the students waiting in line to meet her were in tears, especially those who were Japanese-American. They kept telling her, "Thank you for writing our story. You've inspired me to keep fighting."

It was then that I fully grasped what a writer did. A writer changed lives and told her readers, *You're not alone. Have courage.* At that moment, I became even more committed to my writing and understood the power of storytelling that I had been given. I would have to honor that gift.

When it was my turn to get my book signed, I told her, "Thank you for inspiring me to write my people's stories. To fight against invisibility. To demand that we be seen. Heard."

She smiled and took the book from me.

To Reyna,
  A great pleasure meeting you—and best of luck to a future of writing many books!
                    Con cariño,
                    Jeanne Wakatsuki Houston

I returned to my apartment that night thinking about that book inside of me that I wanted to write but was afraid to. I knew then that I needed to find the courage to do it.

One of the requirements for graduating from the creative writing program was to write a senior project, which could be a portion of a novel or memoir, or a short-story collection. I decided to tell my story—to write that book I wanted to read. I would write about immigration from a child's perspective.

I didn't get very far.

Even though everything I had written came from my own experiences, I had always fictionalized them because being the protagonist of my story was too painful. Fiction allowed me to explore my experiences from a distance.

As I began to write about my father's departure to the U.S., about my mother's departure, about the years of longing for them, of being afraid they would forget me, I realized that I wasn't ready to write about myself. I couldn't. It hurt too much. I was twenty-three years old, trying to understand why those things had happened to me. I didn't have the maturity to comprehend the emotions I was writing about, nor did I yet have the maturity as a writer to craft my story.

In fiction, I knew I could still write about my experiences and bare my soul without making myself so vulnerable. So I began to write a novel about a girl who was left behind in Mexico when her father goes to the U.S. to look for work. By turning to fiction, I created a character to stand in for me so that when the writing got particularly hard, I could tell myself: "This isn't happening to you. It's happening to your character." That way, under Micah's guidance, I managed to get through my senior project. I knew that, one day, in order to be set free, I would have to write that memoir. But for now, this book had to be a novel, so I let it be.

I didn't have a title for my senior project yet, but eventually, many drafts later, it would come to me: *Across a Hundred Mountains*. I never thought that my senior project would one day become my first published book, a book that would change my life forever.

18

Reyna at her graduation, UCSC, 1999

AN IMPORTANT LESSON Santa Cruz taught me was that it wasn't enough just to survive. I needed to thrive, regardless of the difficult circumstances I found myself in. I had been fortunate to have teachers like Diana, Marta, Micah, and Robin—strong, intelligent, hardworking women who helped shape me into the woman I would one day become.

In June of 1999, I became the first person in my family to graduate from college, finishing my time at Santa Cruz with college honors, honors in my major, and Phi Beta Kappa.

To my surprise, everyone came to my graduation. All my siblings were there—Mago, Carlos, Betty, and Leo—and their spouses and children. Diana and my mother came up, too. And so did my father.

I hadn't expected my father to come. I hadn't allowed myself to even dream that he would. When he showed up in Santa Cruz for my graduation, for a moment I thought he wasn't real, just the way I had felt fourteen years before when he showed up in Iguala. Back then, I thought I had conjured him up—like a spirit—after so many years of longing for his return. More than my mother's presence at my graduation, it was my father's that shocked and pleased me the most. My mother had been coerced into coming to the ceremony by my siblings, but since I knew that no one on earth could make my father do something he didn't want to, I concluded that if he was here, it was because he wanted to be.

They all spent the weekend in Santa Cruz, and joyfully I welcomed them into my world, showing them around the place I had called home for three years. The day before graduation, my father invited me to lunch, and I took him to my favorite Thai restaurant to try my favorite soup. He had never been to a Thai restaurant because, of course, he never ate anything that wasn't Mexican.

And the truth was that for the most part, neither did I. But when I lived with Diana she had introduced me to other kinds of food— Italian and Greek. Edwin, who was Salvadorean, had introduced me to his people's cuisine, and here in Santa Cruz I had ventured out to try new things as well—Indian, Chinese, Japanese, and Thai— whenever I had extra cash.

When we sat down at the table and my father looked at the menu, I was nervous. Perhaps it had been a bad idea to bring him here. What if he hated the food? What if he was angry that I had made him waste his money on this? I should have taken him to Taquería Vallarta instead. He looked at the menu, and as I looked at him, I could see his eyebrows pull together into a frown. His forehead wrinkled the way mine always did. I felt myself retreating to the insecurity of my teenage years.

When the waitress approached, she asked us a question, and my father and I looked at each other in surprise. She was speaking to us in Thai!

"Excuse me?" I said in English.

She repeated herself, again in Thai, and my father and I smiled at each other from across the table. "We aren't Thai," I said. "We're Mexicans!"

The waitress laughed, surprised. "Oh, my God, you could have fooled me!"

My father and I laughed as well. He and I could probably pass for Korean, Cambodian, Filipino, Indian, or Thai. We looked so much alike: slanted eyes, round faces, small foreheads, wide noses. We recognized each other from across the table. I was his daughter, and he was my father, and we shared the same blood flowing through our veins, a common history woven from the same dreams and sorrows. For that brief moment, whatever had happened in the past no longer mattered.

I saw my father's shoulders relax. He said, "Why don't you order for us, Chata, since you know what you like from here?"

"All right," I said, and the tension in my own body began to disappear. I ordered chicken pad thai noodles and my favorite coconut shrimp soup to share.

I had discovered this restaurant over a year and a half earlier. Marta brought me here to celebrate Thanksgiving. I think she felt sorry for me when she found out that unlike most students, who had gone home for the holidays, I stayed in Santa Cruz. I told Marta I had no home to go to, and that I was used to it by now. She must have not believed me—or she must have seen past my lie—because it was then that she asked me if I would let her treat me to lunch. That day, as I sat there with Marta, I hadn't stopped thinking about how much I wanted to be home, how much I missed my father. Not the alcoholic and abusive one, but the other father. The one who taught me to be a big dreamer. I had pictured all of us—Mago, Carlos, Betty—under our father's roof, making tamales and baking a turkey together.

And now here we were, my father and I.

"This is a nice town," he said. "So different from Los Angeles."

I nodded. "I've been happy here."

He looked at me for a moment, and I wondered if perhaps he had heard, woven into that statement, that I hadn't been happy at his house in Los Angeles.

"Then you should stay," he said. "Why would you leave then?"

I didn't know how to answer his question. I wanted to stay, but Santa Cruz isn't an easy place to live when you're poor. As a college student, I didn't mind the low-paying jobs that I had found at the Capitola Mall or selling hot dogs and ice-cream cones at the Boardwalk. Those jobs were okay when I was a student and had loans and grants to help me with my expenses. Once I graduated, I would have none of that support.

"My friends who are staying can't find work," I told him. "They're taking jobs in whatever they can find. There are no good jobs here. And I didn't work so hard to get through college to end up at a coffee shop." Maybe I was being arrogant, or perhaps I had unrealistic expectations of what it meant to have a college degree, but I wasn't about to put up with low-paying jobs. "Maybe in L.A. I'll have better luck."

I didn't tell him that Eddie, the guy I had a crush on and had recently started spending my time with, was also from Los Angeles. "Plus, I'll be closer to you," I said. "To Mago, Carlos."

He didn't say I could stay with him if I came back to L.A., and I didn't ask. I didn't want to live with Mila, especially after she had been the reason my father kept us out of his life.

The food arrived and I watched him dig in, observing his face for a clue about whether or not he liked the Tom Kha Goong. After a few spoonfuls in silence I couldn't wait any longer. "How do you like the soup?"

"It tastes like armpit," he said, but he ate it all.

UCSC has an essay-writing competition for graduating seniors. The topic of the essay is to write about a teacher who impacted their lives. The winner gets to read this essay at the commencement ceremony, and the inspirational teacher is presented with the Distinguished Teacher Award. I jumped at the opportunity. Ever since Diana had taken me in and encouraged me to keep pursuing my education, I had made a vow to one day repay her for her kindness. This was the perfect way to do that—to have my beloved university give her an award, to recognize her as a teacher who changes lives. I had never worked so hard on an essay. A few weeks after I turned it in, I received the news that my essay had won!

UCSC paid Diana's airfare and hotel so she could attend my graduation. I hadn't seen her in the three years since I moved to Santa Cruz, and when she arrived, I was filled with pride to show her that everything she had done for me had paid off. I had honored her in every way I could as her former student and mentee.

At the ceremony, I was invited to read my essay before Diana was presented with the Distinguished Teacher Award. I spoke about the circumstances that had brought her into my life.

"As I was growing up with my father, my siblings and I had to deal with his alcoholism and physical abuse. It got out of control and one day he was arrested for domestic violence. That day, I watched my father being handcuffed by the police and taken away to jail. I didn't know what to do. I felt that my life was falling apart. When I told my teacher, Diana, about what had happened, she offered to take me in. She opened the doors of her house to me and provided me with something my own father had not been able to give me—a safe and loving home." As I spoke about my father's alcoholism, the abuse I had experienced at home, and the lack of support, what mattered most to me was honoring Diana. This was my first time thanking her publicly, and I thought I couldn't speak about the impact she had had on me without sharing the situation that led to her rescuing me. I did not consider how it would affect my father, who despite his broken English, knew perfectly well what I was saying about him to the hundreds of strangers at the ceremony. "She was my hero. She saved me," I said in my speech, not realizing the mistake I had made.

After the ceremony, my father retreated once again into his stoicism, his curtness, his indifference. The man I had had lunch with the day before, who had laughed with me and eaten my soup even though it tasted like armpit, was gone.

He gave me a quick hug and seemed unwilling to be in the pictures we took. He had withdrawn into himself, and I could see how much he yearned to leave. If he hadn't come up with Carlos and his family, he would have taken off.

My father was a private man. Through the years, whenever I asked him about the past, he would rarely share anything about himself. He would say, "The past is past. Just let it go, Chata. Move on with your life." He didn't understand that only by knowing about it, and writing about it, could I come to understand it. Only then could I let it go.

"Reynita, I'm so proud of you!" Diana said, joined by Carlos and Mago, my mother and Betty, along with Eddie, some friends, and Marta, Micah, and Robin.

My sisters, my teachers, my boss—these were the women who had been part of my education and were here to see me end this journey and begin a new one.

I looked at my father, waiting—hoping—for the words I had always longed to hear from him. That he was proud of me, that he wanted the best for me and from this moment on would never lose faith in me again. What he said was: "You told everyone I'm an alcoholic. That I beat you." I realized then that despite the fact that I had finally broken the cycle my family had been stuck in for generations—making history by becoming the first in my family to graduate from college—that speech was what my father would always remember about that day.

I opened my mouth to explain, to defend myself, but at seeing the pain so openly displayed on his face, a vulnerability I rarely got to see, I stopped wanting to justify my words and instead I wanted to apologize for what I had done, for the hurt I inflicted by sharing my truth with the world. But I said nothing. Like him, I didn't know how to say I was sorry.

Though he didn't forgive me, my father managed to push his wounded pride aside and did something that deeply touched me. I didn't witness it, but Diana later told me that before heading back to Los Angeles, my father had approached her, shook her hand, and said, "Thank you for what you did for my family."

That day at my graduation, despite what happened between me and my father, I felt elated, relieved, and immensely proud. The three years of working hard—of pushing past my fears, of clutching tightly to my dream with sheer tenacity—had brought me here. I was now a university graduate, a recipient of a bachelor of arts degree. No one could take that from me.

I returned to Porter Meadow, where I had walked on my first day in Santa Cruz, and looked out at the ocean before me and the redwood trees behind me. I breathed long and deep, filling my body, my spirit, with the sweet scent of Santa Cruz, and as the fog slowly rolled over the campus, I said goodbye to my home.

Reyna at her graduation with her family and Diana, 1999

Book Two

THE HOME I CARRY

19

My BUDDING ROMANCE with Eddie helped soothe the sting of my new estrangement from my father after my graduation. Once again, my father and I were back to not speaking to each other, and this made me cling to Eddie in a way I shouldn't have. It made me desperate for Eddie's love and approval to replace the hurt I had felt when my father returned to Los Angeles without saying goodbye.

I had met Eddie the year before when I joined Los Mejicas. He was one of the best dancers in the group. Not only could he seduce an audience with his charisma onstage, but offstage he was even more charming. He was very popular, especially with the girls, since he was a great listener and had a wonderful sense of humor. Unlike other guys, he didn't intimidate me or try to dominate me with his machismo. I had had too many disappointments from the Latino guys on campus who only wanted one-night stands and treated me like just another girl to add to their list of college conquests.

We had become good friends from the moment we met, and though I harbored a suspicion that Eddie might be gay, I never asked and he never said. Besides, you couldn't live in Santa Cruz without ever questioning your sexuality. This is where I had met my first lesbian, gay, and bisexual friends after all. The year before, I'd had my first crush on a girl, but after one kiss with a girl, it was clear to me that when it came to members of my own sex, I just wanted to be friends with them. I liked guys too much, especially Eddie.

When my final quarter had begun three months earlier, I couldn't believe I was graduating without ever once having had a college boyfriend at UCSC to talk to about our future dreams. I wanted someone who was on the same journey as me, who understood me. I was ready for a different kind of love—a guy who didn't remind me of my father for a change. I thought that guy would be Eddie. I felt safe with him, his tenderness and sweet smile; the vulnerable sensibility he openly and unabashedly displayed was something I had yet to see in a man.

One day, a few weeks before my graduation, he and I found ourselves messing around in his room. We did everything but have sex, since he didn't want to go "all the way." He claimed to be old-fashioned and wanted to save himself for marriage. I thought he was a guy like no other, and I was actually glad that he didn't want sex from me.

"Sex just complicates things," Eddie said. He was a big fan of the Mexican writer Carlos Cuauhtémoc Sánchez, and gave me a copy of *Juventud en Éxtasis* ("Youth in Sexual Ecstasy"), about the perils of premarital sex and the purity of marriage and love. Unlike my high school boyfriend, who had harassed me about having sex with him until I consented and lost my virginity under pressure, Eddie spouted the ideals of only giving yourself to someone out of love. At twenty-two, he was still a virgin, whereas I had already slept with a number of guys and felt ashamed of my sexual history. The books Eddie gave me made me even more ashamed.

I wanted to experience that celibate love that he seemed to believe in. Being with him made me want to be pure and innocent the way he was.

Eddie was born in the coastal state of Nayarit, in the west-central part of Mexico, and came to the U.S. as a child. Some of his sisters still lived in Nayarit, and he was planning to visit them as soon as school ended. I told him I had never been anywhere in Mexico except for my state of Guerrero. "Why don't you come with me to my hometown?" he asked me a few weeks before graduation.

"You serious?" I said. He was taking me to his place of birth? That could only mean one thing—things between us were getting serious. He hadn't asked me to be his girlfriend yet, but I assumed that was just a matter of time, or otherwise he wouldn't be taking me home.

"It'll be fun," he said. "So, what do you say?"

Ever since I joined Los Mejicas, I had been fantasizing about traveling through Mexico to visit the states, besides Guerrero, where my favorite dances originated: Veracruz, Jalisco, Michoacán, and Nayarit.

So, after graduation, when my siblings and my parents returned to Los Angeles, I eagerly headed to Mexico with Eddie, planning to spend part of my summer in his hometown. Then I would return to Los Angeles and begin my new life as a university graduate.

We arrived in Guadalajara and took a bus to Eddie's hometown in Nayarit, which was a few hours to the north. I was excited to get a chance to see a new part of Mexico and to share this experience with Eddie. I still couldn't believe he had taken an interest in me, because in my experience popular guys like him never looked at me twice. I wasn't beautiful or remarkably intelligent, just an ordinary girl with extraordinary dreams, which usually wasn't enough to impress the guys I wanted to impress.

Now I was in Mexico with the boy I was falling in love with. As the bus made its way along the highway, I rested my head on his chest, thinking about the wonderful time we were going to have. I hoped we would finally take our relationship to the next level.

As we got closer to our destination, he told me about his sisters, his nieces and nephew, and his hometown. I couldn't wait to meet his family and to explore his home. Then Eddie stopped talking and became serious. His ever-present smile disappeared. He looked at me and said, "Reyna, there's something I want to tell you."

I sat up on my seat to face him. "What is it?"

"Look, don't take this the wrong way, okay? Well, I really like you a lot, and I have fun hanging out with you, but I just want to be friends."

"What do you mean?" I asked. His black hair, as usual, fell over his forehead and partially covered his brown eyes. I wanted to reach over and brush it back, like I had done many times before.

Eddie looked out the window as he said, "I mean, let's just be friends, okay? I know you care about me a lot, and I care about you, too, but I'm not ready for a relationship."

"Why are you doing this? Why here, on this bus? And in Mexico no less?"

"I'm sorry, I don't mean to hurt you," he said, looking down at his hands. "It's just that I'm not ready for a commitment, and well, I feel bad that you seem to be expecting more from this trip than I can give you. I don't want to hurt you, Reyna. Believe me." He finally looked at me, his eyes pleading with me to not make a scandal. "Can't we just be friends?"

I didn't know what to say, what to do. How was I supposed to react? I was on a bus heading to a state I had never been to, where I knew no one, going to the home of the boy I adored who had just broken my heart. I knew he was trying, in the best way he could, to make clear what his intentions were with me and to do away with all those fantasies in my head that I had created, but why the hell couldn't he have ended things with me before I got on the plane with him?

I looked at my hands, feeling like a coward for remaining silent.

"Let's just enjoy our time together," he said. "Okay?"

The bus driver announced our arrival. I took a deep breath, forced myself to swallow my tears, and followed Eddie off the bus. I looked at the ticket office, wondering if I should buy a return ticket to Guadalajara and go back to the U.S. I had to get out of here. I couldn't stay here with him. Not like this.

But Eddie's older sister and nieces and nephew were there, and I had to turn my eyes away from the ticket office and resign myself to the fact that there would be no running away.

"This is my friend, Reyna," Eddie said as an introduction. I winced at the way he emphasized the word "friend."

"Nice to meet you," I told his sister, shaking her hand. And with a big sigh, I went to collect my luggage, swallowing back my tears.

Throughout the following days, I discovered a new level of hurt. Being trapped with him in his sister's house was torture. Eddie, with his jokes and his laughter, brought his beautiful energy into the house. Everyone loved being with him. His nieces and nephew clung to him, and so did his sister. We would swim in the river, explore the cornfields, climb the rocks along the riverbank. We explored the city center, the marketplace, the ruins of the temples built by the indigenous tribes of long ago. His hometown was so beautiful, just like Eddie had said. The earth was a deep crimson, and it was used by the locals for making ceramics. I had never seen anything like it. Even the river was red, like liquid terra-cotta. The town was so different from Iguala. Even though the homes were made of cinder block, simple and humble, this town didn't have the grinding poverty that my hometown did. There was color everywhere: houses painted in bright green, yellow, and hot pink; the redness of the earth; the electric blue of the Nayarit sky. It was idyllic. The perfect place for falling in love.

The beauty of the town only made my pain worse. From that first night on, I would cry myself to sleep, trying to keep quiet and not wake up Eddie's nieces, whose room I shared. With Eddie, I wanted to have a relationship without the turmoil, drama, and psychological trauma of my abusive upbringing getting in the way. I wanted to be an important part of his life, just the way he was in mine.

In the mornings, I would wake up with my eyelids swollen and my eyes red. Eddie's sister took pity on me and gave me fresh potato slices to get the swelling to go down so I wouldn't look like a fool all day.

"I don't know why he did this," I told her as she applied the slices over my eyes. "He brought me to his hometown just to break my heart."

"It's a cruel thing to do to someone. It's so unlike him," she said. "I've never known anyone as sweet as my brother. I really hope you can forgive him."

As the days passed, I kept hoping he would reconsider. You just don't break a girl's heart in a place where she doesn't know a soul, where she has nowhere to go, where she has no one to give her love and help her heal.

Then I realized that I did have a place to go. That I did have someone. "I'm leaving," I told him the next day. "I'm going to Iguala."

"I'm sorry, Reyna," he said. "De verdad. Can you please call me when you get there so I know you're safe?"

I nodded and walked out of the door with my suitcase and made my way south to my grandmother.

It took me thirteen hours to get to my hometown, and I cried most of the way. I was terrified to be traveling alone on a bus at night. The times I had gone to Iguala, I traveled during the day and my bus ride had only been three hours from Mexico City. Nayarit was far to the north, and I had to cross three states to get to Guerrero. I didn't know the route at all. I felt lost in more ways than I could count, a vagabond in a country that felt more bewildering to me than ever before.

When I got to Iguala late at night, my aunt and my grandmother were surprised to see me, even though I had called to let them know of my arrival. It was the way I looked; even the darkness couldn't hide my bloodshot eyes. I didn't want to tell anyone that I had just had my heart broken. But they could all see that I was suffering. When my cousin Lupe cleaned the house, I volunteered to help. She put on the songs of Marco Antonio "El Buki" Solís, and I would burst into tears as I was mopping the floor.

Te extraño más que nunca y no sé qué hacer.
Despierto y te recuerdo al amanecer.

"There's nothing harder than living without you!" I would sing. "Suffering from the anxiety to see you come back."

In the evening, I sat at the dining table with Abuelita Chinta, complaining about my love life. My grandmother told me a story I had never heard before.

"I understand your pain, m'ija," she said to me as she patted my head.

"Thanks, Abuelita. I know you suffered a lot when my grandfather died," I said as I took a sip of the cinnamon tea she had prepared for me. My grandfather, Abuelito Gertrudis, passed away a week before I was born. My pregnant mother didn't go to his funeral because the locals believed it was bad luck for an unborn baby to be exposed to all the dead bodies and wandering souls in the cemetery. Of all my siblings, I was the only one born left-handed, just like my grandfather. I had always believed this was his special gift to me, upon his death.

"I wasn't talking about your grandfather," she said.

My grandmother told me that when she was a señorita, she had fallen in love with a young man, but her father and brothers hadn't approved of their relationship. "Eliseo was poor, nothing more than a simple peasant," she said, "and my family wouldn't allow me to be with him. So I ran away from home and went to live with him, desperate to fight for our love. We loved the way young people tend to do—con ganas y entrega total." She laughed at that before continuing. "But my father and brothers came looking for me, and they grabbed me by the hair and dragged me out of his house. They threatened to kill Eliseo if he came near me again, and that was the end of our relationship."

"You really think they would have killed him, Abuelita?" I asked, holding her hand.

"Yes. They could have easily done away with him, m'ija. You know what this place is like. Here, you can easily disappear and no one would ever know why or how it happened."

As punishment, she was sent to work at her brother's cantina. She spent her days serving beer and tequila to borrachos, drunks. "The bar was no place for a young innocent woman, but my family no longer saw me as pure. So I had no choice but to work there along with the women of ill repute, who always mocked my innocence and naïveté, telling me to stop pretending I was a blanca palomita, a white dove. That was where I met your grandfather. He was twenty years older and had grown obsessed with me. He wouldn't let any of the other women serve him his drinks. He wanted only me to pour his tequila and mezcal. One day, after work, he waited for me to come out of the bar and he pushed me against the brick wall and put a knife to my throat, threatening to kill me if I didn't become his woman. My father and brothers did not defend me. They did not stop him from pursuing me."

"And that was how you ended up with my abuelo?" I said in disbelief.

"Yes. But I never forgot my first love."

I sat there with my grandmother, dumbfounded by the story she had just told me. How was it possible? How could that story be true? I thought about the tales I had heard of the old days, when a man would kidnap a woman by throwing her on his horse, like a sack of corn, and running off with her, taking her away from her family and everything she had known. Many Mexican marriages had begun that way. I knew my grandmother's story was plausible, and yet I couldn't believe it.

I never met my grandfather since he died of alcoholism eight days before my birth, but the years that I lived with my grandmother she had been a devoted wife to him, even in death. She had gone to the cemetery every week to bring him flowers and clean his grave. She placed a framed photograph of him on her altar, where he sat surrounded by saints and La Virgen de Guadalupe. She prayed at that altar every night and looked at his photograph. How could she tell me now that he had forced her at knifepoint to be with him? How could she forgive him and not only give him flowers but be so loyal to him in death that she never remarried?

When I asked her, she simply nodded. "Era mi esposo," she said. "For better or for worse, he was my husband. He gave me five children."

And I suddenly hated her father and her brothers. I hated my grandfather for what he did. I hated my culture for breeding these men who would treat women as if they were merely objects to be used and abused. As Sor Juana Inés de la Cruz had once written, men like that were the cause of all that they blame on women.

My grandmother was so used to being victimized that even after he died she was still a faithful wife. And what about that young man she had loved? I asked her. Did the pain of their forbidden romance eventually wear off?

"He fell in love with someone else," she said.

This was the only time my grandmother ever told me anything about her past, which ended up making my failed romance with Eddie worth the pain. I never learned why Eddie decided to end our relationship without giving it a chance. But thanks to my abuelita, it no longer mattered. My heartbreak had been the catalyst for her revelation—a grandmother's gift of love.

"I'm sorry, Abuelita."

"Me too, m'ija," she said.

My grandmother and I hugged each other and cried for the love we could not have. For what would never be.

Abuelita Chinta as a young woman

20

Carlos, Norma, and Natalia

I RETURNED TO Los Angeles and decided to go on with my life and get over my failed romance with Eddie. I wanted to embrace this next stage with optimism. I was a new college graduate with my whole future before me. It was an exciting time for me, and I was ready to work hard for my dreams.

My brother, Carlos, was generous enough to open his home to me. I moved in with him and his common-law wife, Norma, and their one-year-old daughter, Natalia. They lived in a tiny one-bedroom apartment, and all they had to offer me was a couch in the living room, but I was grateful for the couch. I told them it would be for only a month or so. Soon, I told them—told myself—I would be a published author, sharing my writing with the world and making a difference.

Their apartment was in East Los Angeles, an area I wasn't familiar with. Though I had grown up in L.A., I only knew Highland Park and nearby communities, like Pasadena. I was a little familiar with downtown because that was where my mother had lived for thirteen years. Other than that, L.A. was a big unknown city that seemed to go on forever.

As the days passed and I found myself lying on my brother's couch night after night, I came to the frightening realization that I didn't know a thing about how to get published—I mean published for real, not the self-publishing I had done in Santa Cruz with a school grant. In my writing classes we had never talked about how to approach publishers or how to find an agent, and I was completely clueless about where to begin. In Santa Cruz, I had learned the craft of writing. I learned to take risks and venture out of my comfort zone. What I didn't learn at UCSC, however, was what to do with myself once I was back in the real world.

I looked in the classified section of the newspaper to see if any publishers were looking for writers to publish or if any agents were looking for writers to represent. Maybe I could find someone to hire me to write a novel or pay me to finish the one I was working on. I found a few ads for local newspapers hiring journalists, which wasn't what I had in mind. But as the weeks turned into a month, then two, I ended up responding to those ads because a job writing news articles was better than no job at all. I was told that creative writing was not the same as journalism and that to them my degree was useless, thank you very much. I had written for the school paper at PCC, but that didn't seem to count.

Some of my friends, who had also majored in what I began to think of as useless fields, were heading to the office of the Los Angeles Unified School District to get jobs as teachers, even if teaching hadn't been their original career choice.

"You should check it out," one of my friends said to me after finding a job as a math teacher. It was August of 1999 and the LAUSD was in the middle of a severe teacher shortage. They were giving away emergency credentials to anyone who had a bachelor's degree.

"I don't want to be a teacher," I said to my friend. "I want to be a writer." I continued my search, but then another month passed, and the couch at Carlos's house was getting worn and so was my welcome. I turned twenty-four that September, and my worst nightmare was becoming a reality: I was jobless, broke, and had over $20,000 in student loans to repay. I wasn't contributing anything to household expenses and was becoming a burden, but my brother never complained. He was being as supportive as he could and was grateful that I was keeping Norma company while he worked two jobs. Being a housewife and taking care of a toddler wasn't easy, and at least I was good at washing dishes and entertaining Norma with interesting stories.

I couldn't turn to Diana for help. I told myself she had done enough for me already. I couldn't expect her to keep rescuing me. I needed to take care of myself as I had done during my three years in Santa Cruz.

I missed the city terribly, the smallness of it, the sense of community, the ocean, the redwoods, having my own room and an income, regardless of how meager it had been. I could ride my bike wherever I wanted and feel safe, and wherever I went I was sure to run into a familiar face—a classmate, a teacher, a friend. L.A. was a city of concrete and strangers. It was gray and dull, not the lush, vibrant green and blue of Santa Cruz. It made me feel small and insignificant, lost and alone.

I missed my job in the Kresge Maintenance Department, a job I had truly loved. I was beginning to feel useless. My student loan grace period would be over in January. I had two months left to find a job. Little by little, the realization that my education at UCSC hadn't prepared me for the real world began to frighten me. The plain and simple truth was that I was a storyteller, but I didn't know how to make a living telling stories. I had never realized that there were two sides to writing: the art and the business. Sleeping on my brother's living room couch, I started to feel like an ignorant fool with nothing to show for my college education.

Since I had double-majored in film and video, I went to Hollywood to look for jobs, hoping to have better luck in film than I had had in publishing. I found listings for internships at TV stations and film studios, but all of them were unpaid positions—every single one.

"You want me to work for free?" I would ask, astounded. "I have over $20,000 in debt I need to pay!"

"But just think about how valuable this experience would be," they would say.

In early November, I went to the Pasadena Mall with Norma to window-shop. We saw a "Now Hiring" sign at a clothing store. The holidays would be upon us soon, and they were hiring seasonal workers. All I could think of was that when the holidays were over I would need to start paying my student loan for a college degree that day by day seemed to be losing its value.

"You should apply," Norma said to me. "A job is a job."

"I know," I said. "It's just not what I thought I would be doing by now, you know?"

Norma was seven years younger than me. Like Betty, she was a teenage mother with a maturity that amazed me.

"It's a temporary job," she said. "It'll provide you with some money while you figure out your next step. You have a green card, a college degree. Doors will soon open for you. Just be patient and don't be so hard on yourself."

Norma had come to the U.S. from El Salvador four years earlier, smuggled in the back of one of those infamous trailer trucks where immigrants sometimes die of extreme heat and no ventilation. Once she and my brother were married, he helped legalize her status, but at the time, she was still undocumented, and because of her baby and because she was a minor in an illicit relationship, she had stopped going to school. In addition to the challenges of being a young mom and wife, on a daily basis she had to deal with her fear of being deported and separated from her child, or that her baby's father might end up in prison. I knew that I had nothing to complain about. In the scheme of things, I didn't have it so bad.

"You're right," I told her.

A week later, I had a job steam-ironing and putting price tags on clothes. I also stood at the door greeting customers. "Hi. How's your day going?" I said over and over to customers who pretended not to see me or hear me as they walked into the store. The Christmas songs played for hours on end, burrowing so deeply into my mind I would hear them in my sleep. My coworkers were mostly high school students. At twenty-four, I was the oldest employee in the store, and my manager was a kid who wasn't even planning on going to college.

When I asked her why, she eyed me up and down said, "What for? It didn't do you any good."

At home, things had deteriorated. Though at first they had been supportive, now Carlos and Mago had started making fun of me. "You with your college degree, and now look at you, working for minimum wage at a clothing store as a seasonal worker," they said.

To be fair, I deserved it. Whenever I had spoken to them while in Santa Cruz, I had done nothing but encourage them to return to college for their degrees. "You'll have great jobs—amazing careers. Earn lots of money!" I would tell them, often criticizing Mago for working at a collection agency and Carlos for being an office clerk at a hospital and having to work two jobs just to make ends meet.

I had been a snob, and I became an even bigger snob when I

graduated and framed my diploma, hung it up for all to see on a wall that wasn't even mine to begin with.

As I always did, I turned to my writing and my Mexican community for inspiration. East L.A. had Mexicans—lots of them! It was wonderful to be part of the majority again. On my days off, I would walk around the neighborhood with Norma and my baby niece. We would hear the ranchera music drifting from open windows, smell beans boiling on the stove, see taco trucks on almost every corner.

It was in East L.A. where I discovered an appreciation for the shopping cart. They were everywhere: a woman pushing a shopping cart loaded with dirty laundry on her way to the Laundromat on Olympic Boulevard, a man pushing a shopping cart carrying a large aluminum pot filled with corn on the cob or tamales. "Tamaaaales. Eloootes!" he would say and people would run out of their homes with money in hand. An older couple pushed a shopping cart filled with cans and bottles. I would watch them go down the length of Soto Street, rummaging through trash cans as they made their way to the recycling center nearby. A woman pushed a shopping cart filled with the groceries she had bought at the local market, her three children clinging to each side of the cart, begging her to go faster, faster. A homeless person pushed a shopping cart down César Chávez Avenue carrying everything he owned in the world, turning the shopping cart into a home that he could carry.

Who were these people? What were their stories?

Even though I would come home exhausted, my feet throbbing from standing all day, after everyone had gone to bed I would sit at the kitchen table and write late into the night. I began a second collection of short stories called *The Shopping Cart Chronicles* and continued to work on my novel.

21

Reyna and her couch

IN DECEMBER, PANIC set in. With the arrival of the new year, my seasonal job would end and my first student loan bill would arrive. Though I had promised Norma I would be patient and optimistic about my future, my debt kept me up at night. I wasn't going to default on my loans, no matter what. I had promised to repay this money, and I would keep my promise.

"LAUSD is still hiring," my teacher friends said.

The morning of my day off, I dragged myself off the couch and headed downtown to the school district's office, and turned in an application. In two hours, I had a full-time job as a middle school teacher, earning more than I had ever expected.

Even though I had liked my tutoring job on campus, being a teacher wasn't a career I had seriously considered. Now I was the new remedial English and ESL teacher at a middle school in South Central Los Angeles. Due to overcrowded schools, the district had a year-round system, with tracks A, B, C, and D. I was placed on B track, which meant I would work through the summer. My track started in July, and it didn't dawn on me that by starting in January, I would be coming into the school year late. It turned out I was taking over a class that had already had five different substitutes. I knew nothing about being a teacher, not even how to fill out a roster. All I thought about was the salary. With that kind of money, I could rent my own place, buy a new car, pay my bills, and put an end to Mago's and Carlos's mocking. I would finally have something to show for this college education I had worked so hard to get.

I was finally going to be what my father had once dreamed for us to be—a working professional.

To help me get ready for my new job, Mago took me shopping. If there was one thing my sister could do well, it was picking out stylish clothes. I wanted to look older and sophisticated so that I would be taken seriously. I looked younger than twenty-four, and at five feet tall, I was the size of a child. I didn't have much money, so we went to Ross.

We walked down the aisles, and Mago picked out dresses and skirts, professional-looking jackets and blouses for me to try on. I watched her with admiration because she seemed so sure of herself here, touching fabric, admiring the cut of a blazer, the buttons on a blouse, the waist of a dress. "Oh, look at this one," she said as she held out a red dress with spaghetti straps.

"That's not a teacher's dress," I said.

"Not for you, for me," she said. She looked at her belly and with a shake of her head put the dress back. At twenty-eight years old, she was seven months pregnant with her third child.

"Soon you'll get to go clothes shopping for yourself again," I said.

She smiled, and we continued down the racks. Mago and I had been drifting apart ever since she moved out of my father's house when I was seventeen. When she was planning her escape, she had promised to take me with her, but she had left me behind to fend for myself. Since my father forbade me to see her, we had to sneak behind his back to spend time with each other, and it was always awkward between us. When I left for Santa Cruz, I thought I had succeeded in learning how to take care of myself.

Now as we walked around Ross, there was a part of me that wanted things to go back to how they used to be between us. I missed the special bond that had seen us through our difficult childhood. I wanted to reconnect. I wanted to once again be her "Nena," her little baby, but seeing her swollen belly reminded me that those times were long gone. She had her own children now.

"How are you feeling about next week?" Mago said.

"I'm afraid," I confessed. I had attended a one-week training session hosted by LAUSD staff, where I had been shown how to fill out a roster, prepare a lesson plan, follow the standards, and become familiar with classroom procedures. But the crash course on teaching had left me even more frightened. I had never once taken an education class. At UCSC, my friend Claudia had majored in education. I wished now I had asked her more questions about her classes or gone with her when she did her student teaching. I made a mental note to call her and ask her what pedagogy meant.

"Don't be scared," Mago said as we walked back to her car. "Act confident, pretend that you know what you're doing. They're just kids."

So am I! I wanted to say. I took a deep breath and decided right then and there that perhaps the time had come for me to grow up.

In addition to buying new clothes, I did what I had tried so hard to avoid—I bought a brand-new car. Unlike Santa Cruz, where I could get by with a bicycle, it was nearly impossible to get anywhere in L.A. without a reliable motor vehicle, especially with such a long commute. So I added a car payment to my growing list of debts, and with that new burden, I finally entered adulthood.

In January 2000, a few days after celebrating the new millennium, I drove my brand-new Toyota Corolla from East L.A. to South Central at 5:30 a.m. Classes started at 7:20, and I wanted to give myself enough time to get to my classroom and prepare myself mentally and emotionally for my first day.

I wore a long-sleeved burgundy velvet dress and matching high heels. Mago had said heels were a must if I wanted to be taller than my students. "They'll respect you more if they have to look up at you," she said. But I had rarely worn heels, and as I made my way across the parking lot with my new briefcase in hand, I felt like a little girl playing dress-up.

My classroom was out in the bungalows farthest from the main building. Except for the grassy lawn in the front, the school grounds were nothing but concrete. Since there were no flowers and only a few trees, I put in a lot of effort to make my classroom look beautiful and welcoming. The clock ticked by much too quickly, and I hurried to decorate my classroom with the pretty trimming and posters with inspirational quotes I had bought at a teacher supply store. I had spent the weekend reviewing the English textbook and was optimistic that my passion for reading and writing would more than compensate for my lack of teaching experience. I thought of my favorite teachers—Diana, Marta, Micah—and wondered what it was about them that I could try to imitate. Their kindness, their interest in me that went beyond my performance in their classroom, their willingness to help me reach my full potential—that was the kind of teacher I wanted to be. I would do everything I could to inspire and motivate my young pupils.

The bell rang, and I opened the door and stood there as one by one my students walked in. Who knew eighth graders could be so tall? In eighth grade, I had been four-foot-eight! I stood as straight as I could in my high heels as I welcomed my students into my classroom, but sure enough, almost every kid who walked in was taller than me. They were all Latino, which made me happy until I realized most of them were little wannabe cholos—the very kids my father had kept us away from when we were growing up, the kids I grew up being scared of. But then I thought of Betty, of how the abuse and lack of support at home and school had driven her to want to join a gang. I wondered what kind of personal lives these kids had. I hoped I could make my classroom feel like a home for them and for me.

The kids all knew one another. I was the outsider. There were sixteen boys and six girls. I had heard rumors that boys were tougher to discipline than girls. But as I inspected the girls and took in their heavy makeup and hard-core chola expressions, they seemed just as tough as the boys.

"Good morning," I said, but they continued talking as if I weren't there. "Good morning," I said, trying on my teacher voice. It cracked, and I had to clear my throat to continue, but it worked. The students grew silent and they all turned to look at me. "Hello, everyone. I'm Ms. Grande."

The class erupted with laughter. "Seriously?" someone exclaimed. I was used to the laughter. Growing up with such a grandiose name had made me the butt of many jokes. In that moment I once again hated my name with a passion. Reyna Grande, the little Big Queen. Why couldn't I have a more sensible name, like María González or Lupe Martínez? Or an elegant name like my great-grandmother's, Catalina Catalán. Or how about the name of the heroine in my favorite telenovela, *La Dueña*. Regina Villarreal would have been perfect, strong and fierce, especially if you added an extra roll to the r's.

"Can we call you Ms. Chiquita?" one of the students asked.

The class erupted in laughter again.

"No, you may not," I said. My heart was beating so fast, I felt as if it was going to burst at any moment. "I am Ms. Grande."

"So, Ms. Chiquita," one of the girls said, "where did you buy your dress?"

They eyed me up and down, and I suddenly wished I had not listened to Mago and had bought myself a dozen pair of pants and long-sleeve blouses instead. Not the fashionable dresses and the pencil skirts that hung in my closet. The dress reached my knees, and there was nothing indecent about it, but now I tried to pull the hem down, feeling suddenly exposed. No matter how much I wanted to, the dress would not magically grow in length to my ankles.

"So, Ms. Chiquita," one of the boys asked, "do you have a boyfriend?"

In the teacher's cafeteria, I found terrified faces that were mirror images of mine. Young teachers who, like me, had been thrown into the classroom with one week of training. We were the majority. The minority were the veteran teachers, some of whom had permanent scowls. When I sat with them during lunch and they asked me about my day, and saw how flustered I was, they said, "It gets better. The first year is the hardest."

At first, I believed them and hoped things would get easier, that I could learn how to teach and engage and discipline my students, that I could learn how to follow the standards and create amazing lessons. But everything I tried ended in chaos. I would spend the weekends coming up with classroom activities that I thought would make learning fun, only to be met with boredom and apathy. I tried to channel Diana and Marta, to be kind and giving, to show that I cared, but I realized those things were easier to do when you had students who met you at least halfway. But the worst thing was that they could smell my fear, see it in my face, hear it in my voice, and they took great pleasure in it. The game of the day was *How much will Ms. Chiquita take before she runs off like the others?* Having chased away five substitutes already, why not chase away the new teacher and finish the school year never having to do any real work?

Later I would discover that most inexperienced teachers like me were placed in inner-city schools. The Latino and black kids who lived in these neighborhoods had no say in the matter and were stuck with us. Since we held emergency credentials, we couldn't request a transfer out of the school where we were placed. By the end of the year more than half of those new teachers would be gone, having quit teaching and moved on to another, less rigorous career. They would be replaced with new young faces looking as scared as I had on my first day.

In the evening, I would arrive at Carlos's house feeling emotionally drained and physically exhausted. And I didn't have a room of my own where I could retreat and recharge. I was still sleeping on the couch in the living room. My writing waited for me to return to it, but I could write only a few pages before exhaustion overwhelmed me and I had to put my novel and short stories away, promising myself to return to them another day.

In addition to the mountain of papers I needed to grade, the district personnel had also failed to mention in the training course that I wasn't going to be doing much teaching. In middle school, I soon discovered, it was all about disciplining. Having grown up with a father whose only form of discipline was to insult us or hit us, I was rather limited in my resources. If I didn't want to end up in jail, I knew I had to find a different approach.

When I asked other teachers for advice, they said. "Do time-outs."

"What are those?" I said.

I got a list of discipline techniques: give them time-outs, give them detention during lunch or after school, take things away. I could send the troublemaker to another class if I made prior arrangements with the other teacher. I could call their parents. I could send them to the principal or the dean if worse came to worst.

None of it worked. I grew desperate. My classroom was a zoo. I was so ashamed I kept my doors closed so that no one could hear me trying to deal with the chaos. I didn't want anyone to see the boy who insisted on riding his skateboard across the classroom; or the girls who huddled in a corner putting on their makeup and doing their hair, stinking up my classroom with hairspray and perfume; or the paper airplanes that flew above my head and crashed into the chalkboard before nose-diving to the floor; or the kids who pretended to listen to the audiobooks at the listening center but were actually pulling the tape out of the cassettes.

Another teacher recommended positive reinforcement.

"What's that?" I asked, completely taken aback by the word "positive." Could discipline be done in a positive way? Why hadn't anyone told my father?

"It means you reward them for good behavior," she said. "And the more you reward them for the good things they do, the better they will behave. You can buy pencils, cute erasers, and stickers as prizes."

I tried to picture giving my students those "prizes." They would throw those cute erasers at me instead of the paper airplanes. And did she really think eighth graders would want stickers?

At seeing the doubt in my face, she quickly added, "You can also try popcorn and a movie on Fridays, or pizza parties at the end of the month. Or buy board games and reward them with free time."

"Blah," another teacher said, waving the words away with her hands. "Don't listen to her. That's not discipline. That's bribery." She turned to me and said, "You'll just end up spending a lot of your hard-earned money buying things to bribe them with. Don't. All you're doing is paying them to behave."

"You should go observe Ms. Hoang's class," another teacher suggested. "She runs a tight ship."

I glanced around the cafeteria to see if I could spot Ms. Hoang. I didn't think I had met her yet.

"She never leaves her room," the teachers said. "She keeps prisoners."

During my free period the next day, I went to observe Ms. Hoang. She frightened me. Though she was only a few years older than I was—thirty, at most—she didn't look young. Even though she was dressed in a silk blouse, black pencil skirt, and high heels, she looked like a drill sergeant. She held her body ramrod straight—rigid, tall, imposing. Her hair was pulled back in a bun so tight it looked painful. I sat in a corner by the door and watched the transformation in her seventh graders. The minute they walked into the classroom they stood straighter, their smiles disappeared, and whatever conversations they had been having in the hallways ended abruptly. They walked in complete silence. Chairs did not screech, shoes did not squeak against the linoleum, papers did not rustle, textbooks did not slam onto desks, gum wasn't smacked. None of the sounds in my classroom existed here.

The warm-up exercise was on the projector, and Ms. Hoang told them only once to take out their paper and start the warm-up. Like robots, they sat in unison, pulled out their pens and papers in unison, and got to work without being told twice.

Ten minutes later, no sound had been uttered. Finally, Ms. Hoang broke the silence and said, "Time is up. Please turn in your work," and what happened next was like a dance. The students on the far right passed their papers to the row to their left, and then that row passed the papers to the next row, and the next, until the papers magically ended up at the last desk in the corner closest to the teacher's desk. That girl put the papers in a neat stack and placed them in front of Ms. Hoang.

"Open your books to page 181," she said. "And read to page 185. Be prepared to discuss it in ten minutes."

In unison, the students reached under their desks, took out their textbooks, and set out to do what they were told. Still not a sound, not a word from any of them.

I stared in awe at Ms. Hoang, wondering what kind of magic this was. Surely, it had to be magic. I had only seen such a thing in stories like *Harry Potter*, where teachers literally used their magic wands to discipline their students.

Afterward, when the students had filed out of her room, leaving as quietly as they had come, I approached her, a thousand questions in my head, but all I could say was "How?" I couldn't even finish my thought.

She shrugged. "You have to show them who's in charge," she said. "The first three weeks of school, we do nothing but drills. Drills and drills and more drills until they know the routine. And those who break the rules suffer the consequences. You can't teach them anything until they respect you. Until they know *you* are in charge, not them."

Drills worked in the army, she said, why wouldn't they work in the classroom?

As she gave me a list of suggestions of the many ways I could humiliate my students into submission, her voice sent chills down my spine. She spoke as if she were giving me orders, even though she was giving me advice.

As she recommended, I called the parents of my worst students and had them come sit in the class to observe their children. It backfired on me. Those kids—the ones who gave me the most grief—behaved like saints. I had never seen them so quiet and respectful, so eager to do their work and obey the rules. They even called me Ms. Grande instead of Ms. Chiquita. To make matters worse, the rest of the students, those whose parents were not there, behaved worse than usual.

At the end of class, the three parents confronted me, and I cowered before them. "You made us take a day off work for this?" one of them said.

"There's nothing wrong with my child. Are you blind? He's a great student as far as I can see."

"Didn't you see my son do all his work?" another said. "Which is more than I can say for the other students!"

You should humiliate them, Ms. Hoang had said, but the one who was humiliated was me.

22

Saudade

I DECIDED TO MOVE to my own apartment and I found a place in Boyle Heights. A friend gave me a stray kitten he had rescued from the streets so I could have someone to come home to. I loved my black-and-white kitty, whom I named Saudade, my favorite word in Portuguese. Saudade, a deep longing, melancholy, nostalgia, the Portuguese equivalent to the Spanish añoranza. But even my kitty's comforting presence couldn't take away the harsh realization that this next step in my life, to have my own apartment, came with more bills to pay. Now I had to pay for rent, groceries, my car, my student loans, cat food, and litter. All of a sudden, what at first had seemed like a great salary no longer felt so great. With all my expenses, I didn't have much left at the end of the month. And the job was so demanding that I would come home too tired and too overwhelmed to write. As the weeks stretched into months, I wrote less and less, until eventually I stopped completely. The words wouldn't come anymore.

I would sit down at my computer with Saudade on my lap and stare at the screen, searching for a story, an image, an opening line. But I couldn't drown out the noise and chaos of my middle school classroom, the fear that gripped me every time the bell rang, or the feeling of incompetence that now dominated my every thought.

The screen remained empty. My stories seemed to have left me.

When they learned that I had some experience dancing folklórico, the Latino teachers asked me to volunteer after school to get the students ready to perform a few dances for the Cinco de Mayo event they were organizing.

Every day after school I went to the auditorium to teach the kids some of the dances I had learned at UCSC. Since the polkas from northern Mexico were what I knew best, they were what I taught the students. To my amazement, the kids actually listened to what I said. They worked hard at learning the steps and choreography. They didn't argue, fight, or cause mayhem the way they did in my classroom. What was different? Finally, I realized that the kids who stayed after school were there because they *wanted* to be there and were interested in what they were learning, which perhaps they had never been in my class. Also, they knew that the minute they misbehaved, I could ask them to leave. I suddenly felt confident and capable as a teacher, something I hadn't felt once since I had started teaching.

When the Cinco de Mayo celebrations were over, the kids having put on a great performance, I missed teaching dance. It turned out I wasn't the only one who missed folklórico. Two weeks after the Cinco de Mayo performance, one of my dance students came into my classroom after school and said, "Ms. Grande, do you think you could start a folklórico group here at school? I mean, a permanent one."

His name was Luis Felipe, and he was the kid who had been riding his skateboard in my classroom. When I made the announcement in class that I was looking for dancers for the Cinco de Mayo event, I had been surprised when he raised his hand. I was even more surprised that when the practice started he turned out to be my best dancer.

Now here he was, a thirteen-year-old boy, telling me he wanted to keep dancing.

I could see the enthusiasm in his eyes, and looking at him I knew what had happened to him was the same thing that had happened to me at Santa Cruz—he had discovered the exquisite beauty of the Mexican dance tradition, and he was proud.

Luis Felipe had been brought to the U.S. as a little boy. Like me, he was struggling with his identity as a child immigrant, finding a place to belong in America while at the same time holding on to his Mexican culture. Folklórico was his way to form a connection with Mexico so that he wouldn't completely lose his right to claim it. Folklórico became the bridge that connected him to his native country. I understood that completely.

"All right," I said. "But if I do start the group, will you help me recruit dancers?"

His face broke into a smile, the sweetest smile I had seen in my time at the middle school. "Yes," he said. "Leave it to me!" He ran out of my room to follow through on his promise.

I was left to wonder what I had gotten myself into. I didn't know enough about dancing to have a real group. At Santa Cruz, I had been a beginner. Who was I trying to fool, thinking I could teach kids to dance? I had made a mistake, I told myself. I needed to tell Luis Felipe that I couldn't do what he had asked of me.

During lunch the next day, I mentioned this to one of the teachers, a newbie like me.

"Don't give up on this project yet," he said. "You know, my sister dances in a group in El Sereno. You should check it out. Maybe she can give you suggestions."

El Sereno wasn't far from Boyle Heights. In fact, I wouldn't even need to get on a freeway to get there, so I decided to follow his advice. On Saturday morning, as I walked through the park looking for the community center where practices were held, I simply followed the pounding of a drum, and even before entering the studio, my body felt the vibrations, my heart began to follow the rhythm of the danza. When I entered the studio, the dancers were sitting on the floor or standing around the room. Only one person was doing the Aztec dance. A man whirled around the room to the beat of the drum. His dark brown skin glistening with sweat looked like melted milk chocolate; his black shoulder-length hair whipped the air as he spun around. His face was that of a fighter who fears nothing, no one. He was a real Aztec warrior come to life. I stood there and couldn't move. My breath caught in my throat, mesmerized by that man who danced as if we weren't there; as if he was in a forest with the moon and the gods as his only witnesses. The drumbeats quickened as he spun in place faster, faster, my heartbeats matching the crescendo of the song. With one last bang of the drum he landed on the floor on one knee. The danza ended and the spell was broken. Everyone clapped, and at his command, they took their places on the floor.

"Let's do this," he said, and the danza started again, with everyone following his every step. I wanted to join them, to follow him, the music, the dance, to the divine place of the Aztec gods.

That was how I began a relationship with a man who was fourteen years my senior. His name was Francisco, and he was the co-director of the group I had come to see. He entered my life when I was at my most vulnerable. Even though I had moved to L.A. to be with my family, we were so busy with our lives that it seemed as if we all lived in different countries and not within driving distance of one another. The truth was that I was lonely and becoming disillusioned with our so-called reunification. The miles that once separated us were gone, but the distance had remained.

To make matters worse, I was drifting farther and farther away from my writing dream. The only joy I felt at that moment was starting a dance group and helping my students have something to be passionate about. In South Central L.A., a place where kids were tempted by gangs at a young age, I found myself desperate to keep that from happening to Luis Felipe and to all my students. What he had asked of me that day gave me hope that things were turning around for me at the middle school, and it also showed me a way to make a difference in the lives of my students.

It was with this enthusiasm that I approached Francisco after practice and told him why I was there. When I asked him for advice about how to start a folklórico group at my middle school, he invited me to return to practice as often as I wanted to observe and learn. He shared music and ideas with me and offered to come to my house and show me some dances that I could teach my students. He went as far as letting me use his costumes if I ever needed them. I appreciated his support, though I found him to be intimidating as well. From what I had seen at practice, he was a tough teacher, and he swore at his dancers in a way I found unprofessional and unnecessary.

When he saw that my passion for folklórico didn't match my dance skills, he said, "Are you sure you're capable of taking this on? Having a group is hard work even for the most skilled dancer."

His words shook my confidence. It was true that I didn't have enough dance experience, I told him, but I had nothing but good intentions. That had to count for something, didn't it?

"You'll do more damage teaching those kids to do the steps wrong," he said. "Then someone is going to have to clean up your mess. It's hard to unlearn bad technique."

"Well, unfortunately I'm all they've got for now," I said.

A few weeks later, Francisco came over to my house to begin my training. In my driveway, he taught me a few steps, but he lacked patience, and I lacked the confidence to remain under his critical gaze for long. I felt like an insect under a microscope, and he could see every single imperfection and insecurity I tried so hard to hide.

"Bend your knees more. Your tits are bouncing all over the place," he said.

I was glad when we stopped talking about my dance group, and he dropped the pretense of wanting to teach me to dance. One night as we were listening to his folklórico music in my living room, he leaned over and kissed me—hard and rough—his breath smelling of beer, and the next thing I knew we were on my living room floor having sex to "El Son de la Negra." From that night forward he made it clear that his only intention was to have a good time in bed with me, not to help me master el zapateado or el huachapeado steps, and the private dance lessons came to an end.

"He's not good enough for you," Carlos said the first time he met him. "You can do better."

"He's so old!" Mago said. Francisco was thirty-nine to my almost twenty-five. "I don't trust him. Nena, after you worked so hard for an education, how can you end up with a truck driver?" she asked with disdain. Every time she referred to him, she would call him "your dad."

"How are things with your dad?" she would ask.

I knew she was right, but the more she insisted that he was too old, the more I wanted to be with him. My father had made little effort to have a relationship with me despite the fact that we both now lived in the same city. So the truth was that I was once again trying to find his replacement, and Francisco—with dark skin the exact shade as my father's, hands just as rough and calloused, and breath that smelled of beer—was the perfect substitute. Like my father, Francisco spoke broken English. He had been born into a poor family in Mexico and had to toughen up to survive. He immigrated to search for a better life in the U.S. and had found work as a cement truck driver. In my eyes, he wasn't a truck driver with a limited education. I saw him as a dancer. He was so passionate about folklórico that every time he talked about it I couldn't help admiring him. Surely a man who loved and cared about Mexico's cultural and dancing traditions as much as he did couldn't be all bad.

When I met him, he was going through a divorce. I soon discovered he was a typical machista—he was a drunk, a womanizer, and a liar. He already had four children, each from a different woman, and he had little or no contact with them. I knew that I should have run the other way, but I didn't. My loneliness made me stay.

When I turned twenty-five in September, and Mago and Carlos asked me what I wanted for my birthday, I said, "The only thing I want is for us to be together."

"We'll take you to dinner," they said.

We went to a restaurant in Boyle Heights I had been wanting to try. I had driven past it many times and heard the food was delicious, but I hadn't heard how expensive it was. As we sat and looked at the menu, I heard my family murmuring under their breaths about the prices. There were eleven of us there, including my siblings' spouses and children, Francisco, and my mother. My father once again had gifted me with his absence. Not long before, he had given up alcohol and found religion and, to our dismay, his church made it almost impossible to see him. When we invited him over for his grandchildren's birthday parties or holiday get-togethers, he would never come because he had to go to church, or he had to mow the lawn at church, or do some other repairs his pastor had asked him to do.

It seemed he had simply replaced one addiction with another, so when I called to invite him to my birthday dinner, his church was the excuse he gave.

I immediately regretted choosing this restaurant, but it would have been humiliating to get up and leave, so we stayed. My siblings didn't make much money and they had bills to pay and children to take care of, so I felt guilty for having brought them here. The food was indeed delicious—gourmet Mexican food carefully prepared. I didn't even know there was such a thing as gourmet Mexican food. But when the check came and the waiter set it down before Carlos, his eyes bulged in shock. He grabbed it and said to Mago, "Here, you pay it," and tossed it over to her.

"Goddamn," Mago said at reading the numbers on the paper. She tossed the check back to Carlos. "You pay it." They tossed the check back and forth to each other, laughing and criticizing the restaurant for its prices, and I wanted to sink into my chair and disappear. Playing with his mustache, Francisco watched my siblings with amusement but wisely stayed out of the family drama. Still, it was humiliating that he was witnessing this spectacle. My mother looked at me with confusion. Mago and Carlos were bickering in English so she only half understood what was going on, though tossing the check across the table like a football seemed pretty obvious to me. The other diners tried not to look at our table, but they couldn't help themselves. I wanted them to stop. I looked at Francisco, at Mago's common-law husband, Victor, at Norma, at my mother, praying with my eyes for them to do something. But no one intervened.

"Give it to me," I said. I reached across the table and yanked the check from Mago just as she was going to toss it once again to Carlos. "I'll pay for it." I handed my credit card to the waiter. The habanero salsa I had eaten with my camarones a la Veracruzana was burning right through my stomach lining and making its way up my esophagus like a raging fire.

"We're just kidding, Nena," Mago said. "We'll pay our share." She opened her purse to grab some money, but I refused. Francisco handed me his share as well, but I wouldn't accept it. All I wanted was to get out of there and be done with this dinner. I had never felt like such a fool.

"It's my treat," I said, my anger not letting me think clearly. I was angry at my siblings, at their behavior, but mainly I was angry at myself, for not being strong enough to stop being a victim, for not being strong enough to stop wanting my family around me and insisting that they care. By paying for my own birthday dinner, I was paying for my mistake and sparing my siblings the hardship of paying more than they had bargained for.

"Eso estuvo bien cabrón," Francisco said afterward with his usual bluntness. And later in my apartment, I clung to him more than ever because he was right. What my siblings had done was totally messed up, and I had never felt so alone as I did that night.

After that, I spiraled downward. As the months went by, I found myself feeling lonelier and more insecure than ever before. I should have turned to my writing instead of a man, but I didn't, and that was my worst mistake.

Even after I discovered that Francisco was lying about being at work and instead was really with other women—including his soon-to-be ex-wife—I didn't leave him. I held on to my fantasy of him, dancing Azteca, his mind and body perfectly in tune with the beat of the drum, giving himself completely to a rhythm as old as time. I was in love with the dancer—with his connection to folklórico—not the real man who lied to me, manipulated me, and at times made me feel that I didn't deserve anyone better than him. Being with him left me emotionally and physically exhausted.

To his credit, he never pretended to be something he was not. I was the one who created the fantasies in my head.

In my moments of lucidity, I would tell myself to leave him, that he wasn't the man for me. Then there would be something that would keep me with him, like when he took me to a quinceañera and we danced the night away. He held me in his strong, confident arms, twirled me across the dance floor, and flawlessly led me in cumbias, norteñas, pegaditas, and quebraditas, salsa and merengue. Everyone watching us couldn't take their eyes off us.

Once in a while when he had time, he would come to help me after school with my folklórico group. To my surprise, he was patient with my students as he taught them the steps, and not a single bad word came out of his mouth when he was with them.

I also liked his spontaneity, like the day before Thanksgiving when, out of the blue, he decided to take me to the Grand Canyon because I had never been there. We jumped in the car and drove seven hours straight. We got there late at night, and to our dismay there were no hotel rooms available because of the holiday. We spent the night in the car in twenty-five-degree weather, clinging to each other in the backseat, our breath turning to frost on the windows, and I thought how crazy this man was and yet how exciting it was to find myself freezing my ass off in Arizona simply because he wanted to show me the Grand Canyon.

It had been every bit as breathtaking as he had promised it would be.

23

As the months went by, I couldn't shake the feeling of loneliness that suffocated me. When I dropped in on my sister-in-law, and she gave me the news that she was pregnant with her second child, a thought planted itself in my mind. *What if what I need is a baby?*

I tried to push the crazy thought out of my head, but it took hold the moment it formed, and I couldn't shake it free. If my own family didn't want to be around me, couldn't I create a family that would?

Norma had become a mother at sixteen when she had Natalia. At nineteen, she was about to become a mother a second time. Yet, as young as she was, she had proven herself to be a better parent than most women I had encountered. If anyone had been born to be a mother, it was Norma. She took parenting classes through Planned Parenthood, watched videos, read parenting books, and asked other women for advice. I had never seen anyone work so hard to be a good mother.

My niece, Natalia, now three years old, was turning out to be a sweet, well-behaved girl. When she came running into the kitchen, wanting to be picked up, I could see the joy in Norma's face. Motherhood grounded her and gave meaning to her life. The love she gave her daughter was returned many times over. Natalia was completely devoted to Norma. Nothing was more important to her in the world than the woman who had given her life.

When Mago went into labor, she had asked me to come to the hospital and witness the birth of her third child, my niece Alexa. I soon forgot about the long hours of pain that my sister endured, the fact that I almost fainted at the sight of a tiny human being struggling to emerge from my sister's womb. The image that stayed with me was that when the baby was put in Mago's arms, her tiny eyes had opened, and the way she seemed to look at my sister had been absolutely beautiful. The purest form of love.

To be loved like that, I thought as I sat there in Norma's kitchen watching her and her little girl embrace. I suddenly envied Norma her daughter, Mago her three children, and Betty her son.

Motherhood is exactly what you need, the little voice inside me insisted. *A baby would love you like no one else has loved you. With a baby, you could make a family and not be alone anymore.*

Then another, even scarier thought came to my mind. Francisco was the perfect candidate for the job. He would never fight me for the child, just like he had never fought for the ones he'd had with other women. I would have a baby who would be all mine and no one else's.

The crazy thoughts about wanting a baby scared me, and I knew it wasn't the answer. It was pure insanity. What I should really do, I thought, was take a trip to get me out of my funk and remind myself that I was young and free. Besides my job, I had no responsibilities, and I should keep it that way so that I could return to my writing and pursue my dream without anything to hinder me.

I talked to my friend Delia, whom I'd met at PCC when we were both in marching band, and we decided to travel to Europe together. She had also become a teacher at a middle school, not far from mine, but as a band instructor, she was having a better experience than me. I was looking forward to spending time with a friend my age, to getting away from Francisco, to reassessing our relationship and perhaps, once and for all, putting an end to it.

Aside from Mexico and the U.S., I had never been to any other countries and I was excited to finally have the chance to see something new, to be exposed to other cultures and ways of life. But at the last minute, due to complications with her passport, Delia couldn't come with me. Francisco eagerly offered to take her place. Since I didn't want to go alone, and no one else could go, I accepted. He bought his ticket and there was no turning back.

I left Saudade under Norma's care, and Francisco and I flew to Madrid, the first of the many cities we were planning to visit. I was taken aback when, for a moment, I thought we had landed in Mexico. With its beautiful Spanish architecture, narrow cobblestoned streets, and stunning Catholic cathedral, Madrid reminded me of Taxco, the silver mining town an hour away from Iguala. As usual, I didn't really have a plan about where to go and what to see, and neither did Francisco. The one thing he and I had in common was an adventurous spirit, so we walked along the streets of Madrid to see what we would find. And we saw a great deal—art, architecture, Spanish dances—but what I would always remember about the trip was what Francisco did.

Two days after we arrived, as we were getting ready to split the check for our dinner, he patted his pockets and said, "Oh, shit, I think my wallet got stolen."

"That's unfortunate," I said, really wanting to believe him, but there was a voice in the back of my mind wondering, *What if he's lying?* I thought of the fiasco at my birthday dinner, and wondered if once again I would be the idiot who had to pay the bill.

"I'll pay you back when we return to L.A.," he promised. Even though he called the credit card company from a pay phone to make a report, suspicion still gnawed at me.

After that, the trip took a sour turn. I paid for every meal, hotel room, train ticket, entertainment. In Seville, we watched a flamenco show, but instead of appreciating the Spanish dance influence on folklórico—all I could think about was the cost of the show, and the bottles of wine and Spanish tapas Francisco ordered. We slept on the train all night to save on hotels, and arrived in Barcelona completely exhausted. Maybe it was my grogginess, but Gaudí's church La Sagrada Familia seemed like an ice cream cake left to melt in the sun. In Venice, we found the cheapest places to eat and we stayed in a crumbling, moldy inn. Instead of appreciating the magic of the city with its canals, water taxis, and gondolas, I thought of my dwindling bank account. We took a train to Rome, walked inside the Colosseum, and I wished the gladiator shows still existed so I could throw this man to the lions. We headed to Pisa to see the leaning tower, but by then I didn't give a damn about why it was leaning. Our last stop was Paris, where I wasn't feeling particularly in love with *mon amour* and the Eiffel Tower was just a big hunk of metal. To top it all off, my camera and most of my rolls of film got stolen at the train station. In a way, I was grateful, because part of me didn't want to remember the trip at all. By that point my bank account was completely depleted, and I was paying for everything with my credit card.

When we returned from our trip, I walked away from that relationship. And if it hadn't been for my cat, it might have stayed that way.

Reyna in a water taxi, Venice, 2001

A few weeks after I broke up with Francisco, my cat went missing. The window in my bedroom was slightly ajar, but it wasn't a big enough opening for Saudade to have squeezed through. And yet, after a long search around my apartment, I resigned myself to the fact that the cat wasn't there. I searched the streets for the next two days and didn't find him. Saudade had no claws, and I worried he wouldn't last a week out in the streets with the feral cats that lived around my apartment. I walked through the neighborhood in the evenings calling out Saudade's name but had no luck.

On the third night, as I was about to go on my search, Francisco called me to ask how I was doing, and when I told him about my missing cat, he offered to come help me find him. By then I was too desperate to say no. We ventured out farther than I had before. On the second night of walking with Francisco all over Boyle Heights, I was surprised—and suspicious—when we spotted Saudade running around in the alley behind Francisco's apartment building, which was a mile away from mine.

"It can't be my cat," I said. Yet somehow, I knew it was. "How the hell did he get all the way over here?" I asked Francisco as we chased Saudade down the alley, and trapped him behind some trash bins. Francisco grabbed the cat and held him tight, and as Saudade meowed loudly, he handed him to me. Saudade was filthy and looked nearly starved. As I took him in my arms, I couldn't believe this was really my cat. But it was. The missing claws proved it. As I held him tight, I could feel his rib bones poking through.

"You silly cat," I said. "How did you end up here?" I looked at Francisco, my suspicion growing. I had never asked him for my spare key when I broke up with him.

"Cats can travel far," he said.

"What a coincidence it ended up here, behind your apartment. Don't you think?"

"You don't think I stole your cat, do you?" he asked, seeing the accusation in my eyes. He shook his head in disbelief. "I can't believe you would blame me for this. Cats are good at escaping. It's in their nature. You can't keep him trapped all day, you know?"

Whether he was guilty or not, I will never know.

I slept with Francisco the night of my cat's rescue, either from guilt for wrongfully accusing him of catnapping or gratitude for him helping me find Saudade or because I was dumb. After I slept with him a second time, and then a third, it was clear to me that I was an idiot.

But rather than blame my own stupidity, it was easier to blame my cat.

I found out I was pregnant soon after, and when the realization sank in, I knew what I had done to my child was unforgivable. The truth was that I had my little "accident" on purpose. When I broke up with Francisco, I had stopped taking my birth control pills. The nights I slept with him, I was aware of the risk. I knew exactly what I was doing.

I had once thought I needed a baby. But when I held the test results in my hand, I asked myself how I could bring a child into this world for the wrong reasons. To put so many expectations on a baby—for it to come and rescue its mother from herself, to help her find her way in the world, to give her roots, to give her life meaning because she wasn't strong or mature enough to do it herself.

This is what I had done to my baby.

Worse, I had given it a father who only liked making babies but not raising them, who would not be there to guide it, love it, and teach it how to be a good human being. I had cheated my baby out of a kind, loving, responsible father because I had been too selfish, thinking only of my own needs.

I told myself my baby would want for nothing as long as it had me. But didn't I know firsthand what having an absent father could do to someone? The way a parent's absence could haunt you every day of your life. How it could mess you up in the head and affect the relationships you had with other people because everything you did or thought or felt stemmed from that dark, empty ache your absent parent had left in your life. How could I do that to my child?

"You can have an abortion," Mago said when I gave her the news. "You made a mistake, yes, but you still have a choice, Nena. Why would you want to have that man's baby anyway? And why would you give your child a father like him?"

I lay in my room thinking about what she had said. I had a choice, yes, but the guilt weighed on me. It was my fault. Besides, what excuse did I have not to have this baby? I had a job. I could support it. I was twenty-five. Betty had become a mother at seventeen; Norma at sixteen; Mago at twenty-one; my stepsister, Cindy, had given birth to twins at nineteen. I was surrounded by young mothers. What excuse did I have except that I had done this to myself, and now I was afraid of having a child for the wrong reasons?

When I was at PCC, I had taken a biology class and discovered a room in the Science Building where they had fetuses in jars. It was the most horrific thing I had seen in my life, yet the most amazing. I had never imagined that such a thing was possible—to put babies in jars and display them on shelves, where they would spend the rest of eternity existing and yet not existing. I returned, again and again, spending hours in that room, going from jar to jar containing a fetus at each stage of development. Seeing how a baby looked at two, or three, or five months after conception fascinated me. I imagined that was how I had looked inside my mother's womb, and somehow it made me feel connected to her in a way I never had before. It was in her womb that I had come to exist and had been at my most vulnerable.

But the one that fascinated me the most was the six-month-old fetus. It had eyebrows and eyelashes and seemed as if it were merely asleep. I felt that if I stood there long enough, it would open its eyes. But then I remembered it was dead. That they were all dead. From the poster on the wall, I learned that these babies had come from natural miscarriages, and my heart ached for them, for the lives they would never get to live. For all that was lost. For the dreams they would never dream.

Thinking of those babies in jars now made me grieve for my child. I was two months pregnant. I knew what the baby looked like in my womb. I decided that unlike those babies in jars, my child would get to have a life and dreams to reach for. I would keep my baby and start my own family, just the two of us.

When I gave Francisco the news, I broke up with him once and for all.

24

Reyna and her teacher's assistant

My administrators had shown me a little mercy by giving me sixth-grade ESL for the new school year. I quickly realized how much I preferred these bright-eyed little sixth graders to the eighth graders I had been struggling to connect with. For starters, the sixth graders were small, so for once being short didn't bother me as much. They also hadn't yet lost their eagerness and enthusiasm for learning, and they didn't dare call me anything but Ms. Grande. The sixth-grade girls, unlike the older girls, looked up to me and respected me. They hadn't yet developed the cynicism toward adult authority that some of the older kids had.

What made me feel connected to these kids was that most of them were recent immigrants from Mexico or Central America. I knew that many were undocumented, though I never asked. They didn't speak English, but in their eyes I could see the desire to find a place to belong, a place where they could feel safe. Their stories were so similar to my own. Broken homes, broken families—that was the price we all had paid for a shot at the American Dream.

My sixth graders reminded me of myself at that age, especially the girls. I had been a year younger than they were when I arrived in the U.S., not knowing the way of life, the language, or the culture. My job was to teach them English, but I also knew they needed a patient, loving teacher who would understand that their needs went beyond learning a language. They needed to heal from their trauma first. They didn't leave it at the door. It came into the classroom with them like a ghost haunting them day and night. As I stood before my students to welcome them into my class, I wondered how many of them were living with parents who were complete strangers to them. I told them what I wished my own elementary teacher had told me.

"The first skill for learning English is patience," I said to my students on their first day. "Being in a new country, learning a new language, a new culture, takes time. You will learn. It doesn't feel that way now, but one day you will be just as comfortable speaking English as you are speaking Spanish. But no matter what, don't ever forget where you came from, and don't ever be ashamed of who you are."

"Yes, Ms. Grande," they said, sitting quietly and looking at me as if I knew everything. Finally, I felt confident as a teacher. With this group of sixth graders, the stickers and pencils, pizza parties and popcorn and movies worked! I even let them play their favorite music when we had parties, and I danced to "Mambo #5" with them.

When I could no longer hide my baby bump, the girls screamed their excitement about my baby and asked me a million questions. Had I picked a name? Was it a boy or a girl? Could they have a baby shower for me when the time came? Would I give them pictures of the baby? Would I come show them the baby when it was born, even though I would be on maternity leave?

I felt uncomfortable when I admitted that I wasn't married and that my child would have no father. That wasn't the kind of role model I wanted to be for them, and sometimes I felt ashamed. They never judged me. I told myself that I was quite capable of being a parent, that not having a man wasn't the end of the world. I had made my decision and was going to do everything I could to be the best mother I could be. That was the lesson I wanted my students to take away: honor your responsibilities and do the right thing.

I shared my first ultrasound pictures with my students, and when I learned I was having a boy, they helped me pick out some names. Sebastian, Fernando, Adrián.

When my girls complained to me about the bullying going on in the playground during recess and lunch, I opened my classroom to them and they would come hang out with me during break, away from the eighth graders who frightened them. Soon, even the boys started coming. They played games, listened to music, told me about their lives and families, did homework, cleaned and organized my room, helped me grade papers while I put my swollen feet up to rest. Many of them joined my folklórico group, so I got to see them after school, too. I grew so attached to these kids that when it was time to go on maternity leave, I was truly sad to say goodbye, and I looked forward to returning to them.

There were many moments when the uncertainty and the fear I experienced at becoming a single mother made me feel more scared than I had ever been in my life. But I pushed past those fears, and managed to do something right: I bought myself and my son a house. If I could have, I would have built it with my own hands. Instead, I did the next best thing—I jumped on the opportunity of a lifetime!

A few months before I went on maternity leave, I heard from one of the teachers at the middle school about a program offered by HUD called "The Teacher Next Door." The properties the program offered were foreclosed homes sold by lottery at half the market price. The only requirement was to live there for three years, at which point you were then allowed to sell the house at its full value.

Through the weeks, I diligently checked the list of houses and spent hours after school and on the weekends driving around looking at them and putting my name in the lottery for the ones I liked. Though I was disappointed at the end of each week when my name wasn't on the list of winners, I persisted. Several weeks later, right before Thanksgiving, my tenacity and endurance paid off when my name finally appeared on the list. I was the lucky winner of a two-bedroom house. I hadn't gone to see the house because I hadn't had time and had entered my name in the lottery on a whim. Now I knew it had been intuition.

The only downside was that the houses being offered were all in undesirable neighborhoods. The whole purpose of "The Teacher Next Door" and "The Officer Next Door" program was to bring teachers and police officers to troubled areas that needed to be revitalized. I was worried about moving to South Central, where my new house was located, ten minutes from work. It was an area notorious for its crime and violence from gangs such as the infamous Crips and Bloods; its troubled history, such as the Watts Riots of 1965, and most recently, the 1992 riots sparked by the beating of Rodney King by white police officers who were not held accountable for what they did. In high school, I had stood outside with my classmates watching the distant smoke rising over the city when the riots broke out.

Now here I was, moving into the epicenter of one of the most violent areas in Los Angeles. I told myself it would only be for three years. After that, with the money I would make from selling the house at its full value, my son and I could go anywhere—even back to Santa Cruz. What I wanted, most of all, was to feel part of a community again. I wanted trees and blue skies and clean air. I wanted to surround myself with people who loved nature and were conscious of our impact on the environment. But the biggest reason for wanting to leave was that I felt small living in this big city, just one of millions trying to survive.

When I got the keys three weeks before my due date, I had to call the police to evict the squatters who had moved into the house while it was vacant. The water had been turned off the entire time the house was on the market and the toilet was a disgusting mess. The house reeked of marijuana, urine, and feces. The kitchen cabinets had been ripped off the walls and there was nothing left but huge holes. In the master bedroom, a large burn spread on the corner of the wood floor, as if someone had pretended they were at the beach and lit a bonfire. The outside was no better. The front yard was nothing but dirt covered in holes from the dozens of gophers living underground. A vendor sold fruit on the corner, right outside the chain-link fence, and the view from the bay window in the living room was his blue-striped umbrella, black plastic crates, and the fruit vendor himself rearranging his fruit to make it look presentable.

The house was directly in the flight path to LAX, and every few minutes an airplane flew overhead. And to make matters worse, the house sat on a busy street. There was a bus stop and a stop sign right by the front yard. Airplanes, gunshots, cars, helicopters, police sirens, ambulance sirens . . . these would be the cacophony of sounds I would be hearing every night from the first day I moved in.

I thought it was hilarious—one of life's jokes—to send me the opposite of the dream house I had fantasized about. But with immense pride I stood in the backyard, my hand gliding over my humongous belly, unable to believe that I was twenty-six and now a homeowner! I didn't know that fifteen years later, I would sell this house for five times what I paid for it, and that that money would allow me to buy a real dream house. I didn't know it, but I *felt* it. I knew in my heart that this house was the equivalent of the first draft of a novel. And as every good writer knows, the first draft is always shitty.

The only thing I loved about the house was that it had two huge avocado trees in the backyard, which provided plenty of shade and a good harvest. I looked forward to making as much guacamole as I wanted. As I stood under the avocado tree, I felt someone watching me, and I turned to see a man in the neighbor's yard looking at me through the chain-link fence that divided the properties. He had pitched a tent in the yard, and he was starting to light a fire to cook with. If my son and I wanted to come out to our backyard without being watched, I would have to figure out what to do about that chain-link fence.

In my pregnancy book, I had read about the nesting period, the instinct in moms-to-be to get a home ready for their baby. At that moment, my nesting instinct fully kicked in, and with excitement I went back inside to throw myself into turning this house into a home for me and my baby.

25

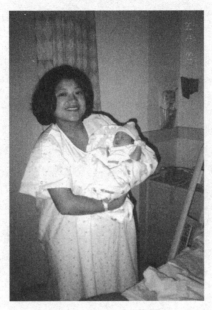

Mother and child

ONE OF THE times I truly needed my mother by my side was when I became a mother. But she wasn't there. Not that I expected her to be. Mago, who had been the only mother I had as a child, showed up at the West L.A. Kaiser Labor and Delivery Unit and stayed by my side, coaching me, calming me, shaking me at times when I was too weak for another push.

"They're going to cut you open if you don't push, Nena!" she would hiss into my ear.

"I can't do it," I cried. "I can't." I writhed from the blinding pain. It was as if an invisible hand was squeezing the base of my spine again and again. I felt I was literally being torn apart. The doctor told me that back labor was the worst kind.

Mago hovered over me, giving me her strength. "Yes, you can push. You must."

The anesthesiologist never showed up, though I had asked for him repeatedly. The nurses said he was busy with a Cesarean and couldn't come to give me an epidural. I was forced to go through every spasm of pain, every tightening and cramping, with no hope for the shot that would take away the suffering. I wondered if I was being punished for being so irresponsible. *You wanted a baby? Well, now suffer.*

I named my son Nathaniel, a variation on my father's name, Natalio. His middle name, Khalil, was for one of my favorite writers, Kahlil Gibran, whose real name, Khalil, had been misspelled in school when he immigrated to the U.S. as a child. I had discovered *The Prophet* six years before, when I was at PCC. It was a book that soothed my soul with its lyricism, spirituality, and powerful words on topics such as love, marriage, and children. But the one that impacted me most was the piece on joy and sorrow.

> *The deeper that sorrow carves into your being, the more joy you can contain.*
> *Is not the cup that holds your wine the very cup that was burned in the potter's oven?*
> *And is not the lute that soothes your spirit, the very wood that was hollowed with knives?*

Gibran's words helped me to look at my sorrow in a different way. Sorrow was what I had known most of my life—and I had resented my sorrow. Life hadn't just given me lemons; it had given me a whole lemon grove. But Gibran's words helped me to think of my body as a vessel hollowed by sorrow so that one day it could fill with just as much joy.

That day in January 2002, when I held my baby boy in my arms for the first time, I felt something pure and beautiful begin to bubble up from the underground spring in my soul. As every nook and crevice of my body filled with an incredible joy at seeing my child's tiny eyes looking up at me, I finally knew what Gibran's words had meant.

Since the repairs to my house weren't completed yet, I went to stay at Carlos's house to convalesce, and Norma, who had given birth to her second daughter three months earlier, helped me recuperate. It took four days for my mother to finally come meet her newest grandchild, and that was only after I gave her a piece of my mind on the phone about what kind of mother I thought her to be.

"The hospital was only twenty minutes away from you, and you couldn't bother to come?" I said. Most of all, I was angry at myself. Furious for wanting her by my side, for expecting her to do the right thing even though through the years she never had. As I watched her hold my baby for the first time, I swore to myself that I would never be that kind of mother to my son. I would be there when he needed me and even when he didn't.

Francisco had been at the hospital when Nathan was born and, to his credit, he did his best to check in on us periodically. But, just as I'd known he would, he eventually stepped aside and left me to care for and raise the baby on my own. He would come by once in a while to visit, but then would disappear for months on end, until one day he would call me out of the blue to ask about our son. I never blamed him. I had known what would happen, but the guilt ate at me as I wondered how having an absent father would affect my son. Would he grow up with that hole in his heart the way I had? Or would my love be enough?

My new identity was that of a single mother. My child would depend on me for everything, and I would do my best to honor my responsibility as a parent, the kind Kahlil Gibran had written about in *The Prophet*:

> *You are the bows from which your children*
> *as living arrows are sent forth.*
> *The archer sees the mark upon the path of the infinite,*
> *and He bends you with His might*
> *that His arrows may go swift and far.*
> *Let your bending in the archer's hand be for gladness;*
> *For even as He loves the arrow that flies,*
> *so He loves also the bow that is stable.*

What I wanted, most of all, was to give my son something that my own parents hadn't given me—a home full of love, stability, joy. In order to do that, I would need to be as strong and stable as an archer's bow, and learn how to bend without breaking.

Not long after I moved into my new house, Mago called me and said, "Let's go to Fidel's for sandwiches."

Since I hardly saw her—she was so busy raising her three kids, working, and dealing with her marriage issues, and I was busy being a new mom and teaching full time—I was elated to get her call.

We met in Highland Park at Fidel's Pizza, a little restaurant where they sold our favorite ham-and-cheese sandwiches on French baguettes. We had grown up craving the food from Fidel's, which was just down the street from our childhood home. We would beg our father to take us there, but he never did. Sometimes when he was in a good mood, he would give us a dollar each, and Carlos, Mago, and I would pool our money to buy one ham-and-cheese sandwich to split three ways. We were always left wanting a whole one for ourselves.

So as adults, we still craved the sandwiches, and now we had enough money to buy a whole one without having to share!

After we finished eating, Mago said, "Do you want to go see him?"

Our father lived right up the street, a mere five-minute walk. Really, it would be so easy to go see him. Wasn't that the normal thing daughters did? To drop in on your father for a surprise visit? But we didn't know whether our father and stepmother would be pleased about it.

"Well, what do you say?" Mago asked, waiting for me to decide.

I longed for my child to have a relationship with his grandfather. Mago longed for the same for her children, and if she, who was even better at holding on to her anger than I was, was willing to go see him and make an effort to connect, then so could I.

"Okay," I said.

With our four children in tow, we dropped in on our father. Mila had gone to the market, so he was alone. We greeted him with big smiles. I wanted to hug him, but none of us had that kind of relationship with him. We had arrived with a positive attitude, but not a minute after our arrival, he said to Mago, "Remind me again what your children's names are?"

And that was enough to trigger Mago's short temper. "Aidan, Nadia, and Alexa," she said through gritted teeth. "Is it that hard to remember your own grandchildren's names?"

"Why do you give your children such hard names to remember?" he said as a justification.

"The names in the Bible are harder, and yet you've managed to memorize them just fine," she retorted. The few times we had seen him recently, all he talked about was his religion, and he had even tried to convert us. It was a touchy subject.

Not wanting to find out whether my father remembered my son's name or not, I quickly said, "And this is Nathaniel."

Mago was fuming, and I could tell she wanted to leave. My father didn't make a big fuss over Nathan. All he did was state the obvious, "He's so little." But he didn't ask if he could hold him. He didn't even reach out to pinch his cheek or ruffle his hair, pat his head or hold his tiny hand, things that even strangers at the supermarket or the mall wanted to do to my baby.

I tried not to care. I was here, with my father, and I wasn't going to leave without at least sharing what was happening in my life, whether he cared or not. "I bought a house, Pa."

My father looked at me with surprise, then his doubt turned to enthusiasm when he realized I was serious. "Really, Chata? That's great news."

Finally, I had done something right. Then, because I couldn't stop myself, I also gave him the other news I had been dying to give him.

"And I'm finally going to get my ciudadanía."

The previous September, on the day that would become known as 9/11, I had gone to the Federal Building downtown to have my fingerprints taken for my U.S. citizenship application. I hadn't listened to the news that morning, so I didn't know what was going on in New York. Mago had called me to tell me and begged me to get out of the government building because downtown L.A. could be the next target. But I didn't leave. It had taken me years to get to this point, and I wasn't about to lose my place in line and not finish the application process. In Santa Cruz, I had sent in my application but somehow correspondence from the INS got lost in the campus mail. The application process was further complicated by the three times I'd moved around in L.A. and more missing correspondence. I'd had to reopen my case and pay more fees. I hoped downtown wasn't evacuated before my fingerprints were processed. U.S. citizenship was another dream that my father had had for us. In two months, I was scheduled for the oath ceremony, and for my child's sake, I hoped that my citizenship certificate would give us the right to finally claim this country as our own.

The way my father looked at me now, with admiration, told me that I had redeemed myself in his eyes. Sure, I was a single mom and had had a child out of wedlock, things he disapproved of. But I was a homeowner. I was a soon-to-be U.S. citizen. I had a college degree and was a working professional. Being a teacher for the Los Angeles Unified School District was a big deal to my father. He hadn't been too impressed when I had told him I was studying to be a writer.

"How do you like your new house?" he asked.

"The house is fine, I just don't like the neighborhood much." I told him about the two times my garage had gotten broken into and the time I was at work and someone cut open the bars on the bedroom window in order to get in. I had to call a welder to repair them. I didn't tell him about the endless airplanes flying over my house, the gunshots in the distance, the tires screeching from drivers who went too fast and barely managed to brake at the stop sign in front of the house. But I did tell him what worried me the most. "The neighbor is letting a friend sleep in a tent in his yard, and he can see into my property all day long through the chain-link fence. He's out there cooking over an open fire, smoking and drinking, and he even pees out there in the yard."

"Hmm, that's not safe for you and the baby," my father said, looking very concerned. For the first time, he really looked at Nathan, and he didn't take his eyes off his grandson when he said, "I'll come build you a better fence."

True to his word, he showed up the next two Sundays and spent the whole day putting up a wooden fence that encircled the property. For the first time, I found myself reconnecting with my father in a way I hadn't since we had gone to that Thai restaurant in Santa Cruz. I came out with a glass of water for him and sat a few feet away as I watched him work. At first neither of us talked. I held Nathan in my arms, and that little bundle against my chest helped me be brave in my father's presence. Every time I saw him, I reverted to my old self. I was tongue-tied and nervous around him. I didn't know what to talk to him about or how to engage him and get him to talk to me. He was a private man and didn't like to share anything about himself, especially with his children. My father was a mystery to me, a puzzle with too many missing pieces that I wished I could find and put together so I could finally fully understand the man whose blood flowed through my veins.

As my father worked, I watched him do what he did best. He was just as good at building things as he was at destroying them. I watched his hands, so brown and strong, shaped just like my own. I admired his skills as he measured and cut, hammered and drilled. The neighbor's friend, a skinny man in his fifties dressed in a dirty T-shirt and jeans that were clearly too big for him, sat on an up-side-down bucket outside his tent, smoking a joint and watching my father build the fence. One by one, the wooden slats went up as he drilled them in place.

A helicopter flew by, and the sound took me into the border-lands, reminding me of the crossing that divided my life into a before and an after.

I remembered so vividly that moment when we were trying to cross, the fear of being caught by Border Patrol, of being sent back to Mexico and losing my chance at having my father back in my life. I remember how my father had been right—at nine years old, I was too little to make the crossing, and I had put everyone at risk of being caught. Sure enough, Border Patrol caught us and sent us back to Tijuana twice. It was a miracle that we made it the third time, although my father had to carry me on his back most of the way.

It was there at the U.S. border that I got my first piggyback ride from my father.

"Do you remember our crossing?" I asked him.

"No," he said. "I've tried to forget." Then he lowered his drill and looked at me. "You shouldn't think about it, Chata. What happened is already in the past. Leave it at that. Olvídalo. Move on with your life." He turned back to the fence and resumed his work.

I didn't tell him that I couldn't forget. The only way I could move on was by remembering my past and trying to make sense of it. Only by understanding and accepting the life I had lived could I free myself from the trauma that still haunted me and kept me prisoner. This is why I needed to return to my writing. It was the only way I would ever be free.

My father, on the other hand, drowned his immigrant trauma in a can of Budweiser. Even though his newfound religion had helped him quit drinking, he eventually started up again. Nine years later, he would die of liver cancer, still a prisoner of his trauma.

"Do you regret immigrating?" I asked him as he turned off the drill to grab more screws from the bucket on the ground.

He looked at me for a long time, as if weighing his words very carefully. "Too many people in this world are living lives full of regrets, Chata. At church, I've learned there is a better way to live—in Jesus. Do you think *He* regrets dying for our sins?"

I looked down at the ground. I didn't know if Jesus regretted anything—all I knew was that I sure did. I was certainly regretting my question, but my father continued. "Jesus died to save you, Chata. And He would die again for you if He had to. Just like I would immigrate again for you, if I had to." He looked at Nathan and said, "You're a mother. Maybe now, you'll understand."

He turned back to his drilling and didn't look at me again. Nathan woke up from his nap and I took him in to change his diaper, pondering my father's words. I buried my nose in Nathan's little neck, inhaling the sweet scent of baby powder. "Chiquito mío, I promise I'll never leave you."

As I held my son in my arms, I began to understand the paradox of our immigrant experience. Despite the trauma I had suffered from my father's decision to immigrate, that same decision would allow me to be the parent he could never be. I would get to watch my son grow up. I would get to celebrate birthdays and holidays with him. I would never have to walk away from my son and go to another country to seek a better life for him. I would get to spare my child the misery of being a border crosser.

When my father was finished with the fence and left, I went out back to run my hands along its surface, admiring his work, the wooden slats as hard and rough as my father's hands.

My father believed in the gift Jesus had given us. I believed in the gift my father had given me—this fence and the time I got to spend with him while he built it. But as I stood there with Nathan in my arms, I realized there was another thing he had given me:

My father's greatest gift to me was that I would get to be the parent who stays.

Reyna and baby Nathaniel

26

AFTER BEING AT the middle school for two-and-a-half years, I had come to discover that one of my biggest struggles as a teacher was that the school kept changing our textbooks. Just when I thought I was finding my way with a textbook, it would get replaced the following school year, and we would be sent off to teacher trainings to learn how to use the new one. Another struggle was that the grade level and subjects I taught kept changing, and I felt I couldn't develop an expertise in any single grade and subject. In July 2002, when the new school year started for those of us in B track, I was given eighth-grade remedial and regular English. Even though I had requested sixth-grade Beginning ESL, which was the grade and subject I was most comfortable with, my principal said there was nothing that could be done about it. What was worse was that to solve the problem of overcrowded middle schools, the school district had implemented the policy that all eighth-grade students would be promoted to ninth grade as long as they had Ds in math and English. They could have an F in everything else. I was flabbergasted. In Mexico, you had to earn your way to the next grade and prove you were ready, which is why my mother didn't graduate from elementary school until she was seventeen.

"Give it your best effort," I would tell my students during class. "Take pride in your work. Your future depends on your education! Education is everything!" I sounded like my father, and I wished he was here to help me convince these kids how important it was to think about their future.

"We don't need to work hard," my students would say, shaking their head at my enthusiasm and overzealousness. "All we need is a D in your class to go to high school, don't you know?"

They looked away from me and went back to their apathy and mischief. Because of the district's low expectations, the students, quick to take advantage of the situation, gave up on good grades the moment they entered eighth grade.

My half brother, Leo, became a victim of these policies. Making his way through school getting the required Ds in math and English had set him up for failure. When he got to high school, he couldn't handle the course work and dropped out. Unlike Betty, he never went back.

My students' apathy was one thing. Rudeness and disrespect were something else. There were some who completely crossed the line, and when I would call the parents, many wouldn't return my calls. I remembered Ms. Hoang's advice to pay home visits, unannounced. So I started showing up at the homes of my worst troublemakers to ask for parental support. "I can't take it anymore," one father said upon hearing my report that his son had taken scissors and cut up all the headphones in my listening center. "Can you help me? Do you know of a place that I could call so they can take him off my hands?"

I sat there thinking, *I came to ask you for help and now you're the one asking me to help you get rid of your son?* I felt helpless seeing this father so desperate. I didn't know what to tell him. I didn't know the details of their lives, of what had led to this, and I felt incapable of giving advice. I thought of my mother and the trouble she had had with Betty. Though it was true that Betty had behavior problems, I thought it had been a reaction to the lack of love and support she had at home. But what could explain her behavior when I took her to live with me, when all I did was to love and support her? She once said to me, *It isn't that easy to start somewhere new with the old you still inside you.* Though habits are hard to break, and although it took some time, Betty did break free of her past, found her way, and managed to take control of her life.

I wished I better understood the dynamics between parents and children. I was unable to offer comfort to this man. "Don't give up on your son" was all I could say. "He needs you to be strong and to have faith in him. He's trying to figure out who he is."

He nodded and said, "Sí, está bien, maestra. Gracias."

Another day, I asked a girl to throw away her gum.

"That's a stupid rule," she said. She blew the huge wad of gum in her mouth into a pink bubble, then burst it with a loud pop. The students erupted in laughter.

"I'm sorry you disagree with the class rules, but you need to follow them," I said, pointing to the trash can by my desk.

She walked up to the trash can, spat the gum out, and looked at me and said, "You're such a bitch."

I sent her to the office, and when class was over, I called her father to schedule a meeting after school the following day to discuss his daughter's behavior.

Instead, he barged into my room the following morning during first period. He hadn't checked in at the main office as visitors were required to do. He came directly to my classroom to yell at me in front of my students.

"It's your fault my daughter said what she said. She was just defending herself. She told me that you're constantly punishing her for every little thing she does. She's not the problem. You are. I'm going to go to the principal and request a better teacher for my daughter."

I was so shocked I couldn't get any words out to defend myself. He stormed out of the room, and I stood in my classroom while my students looked at me, witnesses to my humiliation. I was about to burst into tears, right there in front of them. Thankfully, the bell rang and they jumped from their seats and rushed out of my class-room, leaving me alone with my shame.

That night, I woke up soaked in sweat, my heart racing. I'd had a nightmare where I found myself running from a huge wave, but no matter how fast I ran, I was overtaken by a deep, watery darkness, a bottomless void from which I couldn't escape. I felt an incredible despair wash over me, drowning me, squeezing the last of my breath, my hope.

I sat in bed, the moonlight streaming through the window, the scent of jasmine drifting in from the patio outside. I understood that this dream was a sign. I was treading water, and I needed to do whatever it took to keep from drowning. The truth was, I was running out of strength.

How did my life come to this? I wondered. Being a middle school teacher wasn't my dream, and the longer I stayed, the more it became my nightmare. I opened my desk drawer where I had stored my unfinished novel. It had been almost three years since I had touched it. I took out the pages and leafed through them, thinking of that other me who had once loved to write. Since I was thirteen, writing had been my lifeline. It had been the thing I would cling to when I felt most helpless. It had once been my dream, but I had betrayed it. I had turned my back on it and lost my way.

Now I was twenty-six years old, and I could already feel the years I had lived, the choices I had made or not made, weighing me down, suffocating me, making me feel old and tired. I closed my eyes, thinking of the dream that had carried me through college, the dream of being a writer. Had I let it die by failing to nurture it? I reached into myself, searching for my dream in the deepest recess of my soul, until I found its heartbeat, slow and faint.

Sensing my distress, Nathan woke up whimpering. I picked him up from his crib and sat on the rocking chair to soothe him.

"Once upon a time," I told Nathan as he sucked his thumb and soothed himself back to sleep, "there was a little immigrant girl with a big dream, but then she lost her way . . ."

Nathan started screaming, as if in protest. "You don't like that story?" I asked him. "Well, neither do I."

I looked at my son's face, his eyes half-closed, his little mouth in an "O" as he lost his grip on his thumb. I wished I knew what the future held for him. What kind of human being would he grow up to be? What kind of dreams would he have? Then I realized that I could never encourage my son to pursue his dreams if I hadn't done so myself. When Nathan was older, how could I dare look him in the face and tell him to believe in his dreams, to work hard for them and never let them go, if I had let mine die simply because adulthood had turned out to be too hard? No, my dream was still alive. Barely, but it was alive. It wasn't too late for me. For us.

"I don't like this story, Nathan," I said. "Let's write a new one."

I called Diana the next day and told her about the humiliating experience in my classroom, my disillusionment at knowing that even

Diana and Reyna

though I had tried so hard to do my best, I felt like a failure. She said, "Reynita, you need to transfer to adult school. The difference is like night and day. Middle school is not for you. Plus, all the responsibilities and stress have really impacted your writing. You can't let that happen. Listen to me, you'll love adult education."

Before she began teaching at PCC, Diana had spent several years at an adult school teaching immigrants. "I loved that job," she said. "My students were the most committed students I've ever had. The difference is that they're responsible adults and want to be there. And there are no papers to grade, so you'll have time to write. Reynita, you need to think about yourself and your baby. If you don't take the steps to change the situation you're in, you'll always be stuck there. Don't lose sight of your writing."

Following Diana's advice, I looked into an accelerated teacher credentialing program. It was urgent that I swap my emergency credential for a real one. In a year, once I had a clear credential, I could transfer to the local adult school.

I also looked up writing classes and stumbled upon the UCLA Extension Writers' Program. They offered ten-week courses and weekend classes. Since I hadn't written anything in three years, I decided to start slowly. I registered for a weekend class called Finding Your Unique Voice, taught by María Amparo Escandón, author of *Esperanza's Box of Saints*. I had never taken a class with a Mexican writer, and that added to my enthusiasm.

"Why are you doing this?" Mago asked me when I told her of going back to school. "You have a child. You can't be taking classes. You're a mother now. You need to take care of him. Be with him."

"I'm doing this for both of us."

"How much time are you going to have left for Nathan between work and school?" she asked. And though we were on the phone, I could feel her judging eyes shooting daggers at me.

"Not much," I admitted. Her question made my guilt return. Since I worked full-time, I left Nathan with a babysitter from

6:45 a.m. to 4:00 p.m., while I was at work. And now with me taking credentialing classes, I wouldn't be home until ten three nights a
week, and my weekends would be spent at my writing classes. But if
I didn't do this while he was a baby, it would be much harder when
he was older. *When is the right time for me to reclaim my dreams?* I
wanted to ask Mago. *When he's all grown up and gone?* I didn't think I
could survive those long years of waiting, yearning to piece together
my broken dreams. What kind of archer's bow would I be for Nathan if I was hollow and rotten on the inside?

When Mago and I hung up, I thought about how being a mother
had turned out to be the hardest thing I had ever done. When I became a teacher, at least I had one week of training. When I was dis-
charged from the hospital, Mago had rolled me out in a wheelchair
with my bundle of joy in my arms and a diaper bag full of fear and
self-doubt on my lap. She returned to her life and her kids, and left
me to figure things out on my own.

I couldn't turn to my mother for support or guidance. My sister-
in-law was the woman I admired most when it came to child rearing.
I found it ironic that a teenage mom would be my role model, but
Norma had an uncanny understanding of the complexities of motherhood. She also had something that I was struggling with—unlike
me, she had no doubt that her children should always come first,
and she accepted and embraced motherhood as her first and only
duty. To Norma, her children *were* her dreams. Every time I encouraged her to return to school, get her GED, and pursue a career, she
would say, "Not right now, my children need me."

When I taught Beginning ESL, I had ordered picture books for
my students because even though they were middle schoolers, they
couldn't read English well enough to handle chapter books. One of
the books that came highly recommended to me from other teachers
was called *The Giving Tree* by Shel Silverstein.

As I was putting my new books on the shelves, I sat down to
read the book, and it left me with an awful taste in my mouth. The

story was about an apple tree that plays with a little boy, and he loves her and she loves him and life is perfect. Then the boy becomes a young man and he doesn't want to play anymore. First, he wants money, then a house for his family, then he wants to run away from his problems. The tree gives him her apples, her branches, even her trunk, but it never makes him happy. Years later he returns as an old man—just as miserable as always—and the tree is nothing but a stump with nothing left to give of herself. He says, "I don't need anything. Just a place to sit." So, she offers him her stump to sit on.

When I finished reading the story, I wanted to hurl it out the window and never let my students read it—especially my girls. I refused to believe that to be a good mother I would have to give and sacrifice all until what remained of me was only a dead stump.

So I made my decision. I would go back to school because loving my child didn't mean I had to destroy myself.

27

Reyna and María Amparo

"WHAT IS VOICE?" my new writing teacher asked as we reviewed the course goals for her weekend workshop. "Your voice is the unique way in which you communicate with yourself and with the outside world. It is your spoken and written fingerprint. Hundreds of variables determine your voice from the moment you are conceived. No one in the world communicates the way you do, and what makes your voice unique is that your life's experience is unique."

This was the first time I'd considered that my experiences might be things to celebrate, rather than be ashamed of. Was it possible that everything I had gone through had shaped me into a unique individual with a unique voice?

María Amparo turned out to be a generous teacher, and our

shared country, culture, and heritage made me feel connected to her. Though we had been born into two different social classes—she into upper-class Mexican society, and me, well, let's just say that had my father never brought me to the U.S., I could have been María Amparo's maid—we were both here in a city far away from our homeland, Mexican transplants united through our love of books and words.

In her class we explored the goal of honing our writer's voice. "So, if all writers have a distinct, identifiable voice, why is it so complicated to find our own?" she asked. "Our voice as writers is our own truth. It is the well we all have inside filled with all the moments of our lives. Oftentimes it is a scary place. We are afraid to dip our bucket into the dark waters of that well because painful memories will come out. It is our own fears that don't allow our true voice to emerge."

During breaks, María Amparo sought me out and we talked about Mexico. She was from Veracruz, the eastern state that borders the Gulf of Mexico. It has one of the most beautiful dance and music traditions, one that reflects its European, indigenous, and African roots. My favorite Mexican actress, Salma Hayek, is also from there.

"Have you ever been to Veracruz?" María Amparo asked.

I was embarrassed to admit to her that I didn't know Mexico well.

"Well, I've only passed through your hometown on my way to Acapulco, so I don't know that part of Mexico, either," she said. "But maybe one day you'll have the opportunity to visit my state."

"I do love the dances," I said. "And the sones jarochos!" One of my dance fantasies had been to perform the dances of Veracruz and get to wear the exquisite costume made of yards of white organza and lace, which, when held in a dancer's hands, looked like sea foam.

To my delight, the excerpts María Amparo shared with us were from Latino authors whose work I knew well, and celebrating those authors' unique voices made this class even more meaningful to me: *One Hundred Years of Solitude* by Gabriel García Márquez; the little gem of a story, "Salvador Late or Early," by Sandra Cisneros; and *Pedro Páramo* by Juan Rulfo, the Mexican author whose work Marta, my Spanish teacher, had compared my writing to. His novel was about a man who travels to his dead mother's hometown to find his father, whom he has never met. He discovers that his father passed away years ago, and the town turns out to be a literal ghost town populated by the spirits of its dead inhabitants. The themes of the book—hope and despair—were themes I knew well from my own life.

María Amparo assigned us a writing exercise which was straight-forward and yet difficult to execute. She wrote on the board: *Write as if your parents were dead.*

One of my greatest fears as a child was that my parents would die while they were in the U.S. Through the years I had often asked myself: What would my life have been like if my father had died and never come back for me? Death is the border we can only cross once.

I knew this was a question I needed to explore in the writing exercise. Yet, after almost three years of not writing, I approached the exercise with insecurity. What if I had forgotten how to write? My fear then led me away from the task at hand and I started to think of other things. Was Nathan okay? Did he miss me? Was the sitter paying enough attention to him? Was Mago right? Was I a bad mother for being in class instead of with my child? Should I call the sitter and check on Nathan?

María Amparo looked my way, and I was embarrassed that while everyone had quickly put pen to paper or was typing away on a lap-top, I was staring blankly into space, on the verge of a mini nervous breakdown. She smiled at me encouragingly, and with a deep breath, I opened my laptop. *Focus and write*, I told myself. *Just do it*. As soon as I touched my fingers to my keyboard, it all came back.

Class was over too quickly. María Amparo had helped me reclaim and celebrate my voice. When she dismissed us, I felt a renewed sense of excitement for my unfinished novel. Now I knew I had made the right choice.

I thanked María Amparo for the class, and just as I was leaving she said, "Reyna, have you ever heard of Emerging Voices?" I shook my head, and she continued. "It's a mentorship program offered through PEN Center USA for writers of color. You should apply. I'm one of the mentors."

She explained that Emerging Voices was a seven-month program that would open the doors to the literary community, not only in Los Angeles but also nationally. The chosen participants, or fellows as they were called, met to discuss their work with each other and with a master teacher. They each got their own mentor, received free classes at UCLA Extension, and met with published authors, editors, and agents to discuss craft and publishing tips.

It sounded exactly like what I was looking for—a writing community. María Amparo was the only writer I had met in Los Angeles. If I got accepted into Emerging Voices, that meant I would no longer feel alone and isolated in my writing journey.

"The only problem is," María Amparo said with a worried look, "the deadline is this Friday, which means you have five days to put together your application packet."

"That's going to be hard," I said. "But I have nothing to lose, right?"

She smiled at my enthusiasm and wished me luck. "I hope you get in," she said, giving me a hug, and we said "Hasta luego," not "Adiós," because we both hoped that our paths would cross again soon.

That Sunday night, I called Diana and Micah Perks to ask if they would write letters of recommendation.

"But I only have five days to turn everything in!" I exclaimed.

"No worries," they said.

I spent the next few days working on my application. It consisted of several questions I needed to answer about my writing. *Why are you applying to Emerging Voices? What are your goals as a writer? List any commitments (classes, employment, personal obligations) that could interfere with your participation in the fellowship. How are you locked out of the literary establishment?* I also had to put together my curriculum vitae and prepare a twenty-page writing sample.

On Thursday, just as I was putting the finishing touches on my application, Micah's letter arrived. On Friday, the day the application had to be postmarked, I drove to Pasadena and met Diana at the post office near PCC. She ran up the steps, letter in hand and, after a big hug, I handed her Nathan and she held him while I put her letter in the packet. I sealed it, stamped it, and watched it go into the post office cart with the other packets.

"This is going to change your life," Diana said as we walked away from the post office.

"I don't want to get my hopes up," I said. "I don't want this to break my heart."

Diana had always had an unwavering belief in me and in my future. With no doubt in her voice, she said, "You're going to get it, Reynita. Just watch and see."

28

Abuelita Chinta and Cousin Diana

Every time the phone rang, I hoped it was the Emerging Voices program, but it never was. Instead, the one who called was my mother, delivering the worst news. "Se está muriendo tu abuela," she said to me. "Your grandmother is dying." Her voice sounded weak and distant through the phone receiver, vulnerable in a way that was unfamiliar to me.

"What happened?" I asked, clutching the phone.

A scorpion had bitten my grandmother on her hand. Abuelita Chinta didn't tell anyone. Instead, she did what they do in my hometown—rub alcohol and onion on the sting and eat a raw egg to counteract the poison. Obviously, those home remedies hadn't worked. Two days later, my grandmother fell ill and ended up in the hospital suffering from chest pain, fever, and blood clots.

"We have to go to Mexico. Can you help me with the airfare? I need to go see my mother."

"No te preocupes, Ma. I'll buy the tickets."

Buying plane tickets at the last minute cost more than I had imagined it would. I put them on my credit card and cringed. I asked for time off from work and school, and Mago, my mom, Leo, Nathan, and I left for Mexico the next day.

My mother was on the verge of tears the entire time. I could see her eyes swollen and red, and for the first time I reached out to hug and comfort her. This was new to me, this intimacy. She wasn't the kind of mother who said loving things, and I wasn't the kind of daughter who knew how to comfort. If anything, whenever I saw my mother, I would never fail to remind her of her failures, her mistakes, the many ways in which she had disappointed me through the years. That October morning as I held her at the airport, it was awkward for both of us, yet our mutual grief helped us overcome it.

As we waited to board, we talked about my grandmother. Mago and I shared our favorite memories of her, of how kind and loving she had been when we lived with her. "I should have gone to Mexico more often to see her," I said to Mago as I held Nathan in my arms. He was sleeping soundly, sucking his thumb. "Every time I had vacation from work, I could have gone to see her."

"Me, too," Mago said.

"And I should have sent her money," I continued. That was eating at me the most. My salary as a teacher had been more than enough to send money to my grandmother every month. If my own mother, who was making minimum wage, could do it, why hadn't I?

Instead, I was spending my wages on frivolous things, like a pair of Carlos Santana shoes for $100, highlights on my hair for $120, bags of river rock for $150 to landscape my front yard. I spent money on stupid rocks instead of sending it to the woman who had given me so much love as a child. It hurt so much to realize that I had forgotten that pledge I made four years earlier, that as soon as I finished college and had a good job I would start sending her money.

"How was it that my struggles with adulthood had consumed me so much that I had forgotten about my promise?" I asked Mago.

Mago said nothing. She had her own guilt to deal with. We had turned out to be ungrateful granddaughters, allowing the materialism of the U.S. to infect us and make us forget about our family in Mexico, who had hardly enough to eat.

"She's one of the sweetest and kindest women I've ever known," I said. "The best grandmother anyone could ever ask for. When she recovers from this, I'm going to look into bringing her to the States."

I knew she didn't really want to come. My mother had asked several times through the years and my grandmother had refused. She didn't want to leave her home and die in a strange country, far from the place of her birth. But maybe this time she would realize it was better to come to live with us. We could take better care of her—besides, I would tell her, there are no scorpions where we live!

My mother had been quiet as Mago and I talked, but then she leaned forward and said, "Your abuela wasn't like that with me, you know?"

"¿Qué quieres decir?" I asked.

I could tell she was hesitant to say more, but then, maybe because we still had an hour before boarding, she leaned closer to us and said, "Your abuelita was very cruel when I was growing up. I never knew why. She was just angry and bitter, resentful, but I don't know what caused it. Maybe the poverty we lived in. Maybe it was the life my father gave her. He drank his wages away, and there were many times when we had nothing to eat. She would hit me all the time. Out of her five children, she was hardest on me."

I shook my head, and I wanted to tell her to stop, that I didn't believe her. But there was something in her voice that told me to be quiet and listen. I understood that this was a rare gift my mother was giving us, telling us about her past, letting us see the young girl she had once been.

"When we had nothing to eat, I would go to Doña Caro and beg for a loan," my mother continued. Doña Caro was the only woman on our block who had a refrigerator and a real house made of brick and concrete. Her husband was a welder and made decent money. I remembered Mago, at some point or other, had also asked for loans from Doña Caro. "Your abuelita would get angry at me for going to the neighbor. She would say to me, 'Don't you have any pride?' And I would say, 'Amá, we can't eat pride.' So she would take the pesos from my hand and go to the mill to buy corn dough for tortillas.

"One day, she tried to teach me to make the tortillas, but she wasn't a patient teacher."

As she told us the story, I pictured my eight-year-old mother sitting near the hot griddle, clap-clap-clapping as hard as she could with her little hands, the dough forming into a shape like an amoeba instead of a perfect circle. As hard as she tried, she couldn't get the dough to form the desired shape. My grandmother yelled at her. "You're ruining the tortillas, pendeja!" Once, my grandmother got so frustrated she took my mother's hands and slammed them down on the hot griddle to punish her.

"My hands were covered in blisters," my mom said, looking at her hands, wincing as if still in pain. "It hurt so much to do my chores all week."

When my mother turned into a young woman, and boys began to take notice, my grandmother became very vigilant. Once she caught my mother walking back from the store with a neighborhood boy, and she picked up rocks from the road and threw them at the boy, chasing him away. "I never want to see you near my daughter again!" she yelled.

Another time, she took off her chancla and chased off another boy, hitting him on his butt with her sandal.

"She never let me have a boyfriend and chased all the boys away," my mother said.

"Y mi papá?" I said. Obviously, there was one man my grandmother hadn't chased away. I wondered if my father had been so handsome and charming that he had won over my grandmother. I was imagining a love story straight out of a Harlequin romance novel, when my mother said, "It's her fault I ended up with him."

She said she had met my father at the tortilla mill where she used to work, across from the train station. My father was working on a construction project and would come to the mill every day to buy tortillas for his lunch.

They started seeing each other in secret. Then one day, he invited her to a dance in a town an hour away. She lied to my grandmother, saying she was going to work, and met him at the bus station. They took a bus in the morning, but in the evening, they missed their bus back and had no choice but to spend the night in a motel.

"He didn't touch me," my mother said. "He was very respectful. He didn't take advantage of me that night."

But still, when she returned home the next day, my grandmother was waiting for her. She had already learned my mother had not gone to work, because my aunt had gone looking for her at the tortilla mill. Not accepting her explanation, or her pleas, my grandmother gave my mother the biggest beating she had ever received.

"You're a disgrace to your family," my grandmother said. "Get out of here. We don't want you here anymore. Go live with that man who has already ruined you."

"But he didn't touch me!" my mother said.

"You're a liar. You think I was born yesterday? ¡Vete de aquí!"

So, my mother cleaned herself up as best she could, took her belongings, and walked all the way to La Guadalupe, where my father lived with his parents. She had shown up with a bruised body and her heart in pieces.

"Against your abuela Evila's wishes, he still took me in," she said. "And that was how I ended up with your father."

Mago and I looked at each other. I didn't want to believe our mother, and yet I knew she wasn't lying. My siblings and I hadn't been products of love, but of our grandmother's abuse, mistrust, and betrayal.

I thought about the story my grandmother had told me three years earlier when Eddie broke my heart, about the young man she had loved and how her family hadn't allowed her to be with him. They condemned her to a life with a man she didn't love. Had that made her bitter? Was that why she had kicked out my mother, condemning her to the same fate?

"But she was so gentle with us," I said. "She never hit us, never yelled at us. Not even once."

My mother nodded. "You were her first grandchildren. When you kids were born, things got better between us. She repented for how she had treated me and forcing me to move in with your father, especially once she saw the kind of life he was giving me. He used to beat me because his mother—your abuela Evila—was always telling him that I wasn't good enough for him. That I was a bad cook. A bad homemaker. A bad mother. Sometimes my mother would come visit me and she would gasp at seeing my face, when I had a black eye or a bloodied lip. Then she would cry and ask me to forgive her. And I did."

I knew my mother had forgiven my grandmother. Through all the years she had been in the U.S., my mother had always sent my grandmother money, and my aunt as well. Even though my mother was living below the poverty line in a one-room apartment infested with roaches, she would send half of her wages to Mexico. A year before, she had even built my grandmother a one-room cinder-block house to replace the shack of sticks and cardboard she had lived in for most of her life.

My mother hadn't been a good mother to us, but no one could

say she wasn't a good daughter or sister. I always assumed it was because my grandmother had been a kind and loving mother. Now that I knew otherwise, I was astonished that, despite her mother's cruelty, my mother held no bitterness or resentment toward her. I looked at my mother and wondered if the legacy of the women in my family was to be abused and then become the abuser. My mother had repeated with me and my siblings some of the same behaviors my grandmother had exhibited with her. Would I be expected to forgive her and take care of her when she was an old woman, pretend she had never hurt me? I didn't know if I could be that kind of daughter.

I watched Nathan, sleeping soundly in his carrier. Would I continue the legacy of the women in my family and go from victim to victimizer? As we waited to board our plane, I told myself that since I had already broken one cycle, perhaps it would be possible to break another.

29

TWELVE HOURS LATER, as we arrived at my aunt's house, an ambulance was leaving, its red light slicing through the darkness. Upon hearing our taxi—my aunt, her husband, my cousins, and my uncle Gary came running out of the gate. My mother broke into tears seeing her sister and brother. "We're here," she said, "¿Cómo está mi amá? Is she here? We saw the ambulance."

Tía Güera started crying and couldn't speak. My uncle looked at Mago, at me, then finally at my mother. He shook his head and said, "She's gone, Juana. Our mother went into cardiac arrest three hours ago. The ambulance came to drop off the body."

As I watch my mother and her siblings embrace, I thought about the fact that three hours earlier we had been at the station in Mexico City waiting to board our bus. Three hours earlier, we had been talking about everything we were going to do for her—how she would want for nothing. Now here I stood, learning that I would never have a chance to make things right with my grandmother. I would never see her again, and my son would never meet the woman whom I had been blessed to have as a grandmother.

"Llegamos muy tarde," my mother said, echoing my thoughts. We were too late, and there was nothing to do now but to go inside to plan a funeral, weighed down by the knowledge of what we had lost.

El Hospital Cristina, where my grandmother had died, was charging the equivalent of $1,000 dollars in pesos. I knew my mother and aunt had no money. Carlos was back in Los Angeles and sent enough for flowers and candles but not for the hospital bill. Mago didn't have much to pitch in. The only way my aunt had been able to retrieve my grandmother's body was by turning over the deed to her house as temporary payment. Early the next morning, I walked to the bank to make a withdrawal, and with that money, and the little that Mago could contribute, I settled the hospital bill. The deed of the house was returned to my aunt. She had been worried that on top of losing her mother, she would lose her house as well. I tortured myself thinking about the many ways $1,000 would have made my grandmother happy while she was living and could have enjoyed the money.

At home, we bathed Abuelita Chinta and dressed her for her funeral. She was stiff and incredibly heavy, her skin cold and rubbery, her lips purple, her eyes shut, but her curly gray hair was as soft as cashmere, smelling of almond oil, just the way I remembered it. Thanks to her, my sisters and I had wavy hair that was thick and full.

Mago and I forced our grandmother's hands together and secured them tightly with a rope, then wove a white rosary between them. She would now pray in her coffin, just like she had done her whole life. "I have her hands," Mago said, and she held them out for me to see. I had never noticed before that her tiny hands were the exact shape as my grandmother's.

What else had we inherited from this woman? Her tenacity for life? Her ability to survive in a harsh environment? Her capacity to reinvent herself and go from being bitter and cruel to loving and gentle?

She lay there in her coffin, surrounded by dripping candles, marigolds, and the lamentations of all of us she had left behind. We hired a rezandera, a professional prayer who attended my grandmother's rosary to lead us in prayers. The rezandera's voice was deep and hauntingly sorrowful as she prayed an Our Father and a Hail Mary. I stood in a corner clinging to Nathan, silently repeating her words as I looked at my grandmother lying peacefully in her casket.

"Santa María, madre de dios, ruega por nosotros los pecadores ahora y en la hora de nuestra muerte. Amén."

My grandmother had gone to the cemetery every week to tend the grave of my grandfather and my cousin Catalina. Now she was making her last trip to the cemetery. The procession walked a mile to the holy ground, over the dirt road, past La Quinta Castrejón, the fancy country club where my mother had taken us to sell cigarettes and gum to the partygoers for a few pesos that had kept us from starving. We passed the train station where at twelve years old, Mago had worked at a food stand to help the family. In the 1990s, the government privatized the railroad system, and train service in Iguala was permanently suspended. Now as we walked by the train station, it pained me to see it so empty and lifeless. When I was a child, it had thrived and buzzed with activity—full of vendors selling clay pots and other wares. Food stands had lined the station, and the scent of chicken quesadillas and gorditas wafted through the air; travelers from all the surrounding towns would come here to catch a train to Mexico City, Cuernavaca, or Chilpancingo. As a child, I longed to ride the train to one of those cities, but we were too poor to leave Iguala, and all we could do was stand by the train tracks and wave goodbye to the passengers who were on their way to somewhere else—far away from this broken place.

My grandmother never got a chance to go anywhere beyond the nearby towns we visited on our annual church pilgrimage. Now, as the procession left the abandoned train station behind and veered left toward the cemetery, I suddenly wished we were not burying my grandmother in Iguala. I wished I could take her with me somewhere else—like Acapulco—so that at least in death she would get to visit a beautiful place. Instead, we put her in the same dirt grave where my grandfather was buried. I wondered if this was what she would have wanted, to spend the rest of eternity sharing a grave with her borracho, abusive husband. I never learned if he had ever asked her to forgive him. If he hadn't, I hoped he would do so now, in the afterlife. I no longer believed in Heaven and Hell, but for my abuelita, I wanted to believe that she had gone on to a beautiful, peaceful place, far away from Iguala and its cruel way of life. Perhaps she would find her way to Santa Cruz and find peace in its redwood forest.

When her body had been lowered into the ground, we threw handfuls of dirt over her coffin and said goodbye. I looked at my aunt, uncles, and ten cousins, ranging from babies to teenagers. My little cousin Diana came to stand by me. She was fascinated by me, the cousin who lived in America.

"¿Vives en Disneyland?" she asked me as she grabbed my hand.

I smiled at her, not sure how to answer her question. I didn't live in Disneyland, but I did live in a magical place. I was reminded once again of the privilege of living in the U.S. Though it wasn't perfect, it was a place that allowed me to thrive. It was a place of opportunity, abundance, possibility, and dreams. Living there allowed me to have what I could never have had in Mexico—a college education, a well-paying job, my own house, my writing.

I wondered what life had in store for this sweet little girl. How could I teach little Diana to dream of a bright future here in Iguala where nightmares abounded? What could I do for my transnational family to support and encourage them across the borders and mountains between us?

There, at my grandmother's grave, I promised her that I would do what I hadn't done while she was alive. I would look out for the family she was leaving behind, especially her grandchildren. "This time, I promise I won't forget," I said. "Rest in peace, my beloved abuelita."

Years later, when I would send my cousin Lupe to college, Diana to beauty school, and their brother Rolando to university, I would fulfill my promise.

Mother and Tío Gary at
Abuelita Chinta's grave

30

WHILE I WAITED to hear from Emerging Voices, I continued to work on my teacher credentialing classes. They were intense because a semester's worth of work and lectures were crammed into each month. The accelerated program was demanding, but in a year, I could say goodbye to my job at the middle school and transfer to adult school, as Diana had suggested.

Then, the Emerging Voices coordinator finally called. I had made it to the top 25 finalists. I was invited to go in for an interview. From there, eight applicants would be named the 2003 Emerging Voices Fellows.

I lit a candle next to my grandmother's photograph on my dresser and begged her to look out for me.

"Pray for me so that I get this, Abuelita," I said. "It could change my life!"

The following Saturday, I dropped off Nathan at the sitter's and drove over to the PEN office. There, I was introduced to the interview panel, which included the Emerging Voices coordinator and the PEN executive director. It was the longest twenty minutes of my life, sitting in that small office facing those five judges as they fired question after question at me, questions about my life, my work, why I wanted to be a fellow, how I could contribute to the program.

"Why should we choose you?" they asked bluntly.

"How will your responsibilities affect your participation and commitment to the program?"

"Why do you want to be a published writer?"

My knees quivering and my stomach clenching, I sat frozen in the chair. I swallowed my fear and answered their questions as honestly and passionately as I could.

"Of the books I've read about the immigrant experience, not one has been written by an immigrant herself, as if we were voiceless," I said. "As an immigrant, I have a voice and I want to be heard. This is what Emerging Voices stands for, isn't it? To give aspiring writers a chance to be heard and open the door for us to tell our own stories? Immigrants deserve a place in American literature because our experiences in the U.S. reflect the American experience," I continued. "If you accept me in the program, this is what I will fight for—inclusion and diversity."

Throughout the interview, I was composed and my smile never wavered. Ever since I was a little girl I would drive my father crazy because I smile when I'm nervous. Whenever he would yell at me, I would have a wide smile on my face, which made my father think I was mocking him. He would hit me even harder. I always hated this tic of mine because I couldn't control it. This time, though, it saved me. It wouldn't have done me any good to look terrified.

Finally, the executive director said, "Thank you for coming. We'll let you know of our decision next week." And with that, I was ushered out of the office.

In a daze, I walked past the other interviewees waiting their turn in the lobby with frightened looks on their faces. I was glad it was over for me. I had done the best I could. It was now up to the judges to decide my fate. I told myself that even if I didn't get in, I would still do whatever it took to fight for my dream. The weekend workshop I had taken with María Amparo had been enough to jump-start my writing. With or without Emerging Voices, I would finish my novel and pursue publication. I would write about the immigrant experience in a way that showed our humanity, that told the world we weren't numbers or statistics, but human beings, and that our stories deserved to be told. Still, the road would be so much easier with the support and guidance of this program.

As a Latina writer I knew what I was up against. I had read about the struggles that my literary heroes had gone through to get their works published. Chicana writers such as Sandra Cisneros, Cherríe Moraga, Ana Castillo, Denise Chávez, Gloria Anzaldúa, and all the rest had had to fight not just for racial equality but for gender equality. At a time when male Chicano writers were finding some opportunities with big and small publishers, Chicana writers had to start their own presses because no one wanted to take a chance on them and publish their work. These Chicanas didn't wallow in self-pity; they fought—and won. Several of them went on to get picked up by mainstream publishers. It wouldn't be any easier for me; I knew that. Even though my Chicana godmothers had macheted their way into the publishing world and had blessed me with a path to follow, in the end we all had to go on our individual journeys alone. I had to find my own way and prove my own literary worth.

When I returned home from my interview, I was ready to pray for miracles. Throughout the week, I lit candles for Abuelita Chinta and I asked her to intervene on my behalf. She had spent all her life being a devout Catholic, so I figured she had earned some Brownie points with God. Surely, she had the power to put in a good word for her granddaughter, even if her granddaughter was now a nonbeliever and a cynic and was praying only in her hour of need.

Whether it was my grandmother's help, a little luck, the potential the judges had seen in me, or all of the above, I got a call the following week from the EV coordinator. "Hi, Reyna. It's my pleasure to inform you that you have been selected as a fellow in the Emerging Voices Fellowship program. Congratulations!"

My knees felt weak. I didn't have the energy to walk to the couch, so I just let myself drop onto the floor. "I feel that I'm dreaming. Are you there? Is it real?"

Her voice was firm and clear through the receiver. "It's real. We're really looking forward to having you in the program."

After we hung up, I picked up Nathan and danced around the living room with him. "We're going on this journey together!" I told him. I was one step closer to my dream of being a published writer. I was elated and proud knowing that what I did now would have a positive impact on my son. I was going to help him with his dreams by first honoring mine.

Despite the challenges I was facing being a single mom, the journey to Emerging Voices had turned out to be magical. All the pieces fell together as soon as I made the decision to fight for my writing. For the first time, I didn't feel lost anymore. I had a new direction and had been welcomed into a community of writers. For the first time, I felt there was a place for me in Los Angeles, especially in the literary community I hadn't even known existed.

In January, the 2003 Emerging Voices program began with a beautiful welcome reception at Taix, a French restaurant in Echo Park. I met the seven other fellows in the program and felt proud to be part of such a diverse cohort: There was Ibarionex, a short-story writer from the Dominican Republic; Rocío, a Chicana poet and novelist from Boyle Heights; Adelina, a Tejana poet and performing artist; Colleen, a Japanese poet; Pireeni, a poet from Sri Lanka; Nora, a Native American novelist; Kisha, a writer of Honduran descent. This was the diversity I had hoped to find in my writing classes in Santa Cruz.

Though we were all around the same age and had many things in common, what differentiated me from the other fellows was that I was the only parent in the group, and not just a parent, but a single mother, which added another challenge to meeting my responsibilities in the program. But I told myself that if the committee had chosen me knowing full well I was a single mother, then they believed I could do it, and so I had to honor their trust in me.

I chose María Amparo as my mentor and met with her once a month to discuss my novel-in-progress. She lived in a gorgeous house near UCLA, the kind of house Betty and I had once dreamed about.

"Reyna, I had a feeling you and I were going to work together again," she said when I arrived at her house for our very first meeting. "You don't know how thrilled I am to be part of your writer's journey."

This was my first time at a writer's house, and I was nervous and overwhelmed, but María Amparo's generosity put me at ease. "Gracias, María. I can't tell you how much this means to me, being welcomed here in your home."

Later, María Amparo would tell me that what had struck her the most when she first met me was how driven and how determined I was to finish my novel. She marveled at the resilience of a disadvantaged young girl from Iguala, Guerrero. She said that the more she got to know me, the more she got to know herself—realizing how easy she'd had it growing up in a well-to-do family. Learning my story taught her to appreciate the advantages she had grown up with. She said, "You mentored me as well."

On Sundays, the fellows met to discuss our work and the books we were assigned to read as a group. On Monday evenings, we met with working professionals—writers, agents, editors—for Q&As about the writing profession. Finally, in this program, I was getting not just the lessons on craft but also the much-needed lessons on the business of writing. Sometimes the Q&As would be hosted at a writer's home, and I would get to see more beautiful houses—like the poet's house on the beach where I could see the glittery water from the huge window in the living room and wonder, as I had done in Santa Cruz, how many words it would take for me to build my dream house.

I presented my work for the first time in the city I had lived in for fifteen years when the EV fellows were invited to read at the Los Angeles Times Festival of Books, one of the biggest festivals in the country. I was astounded to find out that one hundred thousand book lovers came out for the weekend to celebrate literature. Though I had lived in L.A. since I was nine, I had never heard of the book festival, and in fact had never been to a book festival before. A gathering of thousands to celebrate books. I thought I was in Heaven. After reading an excerpt of the novel I was working on, *Across a Hundred Mountains*, I was approached by an editor from Children's Book Press, asking me if I wrote for kids. I told her the novel she had heard me read from was for adults, though it had a young protagonist.

"You have captured the child's voice so beautifully," she said to me. "I hope you write a picture book one day."

I hoped I would, too. For now, though, I had to stay focused on my novel, but the editor's praise had given me a glimmer of hope that one day I would find another editor who would be moved by my story the way this editor had been. She had seen something in my writing, and her praise encouraged me to keep going.

After our meetings and Q&As, I would drive through the dark streets of South Central to pick up Nathan from the babysitter, who lived ten minutes from me. As usual, I tried not to look at the homeless people camped out on the streets, or the prostitutes loitering outside cheap motels, the trash heaps along the curbs that even the darkness couldn't hide. I didn't dwell on the world outside of my car. I was too exhausted, and I wanted to stay focused on what I was accomplishing.

One day, Nathan reached for the babysitter, turned away from me, and cried when I took him home. In the car, I cried along with him. Was my son's love the price I would have to pay for my dream? I would lie awake at night thinking about what a fool I had been to believe that having a baby was going to help me feel grounded, rooted, confident. In fact, the opposite was true. I felt incompetent and overwhelmed with the incredibly demanding responsibility of taking care of another human being. Nathan was completely 100 percent dependent on me, and if I didn't do things right, and make the right choices, the consequences would be disastrous.

I'm doing this for both of us, I reminded myself. I stayed in the EV program and pushed past my guilt and insecurities. The last public reading we did was at the beautiful Central branch of the Los Angeles Public Library, which I had also never been to before. As I read from my novel on the stage of the Mark Taper Auditorium, feeling devastated that the program had come to an end, I wish I had known that eleven years later I would be sharing this very stage with my literary hero, Sandra Cisneros. If I had known what the future held for me, maybe I wouldn't have been so afraid of having to wake up from my beautiful EV dream and return to the harsh reality that from that point forward I would have to persevere on my own.

Our very last guest speaker was Jenoyne Adams, writer, literary agent, and former EV fellow. Jenoyne was there to give us advice on how to find an agent, how to pitch our work, how to write a query letter—all the aspects of the business of writing. But the thing that stuck with me the most was when she said, "Make sure that whenever you're in the room with an agent, you introduce yourself."

So when Jenoyne finished her talk, I waited until all the fellows had spoken to her and gathered every ounce of courage I could muster to emerge from the corner. I pushed away my timidity and walked up to her.

"Thank you for your advice," I said. "I really appreciated everything you had to say." Then I forced myself to say what I really wanted to say. "I just finished a draft under my mentor's guidance, but the story isn't where it needs to be yet. I plan to revise the entire thing this summer. I want to keep my momentum going even after EV is over, you know?" She waited patiently while I blurted out what was on my mind. "May I send you my novel when I'm done with my revisions?"

"Yes, of course," she said, smiling. "I'll be waiting."

I was sure she had said that to all the fellows, but those words—*I'll be waiting*—sustained me after the Emerging Voices program came to an end.

*Reyna reading for Emerging Voices
at the Los Angeles Public Library*

31

Reyna hard at work on Across a Hundred Mountains

As if in a trance, I wrote and rewrote through July and August. Since I was teaching B track, I had to work summers and would come home from work exhausted from teaching, exhausted from my credentialing classes and the homework I needed to do. I would grade student homework and spend the evening with Nathan, who at eighteen months was getting into everything and had a limitless amount of energy. But when evening came and Nathan was in his bed asleep, I would spend the night working on my novel, the vessel that I poured my heart and soul into.

Hunched over my computer, I was transported back to Mexico, back to my hometown with its green mountains and cornfields, its shacks of sticks and dirt roads. At UCSC I had set out to write a memoir, which then became an autobiographical novel. But now, under María Amparo's guidance, it had become something different, a novel that was no longer based on the life I had lived, but rather on the life I might have lived.

What would have become of my life if my father had never returned?

I had asked myself that question again and again. The novel I was writing became an exploration of that fear. The story I wrote was about a father who never returns. I rewrote the entire novel in those two months, and I felt as if I were possessed. My character, whom I named Juana, after my mother, was relentless. She wanted me to tell her story. Sometimes I felt as if she were next to me, telling me what to write. The death of her baby sister during a flood is a tragic event that leads to the disintegration of Juana's family. Her father leaves for the U.S. to earn money to build his family a house but in the end destroys his home. When he disappears and is never heard from again, Juana's mother succumbs to alcoholism, her baby brother is stolen by the town's money lender, and Juana has no choice but to head north to search for her father, hoping one day to put her family back together and rebuild her home.

But the pieces weren't fitting together well. There was something missing in the story, and my friend Rosa helped me find it. She was the mother of a former student, and I had become good friends with her and her husband. They lived ten minutes from me, and I often visited them. They were two of the kindest people I knew. In them I saw what my own family could have been if we had done a better job overcoming the distance between us. Though the father had migrated first, and then the mother and children, they had managed to create a home again. They were a close-knit family who, though of limited means, had an abundance of love.

One day while I was visiting, I was talking to Rosa about her job and her frustration and fear of being undocumented in this country. She had to use a borrowed Social Security number to work. At home she was Rosa, but at work she became Gladys. Every day she had to change identities.

"It does something to you, Reyna," she said. "It messes with your head. You ask yourself, which is the real you? Or are there two sides to you, the one they see and the one they don't?"

"Like the moon," I said. "It has two sides, but we only see one."

We sat outside on the steps of her house, hidden in darkness. The moon was not in our field of vision, but I didn't need to look at it to ponder the metaphor and how it applied to immigrants. The duality, the light and dark, the two faces of the moon. I thought about how, upon our border crossing, we take on new identities in subtle ways, and other times in drastic ways—like using a borrowed identity to work or having to lose one of our last names so that we can fit in. Hadn't I gone from being Reyna Grande Rodríguez in Mexico to simply Reyna Grande in the U.S.? Hadn't my sister gone from being Magloria to Maggie? Hadn't Gibran Khalil Gibran gone through a forced identity change when he had immigrated to the U.S. as well?

Marta had once said I was twice the girl I used to be. And she was right. Being split in half had forced me to create two versions of myself. I went home thinking about the duality of being an immigrant, our split identities, the cleaving of our hearts and bodies—half of our heart remained in our homeland, the other was here with us. One foot remained rooted in our native soil while with our other foot we dug into American soil to anchor ourselves and weather the storm.

As with the moon, there is the face that we immigrants show to the world, but our second face is the one we keep hidden in darkness so that no one can see us weeping.

I figured out how to move forward with my story.

When the summer ended, I printed the manuscript for the last time. For nine months, I had done nothing but write late into the night, trying to make up for the three years I hadn't touched the book. Holding the finished manuscript in my hand, I felt I had done everything I could with it. I contacted Jenoyne and said, "I'm ready to send you my novel. It's called *Across a Hundred Mountains*. Do you still want to take a look?"

I couldn't sleep that night or the day after. Then her response came. "I've been waiting."

I mailed her my manuscript, and the next thing I knew, I had an agent.

32

Jenoyne Adams

I N ADDITION TO writing over the summer, I had also been finishing my last requirement to get my teaching credential. The first thing I did upon completing my last class was to apply for a job at Fremont-Washington Adult School, which was five minutes from my house. I was interviewed and hired a few days later as a Beginning ESL teacher. I was elated and relieved. My sacrifice had paid off. Going back to school had helped me to dig my way out of the hole where I had been slowly suffocating.

Diana had been right. The difference between middle school and adult school was like night and day. I soon found myself in a classroom with students who wanted to be there, were not being forced to be there, who, despite working all day, would come into school ready to learn, full of dreams for the future, eager to meet their challenges head-on. Many of the students in my Beginning ESL class were older than I was, in their late thirties and forties, some in their fifties and sixties; a few were younger—all were immigrants.

They came mostly from Mexico, some from El Salvador or Guatemala, a few from Honduras or Nicaragua. The majority of them hadn't finished elementary school in their own countries and had been working most of their lives. In them I saw my parents.

When I had tried to get my mother to learn English, she had shaken her head at me, completely terrified, and said, "El inglés no se me pega." English doesn't stick to me, she said, as if she were talking about a piece of gum. Eventually, she did end up at adult school while preparing for her citizenship test. It if hadn't been for that class, she wouldn't be a U.S. citizen now. When I was in junior high, my father had decided to attend adult school to learn English once and for all. I remember how proud it made me when I would see him go to school after work, textbook and notebook in hand, ready to become proficient in the language of our adopted country and improve his life.

As I scanned the faces of my students, I saw fear and excitement in their eyes. I imagined that this was what it must have been like for my father. I pictured him sitting in the corner of my classroom watching me attentively.

It amazed me that I could give my students an assignment and they would do it without complaint. They only talked when I asked them to practice speaking; otherwise they did their work in silence. I would assign activities that required them to get up from their seats and interact with one another, and to my surprise, there was no chaos. No one was running around the room or pushing. No one saying, "Ms. Chiquita, Juanito spit on me." I never once had to raise my voice. Soon, I realized that I actually enjoyed teaching. At the middle school, I had done too little teaching and too much disciplining.

"Gracias, maestra," they said to me every night as they filed out the door, shaking my hand as they left my classroom.

I had wanted to make a difference in my students' lives. Maybe I hadn't accomplished that in the middle school, but now I could. At Fremont, I discovered that if as a society we want to help children, we need to help their parents as well. When we give parents the opportunity to learn English, to improve their work skills, to get better jobs, to be exposed to new experiences and nurture their minds, they are in a better position to provide for their families. They are able to help their children with homework, or at least able to understand the demands of being a student. Also, their children respect their parents even more, seeing them fight for an education.

This job, although part-time, paid me well enough that I could support Nathan and myself if I was careful with my budget. Now with fewer hours of work, little prep time, and zero grading, I had more time to spend with my son. With my credentialing classes behind me, I also had more time to devote to my writing. Those were the two things I cared most about: my child and my art. Thanks to the decision I had made to sacrifice a year of our lives to return to school, a shorter work schedule allowed Nathan and me to be closer than ever.

While I was learning the ropes of my new job, Jenoyne and I worked together to improve *Across a Hundred Mountains*. Thanks to her insightful feedback, I revised my novel once more and turned it into something I was truly proud of. I decided to play with the identity of my character and write two story lines that merged at the end. I printed the entire manuscript and laid my chapters on the floor to get a clear visual about the order, paying close attention to the transitions and the pacing. Nathan snuck in and started tossing the pages up in the air, laughing. Soon my living room was covered in papers.

"I suppose the story doesn't have to be in order," I told him as I tried to put my chapters back together again. It was all for the best.

After many editorial lunches and home visits, and brainstorming sessions on the phone, Jenoyne and I decided that one of the story lines should be out of chronological order, and somehow it all made sense in the end. I carried my manuscript everywhere I went, even to work. There was something reassuring about the weight of three hundred pages hanging from my shoulder. I patted my tote bag the way I had patted my swollen belly when I was pregnant—with excitement, fear, and great expectations.

One evening, during a long teacher meeting in one of the class-rooms at Fremont, I took out the manuscript and put it on the student desk where I was sitting. There was a scene that was giving me trouble, and I wanted to finish my edits by the end of the week because Jenoyne was ready to send it out. It was now October, and she said that November would not be the best time because of the Thanksgiving holiday. "We need to time it right," she had said. She had made a list of editors for the first round of submissions, and a second. I hoped we wouldn't need the second round. Every little chance I got, I was busy editing and polishing my manuscript, even if it meant half listening during a meeting.

"What do you have there?" a deep voice asked from the desk be-hind me. I turned around and was instantly embarrassed. We were at work, and I was focusing on my writing instead of on my job. What was really mortifying, though, was that it was Mr. Rayala. I hadn't had a chance to meet him, but I had heard from my administrators that he was one of their best and most dedicated teachers, and the handsomest, in my opinion. The first time I saw him was in my job interview. He was in a group photo hanging in the assistant princi-pal's office. I thought he was cute, but on my first day at work, when I saw him walking down the hallway in the flesh, I realized the word "cute" didn't do him justice. The man was incredibly handsome. He was my age, twenty-eight, and six feet tall, with beautiful blue eyes and dirty blond hair. Every time I caught sight of him in the hallway or at teacher meetings I had to keep myself from staring at him.

I had wanted to talk to him before but had felt intimidated not only by his good looks and whiteness, but also by his confidence. The guy walked around as if he owned the world. He seemed so sophisticated and self-assured in his dress shirt and tie, whereas I still felt, in many ways, like a child playing dress up. Four years later I still wasn't used to wearing heels, blazers, and silk blouses.

"Is it a screenplay?" Mr. Rayala whispered, pointing over my shoulder to my manuscript. Even sitting down, he was tall enough to see over me.

"It's my novel," I whispered. "I'm revising it."

"Can I see it?"

The few people I had shown my work to were my teachers. Micah from UCSC had seen the first draft and María Amparo had seen the second. The EV fellows had read a few excerpts. Of course, Jenoyne had read the whole thing. Now here was the handsome Mr. Rayala asking me if he could look at it, and I felt scared and nervous.

In that moment I realized that if Jenoyne was successful, there would soon be many strangers reading my novel. I might as well get used to it. But what if he thought my writing was mediocre? What opinion would he form of me, as a woman and—let's be honest here—a potential date?

With my heart pounding and my hands trembling, I handed my manuscript to him.

I could no longer concentrate at all on the meeting, thinking instead about how frightening it would be to let my book out into the world without me to protect it. In whose hands would it land? What would people say about it? Would anyone understand what I was trying to say about immigration?

I glanced at Mr. Rayala as he skimmed through the first chapter. This was the closest I had ever been to him, and I could see that his eyelashes were long and blond, some of them golden, so that when he blinked, there was a flash of gold. It took my breath away.

I whirled back around to return my focus to the meeting, though

I didn't hear anything the principal said. My mind was preoccupied with thoughts of the man sitting behind me. I no longer cared what readers might think about my book. All I cared about was what Mr. Rayala thought, and how my work would make him feel. I no longer cared whether or not my book would help people to better understand the immigrant experience. What I cared about was whether or not my book would give this man an insight into who I was. Would he understand my struggles and heartbreak? Would he understand who I was by reading the words I had painstakingly carved out of my own sorrow?

Finally, the meeting was over and we were dismissed. I turned to look back at him, and he smiled and handed me back the manuscript. "It looks interesting," he said. "I'd love to read it." I thought he was being polite, but seeing the honesty in his clear blue eyes instead of the false praise I had expected, I knew he truly meant it. I could lose myself in those eyes. Blue like Monterey Bay and the Santa Cruz sky.

"Do you think I could take your novel home and read it?" he asked as we walked out into the hallway.

"You serious?"

He smiled and nodded. He wasn't just trying to be polite. He really did seem interested. Maybe not in me, but at least in my writing!

Letting him read my novel made me feel more exposed and vulnerable than if I had stood naked before him, painfully aware of the flaws of my body, especially the stretch marks and saggy skin on my belly from my pregnancy. I didn't know why, but I felt I could trust him. So I handed the manuscript to him. "You better not run off with my book," I said. "I know where you work."

Throughout the week, before our class or during the break, we would talk in the hallway outside our classrooms and discuss my novel. He said he was impressed with the story.

His first name was Cory, and his last name was a common Finnish surname originally spelled Rajala, with the stress on the first "a," but his great-grandfather, upon arriving in the U.S. from Finland, had changed the "j" to a "y" to make it easier for Americans to pronounce. Immigrants changing their identity to fit in—it was a story I knew well, and it made me feel connected to Cory to know that this was also part of his history.

I was surprised when he told me he had a BA and an MFA in theater. He was from Wisconsin and had come to California to attend UC, Irvine. I thought he was a "real" teacher; that is, someone who had always known that being an educator was his calling. He seemed so passionate about his job, I had assumed he had wanted to be a teacher since he could walk. But his first love had been acting. I was pleasantly surprised that he knew how to talk about plot and structure, scene, dialogue, character arc, pacing. I had never met a man I could talk to about those things, and I found it exhilarating that he spoke my writer's language.

"Where did the story come from? Is any of it autobiographical?" he asked.

I didn't know him well enough to tell him it had come from my childhood fear of never seeing my father again, but I did share with him a little bit of my history, of where I had come from. Just enough for him to know I had some kind of authority to write this book. "The story is set in my hometown, even though I don't name it. Poverty, family separation, children having to fend for themselves because the adults around them fail them, those are things I know firsthand," I said while we stood in the hallway during our fifteen-minute break. "Though it's fiction, it isn't all made up. The heartbreak is real. The pain that Juana feels at watching her family fall apart, I didn't make that up."

"I believe it. It comes across in the writing," he said. "I loved the ending. How did you come up with it?"

"I don't know," I said. "I was struggling with how to end the book and a friend suggested that I just write any ending. He said I could always change it later." I had spent three weeks with horrible writer's block, unable to push through the last chapters. I had called Ibarionex, one of the EV fellows I kept in touch with, and he had listened patiently to me and offered his advice. "I did what he suggested and wrote whatever ending came to me, thinking I'd change it later when I came up with a better one. It turned out that was it."

Cory pointed out a few complications with the plot and suggested some solutions. He showed me where the dialogue was a bit forced, or when a character had acted "out of character." I loved that he would talk about my characters as if they were just as real to him as they were to me. The guy spoke my fourth language, the language of my writer-self that I so rarely got to share with others. And even though he was white, he seemed to grasp the nuances and complexities of my culture, the themes in my novel, my Mexican characters. I imagined that working as an ESL teacher at a school where nearly all the students were Latino had taught him a thing or two. If anything, it had made him empathetic to our struggle. This man, whose great-grandfathers had immigrated from Finland and Scotland, and who was physically the whitest person I had ever met, seemed to understand what my writing was all about.

But though immigration was part of his history, Cory had been born into a different America than I had experienced. Coming from the "right" ancestry gave him privileges immigrants like me didn't have. He was a white man from a middle-class family that had what my family did not—higher education. His mother had a master's degree. His father and stepfather had PhDs. His sister was in a private college getting her BA. His aunts and uncles had BAs, MAs, PhDs. Even his grandmother and grandfather had gone to the University of Wisconsin, Madison. For me, it had always been "*if* you go to college." For him, it had always been "*when* you go to college." He had grown up with that certainty, always knowing what he should expect in life, fully aware that there was a place for him in American society, whereas I had always wondered what life had in store for me and if I would ever reach my goal of a higher education, if I would ever find a place I belonged. He had grown up going to French camp in the summers and having private piano lessons every week, taking trips to Europe or going on cruises in the Caribbean. His stepfather, a Shakespeare professor, had owned a used bookstore, so Cory had grown up surrounded by books—literally shelves and shelves of them at his disposal—whereas I had never owned a book until I turned nineteen and Diana gave me *The Moths and Other Stories* for my birthday. When Cory went off to college, his parents paid for him to go to a private liberal arts college in Minnesota. I had paid my own way through my public college and university, not getting a single dollar of support from either of my parents.

Our lives had been completely different. We had nothing in common. And yet, when I was with him, I felt understood in a way I never had been by any man.

33

M Y ADMINISTRATORS WERE having a Christmas party for the faculty and staff, and two of my colleagues and I decided we should go together. We asked Cory if he wanted to go with us, and he agreed. Two days before the party, the other teachers said they couldn't make it anymore, so I asked Cory if he still wanted to go. "But it will be just the two of us," I said. I certainly didn't mind the change of plans. Truth be told, I was excited about turning this party into a date.

"That's fine," he said. "I'll pick you up."

"Great!" I said.

We were about to part ways in the hallway to go to our classrooms, but then Cory said, "Listen, Reyna, thank you for inviting me to come with you, but I think you should know that I have a girlfriend."

"Oh," I said. I thought of Eddie and that moment on the bus so long ago. He said he wasn't ready for a relationship. Cory was telling me he was already in a relationship. Either way, it meant the same thing: It wasn't going to happen. My fantasies blew away like dried bougainvillea petals in the wind.

"I don't mean to make you feel uncomfortable," he said. "I just want to be honest about where things are with me."

"I get it," I said. What I didn't get was why he was going to the party with me and not her. Where was his girlfriend?

"She's in Egypt," Cory said, as if reading my thoughts. "She's doing research for her PhD."

"That sounds interesting," I said. "How long have you been together?"

"Five years. We met in Minnesota when I was in college. Then we both came to UC, Irvine for grad school."

I didn't know what to say. Five years was an eternity. I had never been with anyone longer than ten months. I felt stupid and disappointed as I walked to my classroom.

Friday night, the day before our winter break began, we made our way to the Radisson Hotel by USC. Throughout the week, I had tried not to get too excited about the evening, but by the time I found myself stuck in traffic with Cory in his Honda, smelling his aftershave, our elbows almost touching, our breaths turning the windows foggy, I let my heart run away to fantasyland again. There were so many qualities I liked about him: his honesty, his frankness, his creativity. I especially loved talking with him about storytelling. Yes, I knew he had a girlfriend, but there was a part of me that hoped that someday, somehow, we could be more than friends. I had always been rather stubborn about my dreams.

At the party, we ate dinner and enjoyed spending some time with our colleagues outside of work. Soon, the DJ started playing music, and everyone at our table migrated to the dance floor. Cory and I sat at the table alone.

He smiled at me and said, "Do you want to dance?"

Our colleagues were dancing the "Funky Chicken," and there was no way I was going to dance that, so I said to Cory, "Let's get out of here."

"You're ready to go?" he said, surprised.

"No. I *do* want to dance," I said. "But somewhere else. Come on." I dragged him to the Latino wedding at the reception hall adjacent to ours. I had taken a peek in there when I had gone to use the restroom earlier in the evening, and I knew that, like most Latino weddings, it was really happening.

"We're crashing a wedding?" he asked.

I shrugged. "They're playing cumbias, come on. No one will know."

Though a six-foot-tall gringo in a sea of brown people sticks out like, well, a six-foot-tall gringo in a sea of brown people, we didn't get kicked out. I taught him the basic cumbia step, and we danced to La Sonora Tropicana's "Qué Bello" among complete strangers. The bride and groom were having a great time and so were we. I wanted to congratulate the couple and wish them many years of happiness. Feeling Cory's hand on my waist, his breath on my hair, the fingers of his other hand intertwined with my own, I wished their good fortune would rub off on me as well.

When the music changed to quebraditas, a Mexican dance that imitated the taming of wild horses, a dance style beyond Cory's skills, we ended up retiring from the dance floor and hanging out in the lobby instead. Neither of us was in a rush to leave, so we lounged on the couch and just talked. I told him about my struggles after college, trying to find my way and almost giving up on my writing until I had that nightmare. I told him about overcoming my doubts and fears, the class I took with María Amparo, getting into Emerging Voices, finding my agent.

"It's like the universe aligned itself to make it happen for you," he said.

He told me about his life in Wisconsin, his student years in St. Paul and Irvine, and the years after graduation when he had headed to Hollywood to pursue a career as a professional actor. "But that kind of life wasn't for me," he said.

"What didn't you like about it?"

"I loved the acting, bringing a character to life, but the real job of a professional actor is to be constantly looking for your next job."

"Yeah, no kidding," I said. I sympathized with him because that was exactly how I had felt with my creative writing degree. All I wanted was to write. I had known nothing about the business of writing. But I was hungry. Determined. Without my writing, my life had little meaning. I had been there already—trying to live without my art—and I wasn't ever going back to that dark place again. Thanks to the Emerging Voices program, I had a finished novel, found an agent, and soon—I hoped—would have a book deal.

"Are you sorry you walked away from Hollywood?" I asked as we walked back to the car.

"Sometimes, but when I'm teaching, I feel like the kindest, most patient, best version of myself."

I realized then why he was considered one of the best teachers at Fremont. He truly had a passion for it. "They're lucky to have you," I said.

Perhaps Hollywood had lost out on a great actor, but the students at Fremont had gained a great teacher. And selfishly I thought, had Hollywood received him with open arms, our paths would have never crossed.

Cory went to Wisconsin during Christmas break, and I stayed in L.A., trying not to think about him, but of course, he was on my mind day and night. *He has a girlfriend. He's unavailable.* I repeated this again and again, hoping it would sink in.

I took Nathan to buy a Christmas tree, and we came home with a little one that seemed even smaller and more insignificant as it sat in a corner of my living room full of mismatched thrift-store furniture. Holidays were the worst, especially Christmas, when all I could think about was that I had failed miserably to create a home for myself and my child. I wanted this to be enough—my son, my writing, my house. But something was missing. Love? Companionship? I wanted to deny it. *Love is overrated,* I would say with cynicism, re-

Reyna and Nathan at Christmas

membering how my mother had yearned for this very thing and had gone so far as to abandon us in her search for it. But the truth was that like her, I longed for a partner, someone to share my life with. I came to realize what perhaps my mother had also discovered long ago: Just because I was a mother didn't mean I wasn't also a woman with needs and desires.

But by falling for a white man, was I betraying my people?

I was like la Malinche! The indigenous woman who aided Hernán Cortés to bring down the Aztec Empire. Malinche, the Mexican Judas. In Mexico, her name stood for treachery and betrayal. In Marta's Chicano studies class, we had learned Malinche's side of the story—how she had been sold into slavery by her own family and later was given as a gift to Cortés, as an object for him to use and abuse if he so desired. Instead, she became his translator, advisor, and lover. "Her people betrayed her first," Marta had declared.

I liked Cory, but aside from his ethnicity what was really insurmountable was that he was in a committed relationship. I needed to respect that. I told myself that if it was meant to be, then it would be. As Kahlil Gibran had written in *The Prophet:* "Think not you can direct the course of love, for love, if it finds you worthy, directs your course."

I hoped that this time, finally, love would find me worthy.

"Come on, chiquito," I said to Nathan as we finished decorating our Christmas tree. "Want some hot chocolate and pan dulce?"

After he fell asleep, I sat in the living room, watching the lights on the tree turn my world blue, green, yellow, and red, and I closed my eyes and pretended Cory and I were dancing cumbias under the disco lights.

Enough! I told myself.

I remembered the folklórico performance in Santa Cruz, dancing onstage under the bright lights and how happy I had been. It wasn't a man who had given me that joy. It was the beauty of the dance. I went to my desk, opened my laptop, and stayed up all night to start a new novel about dancers which I would eventually title *Dancing with Butterflies.*

This is what it comes down to.

The sweat. The blisters on your feet. The aching of your arms from practicing the skirtwork. The hours and hours rehearsing the same song until the music buries itself so deeply in your brain you hear it even in your sleep. The constant need to coax your body to move past the hurt, the frustration, the exhaustion, and convince it that it can do more . . .

All that is worth this moment.

To be up here onstage, bathed in the red, blue, and yellow stage lights. A thousand eyes looking at you, admiring your flawless movements. Your feet seem to float over the floor as you twirl and twirl around and around before jumping into the arms of your partner.

Applause erupts out of the darkness, and you close your eyes and listen to it, let it envelop you. It gives you strength.

34

I RETURNED TO WORK after the holidays, grateful for my students who said "Buenas tardes, maestra. ¿Cómo está?" as I passed them in the hallway. They shook my hand and wished me a Happy New Year. I went into the office and said hello to the staff there, to my administrators, who seemed pleased to see me. "How's Nathan?" they asked.

I went to the copy room, where I ran into the teachers and we exchanged stories of our winter break. Then Cory came in to make copies, and I tried to hide how excited I was to see him.

"How were the holidays for you?" he asked.

"Great," I said. "I started a new novel and wrote eighty pages. How about you?"

He shook his head and said, "You're so prolific. The only thing I did was put on weight. My mother always welcomes me home with piles of Christmas cookies."

I tried to picture his mother, the mountain of treats she had lovingly baked in anticipation of his arrival. I had grown up in a house where we never got treats. My father and stepmother were not big on fulfilling our cravings. Neither Mago, Carlos, nor I had much of a sweet tooth, which we were thankful for. Yet I wondered what it would be like to arrive at your parents' house and be offered a cookie, a warm cup of milk, a hug, and a smile.

"Well, at least you got to spend the holidays with your mom," I said. "So, it's worth the few extra pounds."

"You're right. It was worth it," he said. Then it was time to get to class, and just as we parted ways in the hallway, he stopped and said, "Reyna, maybe we can grab lunch sometime this week."

"That'd be nice," I said in a nonchalant voice, and I headed to my class with my heart pounding in my chest.

He came to pick me up the following Friday. We taught only a morning class that day and there were no evening classes. I debated about whether or not to take Nathan with me. Part of me longed to go out alone, to enjoy my time without a baby in tow, and yet there was another part of me that wanted Cory to see my reality—I was a single mom with a two-year-old. So we went out to lunch with Nathan, and I was nervous the whole time that he might throw a tantrum, that I would lose my patience, that Cory might think I was too much trouble to bother with and did he really want to spend his time with a woman and a toddler?

But things went smoothly, and Nathan was on his best behavior. After lunch at my favorite Chinese restaurant, we returned to my house and Cory didn't just drop me off and leave, as I was expecting him to do. Instead, he came in and sat down in the living room. We talked for hours, and he played ball with Nathan in the yard. At some point, he asked me if I had any board games. "Do you like Scrabble?"

I had never heard of Scrabble. I hadn't grown up playing board games, except Lotería, Mexican bingo. "I've never played it before," I confessed.

"We'll have to play someday," he said. We talked a little more, about our mothers, our fathers. His parents had divorced when he was three years old, and he had been raised by a single mother until she remarried. Through the years, he hadn't seen his father very often, just like Nathan rarely saw his dad. What surprised me though was that Cory wasn't resentful toward his father for not making a bigger effort to be part of his life, whereas I still struggled with my resentment toward my own parents for having left me. Of course, their repeated "abandonments"—emotionally and physically—hadn't helped me heal from my first traumatic experiences. Cory seemed good at letting go of what he couldn't control and couldn't change, focusing instead on living a happy, healthy life and making the right choices.

He was literally the most "no trauma, no drama" man I had ever met. I hoped Nathan would grow up to be like him one day. It was possible, I thought, to not grow up with a hole in your heart when you have an absent father.

Before we knew it, it was dinnertime and he looked at me and said, "Do you want to go out to dinner?"

It felt like two dates in one day, though officially, I reminded myself, we were *not* on a date. This time I decided that Nathan didn't need to come along. We dropped him off at my mother's house. It was the first time I had asked her to babysit for me, but what surprised her more was to meet my gringo friend. My mother was four-eleven. Next to her, Cory seemed like a giant. Since she didn't speak English and he didn't speak Spanish, the introductions were very brief and there were no embarrassing questions for either one to answer.

We headed off to Old Town Pasadena and strolled along Colorado Boulevard, ending up at a Thai restaurant. Cory accidentally ate a chili pepper thinking it was a bell pepper, and his face turned as red as the chili pepper he had just eaten. He reached for his water and choked out the words "I think I'm in trouble, Reyna." I watched his face, flushed a deep red, his blue eyes watery like an ocean. He was trying so hard to hold himself together and there was nothing I could do to help him. I could almost see the steam coming out of his ears. I was immune to spicy stuff, but I could sympathize. "I'm so sorry," I said.

Slowly the redness went away, leaving only a soft flush on his peaches-and-cream complexion. He got through it so bravely, never losing his composure. I wanted to laugh. I wanted to hug him. I wanted to tell him, *I think I'm in trouble, too, Cory.*

I told him I loved to hike, and a week later we went to Malibu Creek. I dropped off Nathan with the sitter because my kind of hiking was not really for babies. I preferred to not follow trails. The goal was to get to the top of a cliff that overlooked the creek, high aboveground. There was a log that stretched from the edge of the creek to a boulder in the middle of the creek. From there you could get to the other side by jumping from rock to rock, and then go up the creek by scaling the rock face along the bank. Except that day there was no log.

"Let's just jump in," I said, ready to throw myself into the creek, jeans and all.

"There must be another way to get across," he said.

"There's no other way," I said. "Let's jump in."

"Wait," he said. "Let me think."

I jumped in and swam to the other side. After what felt like half an hour, he jumped to the boulder in the middle of the creek and then the next and the next until he made it to the other side without getting wet.

"You're soaked," he said. I shrugged and continued the hike, hopping from rock to rock, scaling the rock walls along the creek. As we were about to get to dry land and begin our ascent to the cliff, Cory slipped and landed in the waist-deep water.

"You see, you wasted your time trying to avoid jumping into the creek and now you're wet anyway," I laughed.

"No kidding," he said. And he laughed, too.

In wet jeans, I had him scaling rocks and clinging to bushes for dear life. I worried that I would traumatize the poor guy and then he wouldn't want to hang out with me again. But I had a sense that Cory needed a little excitement in his life, something different than the monotony of the safe, stable, normal life he had always had. I could surely give him that. My life had been anything but safe and stable.

Wouldn't it be nice to do this every weekend? I thought. I knew I shouldn't be feeling what I was feeling, but I couldn't help wishing for more than friendship from him. I was fully aware that he had a girlfriend, but she had left for Egypt. In Mexico, there's a saying that I thought of whenever I was with Cory. "El que se fue a la villa, perdió su silla." Basically, if you abandon an opportunity, someone else will jump on it, or to put it another way, if you don't take care of what you have, you will lose it. To ease the guilt I was feeling, I told myself that if the girl had left him for the land of camels and pyramids, it was her own fault if she lost him.

His pale complexion was now as red as when he ate the chili pepper, but not once did he complain. Every time I turned around, he was still there, following me. Sometimes, I expected him to not be there anymore. That he would give up and say it was too much trouble. "You okay?" I asked.

He caught his breath and smiled. "Yeah, this is fun. I feel like

Reyna getting hooked on Scrabble

Indiana Jones." He was a trooper, and I liked him for that. "You're a mountain goat," he said to me with admiration.

"I know how to cross mountains."

We finally made it to the top of the cliff and we sat on a boulder, our feet dangling in the air, with the creek below us and the blue sky above. *Azure.* That was the word I had played in one of our first Scrabble games, and Cory had been impressed. The Z tile had landed on the triple letter and the entire word itself had gotten a triple score, for a grand total of 120 points. "You're a quick learner," he had said with approval. Now here we were surrounded in azure, Cory and I. A hawk soared over our heads and I closed my eyes, my heart beating hard and fast. I had never felt as alive as I did at that moment. I felt exhilarated, exuberant from the hike, the endless blue sky, and the man by my side.

"That was a hike like no other," he said. And we both laughed.

35

THE FOLLOWING WEEK was Cory's birthday. I invited him over to my house and made him mole with chicken, the national dish of Mexico. This was the first meal I'd made for him, and since it was his first time having mole, and it was his birthday, my cooking had to be extra delicious. I was determined to make my favorite dish from scratch, refusing to use the store-bought kind. I spent an hour stemming, seeding, roasting, boiling, and pureeing four different kinds of dried chili peppers: guajillo, New Mexico, pasilla, and negro. I fried and then ground other ingredients, such as shredded almonds, sesame seeds, cinnamon, and raisins. Mago had taught me how to make this mole several years earlier, when she had learned it from her mother-in-law. I hadn't made it often myself, just a couple of times in Santa Cruz. I racked my brain trying to remember all the ingredients. I was tempted to call my sister and ask her for instructions, but decided not to. I had to do this on my own.

"Thanks for taking the time to make this for me. It smells delicious," Cory said. He and Nathan sat at the dining room table playing with Mega Bloks. I didn't want to take so much pleasure in watching him play with my son, but I did. Cory seemed to truly enjoy it, and he was good at playing with children, which was something I was not.

"Thanks for giving me a reason to make it," I said as I inhaled the aroma of cinnamon, garlic, and raisins frying in the pan. "It's too much effort to make it just for me, so I never do. But it's my favorite dish."

"I can't wait to try it. Any word from your agent yet?"

"No. I think she's tired of giving me bad news," I said as I pureed all the ingredients in a blender. Jenoyne had been sending out my manuscript over the past few months but had received nothing but rejections. She felt so bad for me that eventually she stopped telling me about them. I hadn't heard from her in weeks. We were now in our second round of submissions, but I had been so distracted by Cory, I hadn't wallowed much in the rejections that kept coming in. She had warned me to prepare, and I had. Though rejection will always penetrate through the armor you put on to protect yourself—no matter how impervious you try to be.

I looked at Cory and thought about the potential rejection I was facing with him. I needed to get ready for that one, too. I wondered which would hurt more—to be rejected in love or in art. Either one might undo me if I let it.

"Don't lose hope," he said.

I didn't know if he was talking about him or the editors, so I decided he meant both.

"I know these things take time," I said. "And all I need is for one editor to say yes. Just one yes out of all the nos. That's what I'm clinging to."

"That's a good way to look at it," he said.

I strained all the ingredients and put them in the pot. As the mole simmered, I remembered that Cory had a sweet tooth, so I added extra chocolate to the sauce. The end result shocked me. My mole was the best I had ever tasted. It was perfectly sweet and, to my relief, it wasn't too spicy. It was rich and smooth and had just the right kick.

I presented him with a plate of chicken smothered in mole sauce with a side of rice.

"This looks amazing," he said.

"Thanks. Want to hear a funny mole story?" I asked as I sat across from him. I told him that during my last quarter in Santa Cruz I had rented a room from an old white couple. "I wanted to do something nice for them, so in the morning I left a note saying I was going to make them mole for dinner. They didn't know it was a Mexican dish pronounced mo-leh. They thought I was going to make them mole, you know, the rodent! They spent the whole day dreading dinner-time. Imagine? They thought Mexicans eat moles!"

He laughed and dug into his food. "Wow. This is delicious." He took a piece of tortilla and scooped up more sauce into his mouth.

As I watched Cory eat his birthday meal with Nathan sitting next to him in his high chair eating his own rice and chicken, being silly and making a mess, the thought that came to mind was this: *We could do this every night.* He and I and Nathan, playing with toys, cooking dinner, eating together while talking about how our day went. Making plans for the future. We could be a family.

But before I got carried away, I shook those thoughts away and remembered that Cory was with someone else. His was a "yes" I should not wait for, because as long as he had a girlfriend, the answer would always be "no."

After his birthday, spending time with Cory became painful. I knew that he liked hanging out with me, but he never hinted at wanting more than friendship. If he had been a woman or a gay man, we could have been the best of friends. But he was a straight man I was deeply attracted to, and every minute I spent with him was torture. Fighting against my desire for intimacy with him—sexual, emotional, psychological—was like swimming upriver. He never made a move on me, and as much as I wanted him to—and God knows I tried to tempt him—I also appreciated that he wasn't taking advantage of me.

After Francisco, I was finally ready to give nice guys a chance. I wanted someone who would truly love me, who didn't want to play games with me (unless the game was Scrabble). I was ready for a man who was confident enough to treat me as an equal, who didn't need to be saved, and who didn't need to save me.

With Cory, I wanted all or nothing.

But he had never hinted at leaving his girlfriend, and I wasn't going to push. If he wanted my friendship, I would give it, but perhaps we would need to see less of each other. Whoever said that men and women can't be just friends was right. Sooner or later, one of them was going to fall in love. Unfortunately, it was me.

One night, we did a movie marathon. Cory had me watch his favorite movie, *Casablanca*, and I had him watch my favorite, Alejandro Jodorowsky's *Santa Sangre*. We were lying on the floor side by side, and in a moment of weakness I started nibbling on his ear, pressing my body against his. He inhaled sharply, and he turned to face me, his arms reaching for me. But just as we were about to kiss, he pulled away and said, "I'm sorry, Reyna. I can't do this."

"I know," I said. "I shouldn't have done that."

I turned off the TV, and we sat in the darkness for a few minutes, not saying anything. Then Cory said, "I think I should go home."

"Okay," I said. I walked him to the door, and we said good night. He left my house, and I watched him walk away, wondering if that was the end for us.

I couldn't sleep all night, admonishing myself for my behavior. I called Mago to ask for her advice. Because at times like these, I needed my sister.

"It was bound to happen, Nena. Now what you have to do is give him an ultimatum." Mago was as drastic as always, but I knew she was right. "You can't spend all your free time with the guy just to be friends with him, especially because of how you feel for him. He's lonely, so he's using you. What's going to happen when his girlfriend comes back? You're the one who has the most to lose in this situation, Nena. Send him away and tell him to make his choice."

Following Mago's advice, the next day when Cory called me, I said, "I'm sorry about what I did last night, but the truth is that I like you too much, and I've gotten attached to you. I need you to decide what you want, not just for my sake, but for my son's. I value our friendship, I truly do, but I want more."

"I understand," he said. "And you're right. I know it's not fair to you or Nathan."

We hung up. I told myself that if all he wanted was my friendship, I would have to accept that. I didn't want to lose a good friend.

The next day Cory asked if he could see me. We went to the Huntington Library for a walk in the botanical gardens. The gardens there were exquisite, transporting me to places I'd never been to: China, Australia, Africa. Spring was arriving and everything was verdant, lush, about to burst in bloom and splendor. This was the season of new beginnings, but the emerging beauty around me didn't lift the heaviness in my heart. My head drooped, and my steps lacked the vigor I usually felt in the sunlight. I felt like a flower that, instead of blooming, was on the verge of withering.

"I had a long talk with my girlfriend," he said to me as we walked around, pushing Nathan in his stroller. I was too nervous to enjoy the beauty around me, the rich, earthy smell of the trees, the perfect sunny weather.

"And?" I asked, bracing myself for what was to come. He was going to tell me we couldn't even be friends. That we needed to put some distance between us.

"We broke up," he said. "I told her I was falling in love with you."

My legs grew weak, and if I hadn't been holding on to Nathan's stroller, I might have sunk to the ground. "Can we sit down?" I asked.

We sat by the pond, where Nathan fed his Cheerios to the ducks, my thoughts swirling.

"Are you sure about this?" I asked. He leaned over and kissed me, and as I felt his soft lips on my own, I got my answer.

Reyna and Cory

36

Natalio with his grandchildren

WHEN MY FATHER called, I was completely taken by surprise. Not only that he had called me, but that he was asking for a favor. This was the man who had said he didn't want us asking anyone for favors. Yet here he was.

"Chata, I was wondering if I could stay at your house until I find a place of my own. Maybe for just a month."

Not long before, my father had made a bad investment. He sold his house in Highland Park and moved to Adelanto, a small town over an hour and a half east of L.A. My cousin's husband had told him that houses were dirt cheap in Adelanto and he could have a nice big house with a big yard for half the price. He and my step-mother bought a house there, the nicest they had ever lived in. It was almost brand-new, zero repairs needed, unlike the run-down fixer-uppers they had always lived in. But my cousin had failed to mention that there were no jobs in Adelanto, and my father used some of the money he had made from the sale of his house on a risky venture—he opened a water store. The dream of having his own business quickly evaporated when he realized that selling clean drinking water at a few cents per gallon didn't make much profit in a sparsely populated town. After months of struggling to figure out how else to make a living, my father had no choice but to ask for his former job back in Culver City. "It's too long a drive," he told me.

That was an understatement. Without traffic, the drive from Adelanto to Culver City was almost 2.5 hours each way.

"You can have Nathan's room," I said.

"I'll take the garage," he replied.

The garage was nothing but studs and stucco, barren and dark. It was not a finished room, not comfortable in the least, but he said he was used to worse. As a child, he had lived in shacks where he had slept on a straw mat over a dirt floor. In the U.S., he had never gotten used to beds. Often, through his years living with my step-mother, she would wake up to find him sleeping on the hard, unforgiving floor. It was one of the ways his childhood still haunted him.

At my house, he kept mostly to himself, especially when Cory was around. He was polite and made small talk with Cory in his broken English, but only for a minute or two before he excused himself. I could clearly tell how uncomfortable he felt around us.

Since he made a point to leave the house as early as possible, I rarely saw him, although at times I would wake up and hear the shower running at 5:00 a.m. That was the only way I knew he was actually here. He would come back late, entering through the patio door and wouldn't come into the house. On Fridays, he would go home to Adelanto, and I wouldn't see him again until Sunday night when he returned. It bothered me that he went out of his way to avoid me. I knew he did it so as not to inconvenience me. He thought that staying away would make things better, so that I wouldn't think of him as a burden. Funny how much my father and I were alike. When I had lived with Diana, I had done the exact same thing. I had stayed away as much as I could, and then locked myself in my room so that she wouldn't consider me a burden. But Diana would have none of that. She would knock on my door and say, "Why don't you join me in the living room, Reynita?"

I wished I had the guts to knock on the garage door and say the same thing to him. *Why don't you join me in the living room?* I didn't know how to tell him that I wanted his company, that I yearned for it. That I wanted to sit and have coffee with him in the mornings, and in the evenings, I wanted to make him dinner or sit with him out on the porch or on the patio and watch Nathan play with his toys while we talked about the future. It had always been my favorite topic of conversation with my father: the dreams that we dreamed.

But he made no effort to connect with me or Nathan, and although it hurt, I let him be. I convinced myself it was better to keep our distance. If I didn't see him, I could pretend he wasn't there. I could keep living my life the way I had been living it ever since I left his house and had to take care of myself. I could continue to pretend that I didn't need him.

When a month turned into two months, and I wouldn't accept money from him for rent, he started to come home straight from work to do things around the house. He unclogged the bathroom sink, fixed the leaky faucet, replaced a bad light, pruned my plants, watered the grass. Once, while he was tending to my rosebushes, I mentioned to him that I would like to have a pergola—but not knowing that it was the same word in Spanish, I called it a little house, "una casita," over the brick patio.

"I'll build it for you," he said.

Just like when he built the fence, I would come out to watch him work. I didn't know what to talk to him about, so I just sat and watched. He measured the wood, then cut it with an electric saw. Little by little the pergola began to take shape. I admired how skillful he was.

"Where did you learn to build like that?" I asked him one day.

He continued drilling, and I thought he hadn't heard me, or that he didn't care to answer. But after a minute he turned off the drill and said, "Mis papás me pegaban mucho. Todo el tiempo. Hasta que un día, me cansé." He said that both his parents were so abusive with him, constantly beating him and insulting him, that one day, when he was seventeen, he couldn't take it anymore and he ran away to Mexico City. I tried to picture that boy, and how much courage it must have taken to leave Iguala and go to the big city where he knew no one, where everything was different—the tall buildings, the wide paved streets, the cars, the metro, the millions of people. It must have been a scary place for a young country boy like him with a third-grade education, having known no life outside of Iguala's dirt roads and fields and shacks. "I was lucky," he said. "I found a job in construction and that was where I learned how to build, how to use my hands to lay brick and tile, to stir mortar, to measure and cut, to hammer and drill. To survive."

"How did you end up back in Iguala?" I asked.

"My father came to look for me and take me home. So, I returned. But I told him that if he ever laid a hand on me again, that would be the last time he ever saw me."

He resumed the drilling, and I knew the conversation was over.

I thought about the abuse he had grown up with, and the abuse my mother had experienced. This was our history, a history of violence where abused children turned into abusive parents. I was trying to break that cycle with my son, though I had come dangerously close to hitting him, and through the years there would be a few times when my upbringing got the better of me. This inherited violence was something I didn't want and fought hard to crush.

*Grandfather and Father at the Capilla
del Cerrito del Tepeyac (Mexico City)*

As the pergola took shape, I thought about that dream house my father had wanted to build for us in Iguala, the reason why he had gone north. If he had had the money to buy the material, he could have built us the house with his own hands and stayed. Maybe then I would have been able to talk to my father, ask him more about his life, about who he was, and not feel afraid to do it. I was so hungry to ask him for details of his past, the ghosts that haunted him, the reason for his rage, the source of his sorrows, his regrets. I wanted to ask him, *If your own parents treated you so badly that you ran away, why did you do that to your own children? Where do you think that comes from? What can I do to not be like you, Papá?*

For several more days, he worked on my casita. He never told me any more stories about his past, and I didn't have the courage to ask my questions. As the pergola continued to take shape, I pretended that he was building us a dream house, like the one in Mexico. I pretended that he was going to stay with me forever. That we could rebuild our relationship, erase the past, and this time he would finally stay.

A few days later, he told me that he and my stepmother were moving back to L.A. "I'll hurry up so I can finish the casita before I move out," he said. True to his word, he finished the job, and then he was gone. If I didn't have the pergola as proof, I would have felt that my father living with me had been a dream.

In the afternoons, Cory and I would take Nathan out to the patio and watch him ride his tricycle around and around, laughing with joy beneath our new pergola. And as I sat on the patio with my child and the man that I loved, the casita rising above us, I realized that for the second time in my life, my father had built me a house, but I was the one building myself a home.

37

"YOU READY FOR some good news?" Jenoyne finally said to me on the phone. I held my breath in anticipation, trying not to get too excited. It had been over five months that she had been sending the book out with no success. She said she had sent my manuscript to a Latino editor a few weeks ago and it looked promising.

"He really likes your writing," she said to me. "He's thinking about making an offer."

I felt elated for the rest of the day. This editor worked for a big press in New York City. There were few Latinos working for mainstream publishers, and the fact that he liked my work was a big deal to me. Being a Latino himself, I knew he would understand my story and know why I wrote this book.

A few days later, Jenoyne called me again to tell me that the editor had finished reading the book and wanted to move forward with an offer.

"You serious?" I sat on the couch. Could it really be happening? It had been five months of rejections, and though it had felt like an eternity, the reality was that sometimes it can take years.

"He likes your work, Reyna, but he wants you to make some changes to the story before he can make an offer."

"Sure! Like what?" I asked. I knew the book wasn't perfect, and I was excited that with his help, we could get the story to where it needed to be.

"He wants you to change your main protagonist. He wants a novel about a U.S.-born Latina, not about a Mexican immigrant girl."

"But that's what the whole story is about!" I said. "I can't get rid of my main character. Tell me what he said exactly."

I could tell she was hesitant. She hadn't told me much about the other editors who had turned the book down. I knew she had done that to protect me, but this was different. This was an editor who was willing to make me an offer. But he was asking me to do the unthinkable.

"Well, he said that no one is going to care about the story of an immigrant girl looking for her missing father."

I was glad I was sitting down because those words sliced through me like a machete. "He's willing to work with you, Reyna. He's said as much, but it would take major revisions on your part. He's not interested in immigrant stories. He wants a more mainstream story. Chica Lit is really popular right now. Everyone's looking for work by Latinas but in that genre."

"What exactly is Chica Lit?"

"Books about middle-class Latinas who have assimilated into American culture. Not too ethnic, more mainstream. Like chick lit but with a Latin flavor. You want to think about it?"

No, I don't want to think about it, I wanted to say. But I said, "Yes, let me call you later."

When I hung up, I lay down on the couch and cried. He was willing to take a chance on my writing, but not on the story I had written, only on the story he thought I should write.

But what about my novel? What about Juana and her struggles? Even though it was fiction, those struggles were real. How many children in the world—not just in Mexico or Latin America, but in the entire world—had been forced to say goodbye to a father, to watch him walk away and seek a better life in another city or country, wondering if they would ever see him again? How many children had parents who emigrated and, when they didn't return, were forced to leave their homes in search of them, desperate for an answer to the question, "Do you still love me?"

The psychological violence of watching your parents walk away from you was a wound that never healed. I had to honor that experience by standing up for my vision and holding fast to what I believed in.

I called Jenoyne the next day and asked her to decline on my behalf. I knew that might be my only shot at getting published, but I was willing to take the risk. I didn't want to write for a trend, even if it was my ticket in. I wanted to write a story that mattered. *No one is going to care about the story of a Mexican immigrant girl looking for her missing father*, the editor had said. Could I prove him wrong?

Even though I tried not to let it get to me, the rejection hurt me so much that I wallowed in my misery for days. Even Cory couldn't get me out of my funk.

"Don't you know what this means?" I told him. "If a Latino editor doesn't understand my story, then what chance do I have of a non-Latino editor taking a risk on my book?"

"I know what you need," Cory said. "Come on, get out of your robe and get dressed."

By then Cory knew me well enough to know that when I was down, I needed comfort food. He drove me and Nathan to San Pedro, to my favorite seafood market, where they cooked the food in front of you and served it with delicious garlic bread. But as I peeled my shrimp and licked the spicy sauce from my fingers, my mind returned to my disappointment and fear. The shrimp suddenly took on the metallic taste of failure.

A few weeks later, as I was driving down Florence Avenue, Jenoyne called me. "Are you sitting down?" she asked. "We have an offer.

Atria Books, a division of Simon and Schuster, wants your book."
Simon & Schuster was one of the biggest publishers in the country,
Jenoyne said. The editor, Malaika Adero, was an African-American
woman who had fallen in love with my novel.

"What changes is she asking for?" My stomach was already
churning at the thought that once again I would be faced with com-
promising my vision. Would I be strong enough this time to say no?
Would my desire to see my work in print get the better of me?

"No significant changes," Jenoyne said. "You will still need to go
through edits and copyedits, but essentially she's publishing your
book as you wrote it."

"Oh, my God," I said. "I can't believe this is happening." I
wanted to jump out of my car and dance on the sidewalk, scream
at the top of my lungs that I had an offer, that out of twenty-seven
editors we submitted to I had finally found one editor who understood the story I had written, who would publish my book the way
I had envisioned it. But I didn't get out, and I didn't scream. Instead,
I pulled over and called Cory.

"It happened," I said. "It really happened."

"What?" he asked. "Are you okay?"

"I'm going to be published!"

Reyna with her first book contract

38

To celebrate, I decided to visit the place that had inspired the story—my hometown.

"I'd like you to come with me to Iguala," I told Cory. "I want you to see where I come from."

I believed the only way he would really know me completely was if he saw where my journey had begun. Although our relationship was getting stronger every day, to the point where he spent every day and night with me and only went to his apartment in Long Beach on Sundays to get his mail, I felt that Cory only knew one part of me.

He had been to Mexico as a little boy when his grandmother had taken him on a cruise to Cancún. I warned him this trip was going to be completely different. "Iguala is only three hours from Acapulco, but it's the exact opposite of a beach resort," I said.

"I've read your book," he said.

But I worried about his reaction once he really saw it. His ex-girlfriend had taken him to her hometown, too, but she was from an idyllic island country called Cyprus and he had gone swimming in the Mediterranean Sea, and snacked on figs and halloumi cheese every day as he tanned under the Cypriot sun. In my insecurity, I worried that this trip would make him regret his decision three months before—but it was a risk I was willing to take because I needed to go to Mexico, and I knew he had to come along.

When the school year ended and our summer break began, the three of us took off. But as soon as we landed in Mexico City, doubt set in. What if instead of bringing us closer, this trip tore us apart? What had I been thinking, bringing this middle-class gringo to a place where there were no luxuries, not even the simplest things he was used to? I told myself I was being ridiculous. Cory knew how to adapt to new environments and handled meeting new people better than I did. He also wasn't easily upset the way I was. When there was a drive-by shooting in front of my house while we were playing Scrabble, and we went out to find his windshield shattered and bullets embedded in his car door, he hadn't made a fuss or gone running back to his Long Beach apartment.

When he met my brother for the first time, and Carlos said to him, "Aren't most serial killers white?" Cory handled the situation much better than I did. I wanted the earth to swallow me whole from the humiliation, but Cory simply laughed it off and said, "Don't worry. I'm not going to kill your sister."

I started to feel better and even fell asleep on the bus ride to Iguala. But as the bus entered the city and it rocked back and forth on the uneven road, I woke up and my worries returned.

"Ready?" I asked as we walked out of the Iguala bus station and hailed a taxi to take us to my aunt's house.

"Yeah!" he said enthusiastically, taking it all in—the hustle and bustle of the marketplace across the street; the taxis and minibuses inching along, picking up passengers laden with groceries; the vendors selling their wares along the sidewalks, pushing wheelbarrows full of dried hibiscus flowers, peanuts, tangerines, or jicamas.

We jumped into a taxi and made our way to my aunt's house. I wondered what Cory thought as we drove along the narrow streets rife with potholes and trash, passing by the river with its fetid water, the empty train station with its abandoned, rusty freight trains, the dirt roads lined with shacks and crumbling houses.

"That's where my uncle Gary lives," I told him as I pointed to one of the shacks along the tracks. "Remember in my novel there is a little boy who dies in the bus in his mother's arms while they're on their way to the doctor?"

"I remember," Cory said.

"Well, that was my tío Gary's son, Chucho."

When we passed La Quinta Castrejón, I pointed to it and told him, "That's where we used to sell snacks with my mom. Maybe I'll take you to the pool in there." I looked at Nathan and said, "Won't that be fun, to go swimming?"

"Pool!" Nathan said, clapping his little hands enthusiastically, but I was suddenly weighed down with worry again. I worried about him or Cory getting diarrhea from the food, or being stung by a scorpion, or stepping on a rusty nail, or ending up with lice or tapeworm. Nathan's vocabulary was limited, so I was used to anticipating his wants and needs. I had brought Cory to a place where his vocabulary would be limited, too, so I would have to do the same for him to ensure he didn't feel out of place.

Finally, my aunt's green gate came into view. Hearing the taxi, my aunt, her husband, and my cousins came running out. At the sight of them, especially my favorite cousin, Diana, I felt the long hours of travel fade away. The hassle had been worth it. I was with the family who lived on the south side of the border—the warm ties I had with them kept me even more connected to this place.

"Ya llegamos," I said, stating the obvious.

I introduced everyone, and Cory shook hands and smiled politely, but there was really no conversation to be had with any of them since all he could say was "Mucho gusto" and "Gracias." My cousins—Lupe, Angel, Diana, and Rolando—gawked at Cory with blatant curiosity. My aunt and her husband tried to be more subtle, but they stared at him in astonishment. Of course, they had never seen a gringo in person before! Iguala had no tourism. Foreigners—

especially gringos—never visited. So this giant of a man, with his sparkling blue eyes, pink skin, and golden lashes, was someone they couldn't help staring at. Cory just stood there and smiled, allowing himself to be gawked at. My aunt and uncles looked like our students at Fremont. I hoped those years of interacting with Latino immigrants would help him feel somewhat more at ease with my family.

"Well, I'm so glad we're here!" I said, trying to end the awkward moment.

"Pásenle, pásenle," my aunt said and ushered us into the house. She immediately began to serve us the meal she had prepared. Cory looked around, taking in the concrete floor that should have been tiled but wasn't, the cracked cement walls with the faded paint and crumbling stucco, curtains where doors should have been, the plastic bags hanging from nails punched into the walls. Since storage space was limited, my aunt used grocery bags to store things.

Tía Güera set a plate before Cory, and he looked at its contents in surprise. The sauce looked a bit like baby throw-up, but at least she had served him the drumstick and given the chicken feet to my cousins. Chicken feet on his first dinner in Iguala would not have been a good idea.

"It's mole," I said.

"But it's green," he said.

"Yeah. There's all kinds of mole—green, black, red, yellow. Trust me, you'll like it," I said, in a voice that warned him that he'd better eat it all. Green mole was a favorite meal of mine because my aunt served it with tamales that weren't found in the U.S.—tamales nejos, which were made of corn dough, lard, and a special kind of rock salt called tequesquite which gave them a smoky flavor. Her husband had made them that day, adding nasturtiums to the dough for added flavor, and they were hot and delicious. I dipped a piece of one into the mole and popped it in my mouth. The sauce was thick, similar to the curry sauce in Indian dishes. It tasted of pumpkin seeds and epazote, with a little kick from the pureed jalapeños my aunt had added.

Cory peeled off the banana leaf and was surprised to find that the tamales were nothing but dough, no meat and sauce inside of them.

"Instead of tortillas we eat these special tamales with our mole," I said.

Everyone watched as Cory took a piece of the tamal nejo, dipped it into the mole, and had his first bite. I knew he was not going to like the green mole. He loved the red one I made because it had chocolate. But the green mole was thicker, spicy without the sweetness, and a bit grainy.

But still, Cory put his acting skills to good use and pretended that it was the most delicious thing he had ever eaten. His eyes shone with approval, and my aunt and everyone at the table dipped their own tamales into the mole and enjoyed their meal.

Conversation at the table was in Spanish, and I tried to translate what was being said to Cory—mostly answering questions about my mother and siblings—but at some point I became exhausted from all the effort it took to say everything twice. Finally, we said our good nights and retired to the room my aunt had prepared for us. "Buenas noches. Gracias," he said to everyone, and my aunt smiled at his funny accent.

The bed was so old it dipped and the metal springs poked through as soon as Cory sat on it. The sheets were stiff and scratchy, made of poor-quality cotton. He picked up a pillow and was surprised at how heavy and lumpy it was. "What's this thing made of?" he asked.

"Well, they're not real pillows," I said. "They're pillowcases stuffed with old clothes."

"They're hard as rocks," he said, "and weigh a ton." I shrugged. I had forgotten about those pillows.

I showed him how to fill up a bucket of water from the outdoor tank to flush the toilet. I showed him where to get a glass of purified drinking water to brush his teeth. "Don't drink the water in the tank," I said. "You'll get sick."

As we stood on the patio brushing our teeth and spitting the water on the ground, he exclaimed, "This is like camping!"

"Yes, I suppose it is," I said. I had had little experience with camping. Cory had grown up going to summer camps, and I supposed it had been fun to pee in the bushes and escape "civilization" for a few days.

Back in the room, as he was about to jump into bed, I stopped him. "Make sure you shake the bedcovers," I said as I demonstrated. "Don't lean on walls. Shake your shoes in the morning before putting them on."

"Why?" he said.

"Scorpions," I answered. I pulled the mosquito net hanging above the bed and wrapped it around the entire mattress, making sure there were no gaps. Mosquitoes could be merciless at night. We lay down to sleep, with Nathan between us so that he wouldn't fall off the bed and hit his head on the concrete floor.

"I liked going to camp and roughing it for a few days," Cory said. "I can't believe people here have to live like this on a daily basis. Do you ever get used to it?"

"I suppose people can get used to anything," I said, "especially when they don't have a choice."

The next day, I took him to see my father's house. I had told him so much about that house that he wanted to see it. We walked along the dirt road with Nathan in my arms. Cory massaged his neck as we walked. He had woken up with a terrible sore neck due to the hard pillows, and despite the netting, his legs and arms were covered in mosquito bites. I wondered how long it would take him to ask if there were any hotels in the area and demand that we check into one. We walked to the main road and hailed a cab. As we stood before my father's dream house, the one his sister had stolen from him, I told Cory how when I was a child, the house had seemed like a dream come true. But now as I looked at it with him there, the house seemed small and simple, reduced to what it was—a plain, cinder-block, three-room house. It had meant so much to our family and now was nothing but a sad reminder of what had happened to us all.

"It's not much to look at, is it?" I said.

We went to the cemetery to take flowers to Abuelita Chinta and pay our respects, getting lost in the labyrinth of decaying graves and overgrown weeds. Cory was enthralled by the cemetery, with its spooky angel statues with broken wings and blank eyes that stared at nothing. "Not like the cemeteries back in L.A.," I said, thinking about Forest Lawn with its lush green manicured grass, artificial ponds, and graves that were in neat white rows. Years ago, my father had bought a plot at Forest Lawn because he wanted to be buried in a beautiful place, never mind that its beauty was artificial. Seeing this cemetery, I understood why. Who would want to be buried here where even in death you were stuck in this ugly place? Years later, as he was dying, he changed his mind and asked to be cremated and his ashes to be taken back to Iguala. Despite its broken beauty, it was still home.

"This cemetery has character," Cory said, snapping away with his camera. "I've never seen anything like it."

We finished the day by going up the hill to see the Mexican flag that flies over the city of Iguala.

"It's the biggest flag in the country!" I said with sudden pride. Finally, here was something beautiful and breathtaking about my hometown besides the mountains.

As we stood up there on the hill, the giant flag flying above our heads and the city spread out before us, the mountains a deep purple against the afternoon sky, Cory looked at it all and said, "Thanks for bringing me here, love." He put his arms around me and held me close.

When we got back, my aunt had another surprise for us. For dinner she was going to make another of my favorite dishes—pigeon in red guajillo sauce. She and my cousins sat in the patio plucking away, gray feathers scattered everywhere. My aunt's husband chopped wood and prepared the fire for cooking the pigeons. Nathan was enthralled with the dead birds. In L.A., he loved to chase the birds around whenever he saw them in the park. When we had left this morning, I had given my aunt money to buy the ingredients for the day's meal. I hadn't expected such a treat. Pigeons were a delicacy in my hometown. These were not the pigeons that fly around in the streets. These were raised by a pigeon breeder in the neighborhood. During my last visit, I had gone with my aunt to purchase pigeons from the breeder. She had taken the pigeons out of the cage one at a time, held them with a firm grasp, whispered something in their ear to calm them, and then, to my shock, pressed each pigeon against her hip and smothered it. She killed each one this way, not by violently twisting or wringing its neck, but by gently pressing the soft spot on its throat and suffocating it with her own body.

Nathan was so fascinated by the dead birds, my aunt handed him a pigeon, and he ran to show it to us, smiling with glee.

"Papa, Papa!" he said as he shoved the pigeon at Cory. "Birdie."

The look on Cory's face as he looked at Nathan was priceless, and I didn't know if he was more shocked at being called "Papa" by Nathan or by the dead pigeon in Nathan's hand.

"You eat these?" he asked incredulously as he held Nathan on his lap and looked at the pigeon with the same fascination as Nathan. I couldn't tell how he felt that my son had called him Papa, but the loving way he was holding Nathan on his lap told me he didn't mind.

"They're delicious," I said. "I can't wait."

Later, when he had eaten two of the pigeons, he agreed.

The next day, I took him to Tío Gary's house to deliver the things I had brought him, mostly clothes for him, his wife, and his five children. The three youngest were playing marbles out in the dirt road, their bare feet and hands covered in dust. The youngest boy was completely naked. His little penis waggled from side to side as he ran to tell our uncle we had arrived. Tío Gary lived in a tiny shack near the train station. As he entered the shack, Cory had to duck because the door frame was too low for him. My uncle was skinny and short, a mere couple of inches taller than me but many pounds lighter. As he shook Cory's hand, he seemed smaller and older, the years of hardship marked all over his wrinkled, sunbaked face.

"Mucho gusto," Cory said.

"Te ves más gorda." You look fatter, my uncle said to me with his usual bluntness, making me feel even fatter than I already felt in his presence. I was 120 pounds and I knew I wasn't fat, but here, where everyone was undernourished, I felt like a glutton. My uncle offered us a soda and Cory sipped on it, being careful not to stare at the bottle caps embedded in the dirt floor, the walls made of sticks, the two small beds where my uncle's whole family slept in this one-room shack. My uncle asked about my life in the U.S., and as usual, I kept the details to a minimum.

"And where did you meet this guy?" he asked, as if Cory weren't there. "Does he treat you well? Aren't there any good Mexican men over there in the U.S.?"

"There are plenty of them, but they've never treated me as well as he does," I said, and left it at that, feeling uncomfortable talking about Cory. By the look Cory gave me, I knew he had understood every word. Just because he couldn't speak Spanish didn't mean he didn't know we were talking about him. "And how's your job, Tío?" I said, to change the subject.

Tío Gary worked at a building supply store where he carried, on his back, cement bags and other heavy building materials onto delivery trucks. "It's getting harder," he said. "I'm not young any- more."

I didn't know what to say to him. He had no skills, had learned no trade. He had grown up depending on his body and physical strength, and now his aging body could no longer be depended on for a livelihood.

"What if you learn to drive, Tío? You can become a cabdriver. They make decent money and the work isn't too demanding. I can pay for driving lessons for you."

My uncle blushed and shook his head. "Me da miedo," he said. "I'm too scared and too old to learn to drive."

"Let me know how I can help you," I said as I stood to leave.

I left him some money, and I later learned he had used it to buy himself a used tricycle cart and gone around the neighborhood from house to house picking up the daily trash for tips. When we left and were walking back to my aunt's, Cory reached to hold my hand. I wondered if he had had enough of Iguala. I knew I had.

"It hurts to see them living like this," I said.

"Yeah, I know. How could it not? You're carrying so much on your shoulders, trying to help your family. You've had to work so hard to get to where you are now. You should be proud of yourself, love. I mean, look at you. You started here, and now you're about to be a published author."

I squeezed his hand and held it tight as we walked, grateful that he was here to share my hometown with me. Iguala was me, with all the imperfections and broken beauty. Cory saw me for who I was, just like I had hoped he would. But he also saw me for who I would become. I was glad I had brought him to my hometown. Now I knew that for as long as we were together, whenever I shared with him my sadness, my frustrations, my pain, my worries, my fears, my traumas, he would know the source and understand.

When we returned to Los Angeles, Cory decided to give up his apartment in Long Beach and move in with me and Nathan. I had been afraid we would lose him if I took him to Iguala. Instead, my hometown had brought us closer.

Nathan, Reyna, and Cory

39

Whenever I went to Mexico, I would return feeling guilty about buying into the materialism of the U.S. Did I really need all those clothes crammed into my closet? Did Nathan need all of those toys scattered around his room? I decided to have a yard sale and de-clutter my house. My mother came to help me with the sale. She hardly ever came to visit, and I was grateful for the extra pair of hands. She showed up with her little dog and instantly struck up a friendship with the fruit vendor. She even took him a plate of food when she made us lunch.

I felt ashamed that in the time I had lived here, I hadn't talked much to the man aside from saying "buenos días" and "buenas noches." Before Cory moved in, I had been living alone with a toddler in South Central L.A. I kept to myself and tried to keep my baby safe. I had bought fruit from the vendor, though he always gave me an extra bag or box of fruit and refused to take my money. He would say, "I'm really grateful that you let me stay."

I would wave my hand, dismissing his gratitude, and reply, "The street doesn't belong to me." I should have told him instead that I understood. I, too, was an immigrant. When I bought the house, I hadn't had the heart to ask him to leave, even though it affected the curb appeal of my house. I admired his work ethic. In an area full of homeless people, I preferred to see him out there selling fruit than asking for alms in the street. To hell with curb appeal, I told myself, and so I had let him stay.

Now here was my mother chatting with the fruit vendor and feeding him her pork adobo and corn tortillas. Later that day, she told me that his name was Clemente, and that he was undocumented. He had a wife and four children in Mexico whom he was putting through high school and college by selling fruit. He rented a little room up the street. Every day he woke up at 4:00 a.m. to go to the wholesale market downtown to buy his fruit. He hadn't seen his children or wife in twelve years.

In a few hours, she had learned his story. I thought of his children in Mexico and understood the pain they must feel at being separated from their father. But I also understood his pain as well. My job as an adult school teacher had shown me there were two sides to the story—the experiences of the children who stay behind and the experiences of the parents who leave. Both sides of the immigrant story were equally heartbreaking. I had watched him sitting on a crate in front of my house, surrounded by his fruit, with no one to talk to, but I hadn't known about the children who were growing up without a father. I wished his children could see what I saw day after day from my window: a solitary man who sold bags of oranges and bananas to put them through college and give them a chance. I hoped his children appreciated his sacrifice.

By the end of the day, I had made about $250 from my yard sale. Considering that I really didn't have anything valuable to sell, I thought it was pretty good money.

"You know, yesterday we only sold about $50 at the swap meet," my mom said to me as we were cleaning up the yard. Her husband, Rey, was just pulling up at the curb. He had come to pick her up after spending all day at the Starlite Swap Meet in Rosemead, where they had been vendors for years, selling Avon, Jafra, and Mary Kay products, hair oil, and plastic sandals.

My siblings and I had tried to convince my mother to get a job that would give her a steady income and a retirement plan, but she refused. She loved to sell and wanted to be her own boss. She had done it in Mexico to survive—selling not only Avon, but also popcorn, frozen popsicles, tamarind pulp, and cigarettes. She sold door-to-door or at the fancy club by the house, and that was what she wanted to keep on doing in this country. But her booth at the swap meet kept her living below the poverty line. What frustrated me was that she had options. She wasn't like my adult students, who despite their lack of legal status, were hungry to learn English, to gain work skills, to improve themselves. Thanks to the amnesty of 1986, the Immigration Reform and Control Act (IRCA), my mother, like my father, had gotten a green card and later became a naturalized citizen. What wouldn't my students give for the opportunity that my mother had been given? What wouldn't they *do* with a green card, with U.S. citizenship?

That was what I wanted my mother to understand and to appreciate, but her refusal to do so infuriated me. "You and Rey should get a real job. You are U.S. citizens, I don't understand why you insist on selling at the swap meet when you know it isn't worth it," I said.

"Do you mind if I have a yard sale of my own next week?" she asked.

I was surprised she wanted to do this. For years my mother had been a pack rat. She had a habit of picking up things people threw away. On trash days, she would roam around her neighborhood picking up discarded items meant for the landfill. She would take some to Mexico, and the rest she just kept in her apartment until there was hardly any space to move.

I was willing to help her clean out her house, so I agreed.

The following week, she showed up at my house to have her yard sale. She and Rey unloaded boxes and boxes full of used clothes and kitchen supplies, shoes, tools, toys, car seats and strollers, coffee tables and dressers she had picked up off the street. Once he was done helping her set up, Rey took off to go to the swap meet by himself.

My mother happily chatted with the fruit vendor, Clemente, or with her customers, her fanny pack tied around her waist, her dog running in circles around her. When she made a sale, she would make the sign of the cross before putting the money in her fanny pack. I had never seen her so happy, so relaxed. Watching her, I realized how much she really did love to sell.

In the evening, Rey came back to pick up my mother. He said that after the $30 booth rental, he had only made a measly $15 at the swap meet. My mother had spent no money on the use of my yard and made $150.

I should have seen it coming, but the next thing I knew, my front yard was turned into a swap meet. I had Clemente under the tree at his usual spot on the sidewalk, selling his fruit, and my mother with all her stuff spread out across my front yard. She started to come three times a week to take advantage of the parents who were on their way to and from the local elementary school. I closed the curtains of my front windows. I had never had a great view, and now it was worse. I only hoped she would sell all her stuff quickly and be done with the yard sales.

"Rey and I are thinking about not going to the swap meet at all," my mother said to me a few days later. "Sales just aren't like they used to be. We could have a yard sale here every day."

"I don't know if that's a good idea" was all I managed to say. I couldn't say no. I knew my mother was struggling with money, and I wanted to help her. For my grandmother's memory, I wanted to be as generous with her as she had been with my abuelita. The days she didn't come to my house to sell, people knocked on my door and asked me when she would be back. She smiled when I told her this. "I have many customers now," she said. She took over my kitchen and cooked a quick meal for everyone, even the fruit vendor. If he was lucky, she even fed him dinner. I parted my curtains to peek outside. I saw her talking to her customers, laughing with the fruit vendor, trying to figure out the best way to display her wares.

"I thought she would only have a few yard sales before she got rid of all her stuff, but every week she comes back loaded with more," I told Cory one night as we were lying in bed. He had said he didn't mind the yard sales, and of course, since this was my house, I knew that even if he did, he wouldn't say anything.

"I think she's collecting more stuff," he said. "It looks like she's starting a business."

"I know I need to decide what to do about it before it gets out of hand," I said. "I have to put a stop to this madness. But it makes me sad to know that once I do, she'll no longer come over. Things will go back to how they were before. Ever since I let her set up her yard sale, I've seen her more than I have in years."

I felt as if I were on a roller coaster ride. I was happy to see her and spend time with her, and it felt good to help her make some money, but at the same time I was angry and disappointed that the yard sale—not me, not Nathan—was the reason she came over. Also, I knew my house was not much to look at, but I had done my best to fix it up and make it cute and cozy. I felt that my mother's yard sales tarnished my home. In truth, she was becoming a trespasser. All her stuff strewn across my yard, her constant comings and goings disrupting the precious peace and tranquility I had managed to create despite living in this area, had made me resentful. I felt as if little by little I was losing control of my own home, and I wanted her to care enough to notice how uncomfortable she was making me. But she didn't.

My mother's dog was white so she had named him Güero. Since she lived in a cluttered one-bedroom apartment with her in-laws, there was no room for Güero. He spent his days trapped inside her van. Only at my house did he have a yard to play in, and a playmate—Nathan.

Ever since he was a puppy, my mother and Rey had disciplined

Mother's yard sale, with the fruit vendor

him by hitting him. They even told Nathan to hit Güero if he got too excited. "You will not hit that dog," I told my son. "You must never hit animals."

"Abuela hits Güero," Nathan said.

"Don't do what your grandma does," I told him. "Ever."

One day, Nathan was petting Güero, and he turned around and tried to bite him. "Güero!" my mother yelled from across the yard. "Pégale," she told my son. "Hit him." My mother looked at me and said, "When he was little, that dog wasn't like that. He was a sweet little puppy. Now that he's grown, he's turned vicious. Now, when anyone tries to touch him, he bites."

That's because he's had enough of your ill treatment, I wanted to say. *One can only take so much, even a dog.*

There were times when I was like Güero, when I wanted to bite and snarl at my mother. I wanted to understand, to forgive her the way she had forgiven my grandmother, but one day I'd finally had enough and my rage got the better of me. I turned on her.

That day, Cory and I had gone to work and left my mother to her yard sale. I closed my eyes and tried not to look at what had become of my front yard. I had recently started composting, so I had a small cooler in the kitchen where I put all my kitchen scraps meant for my compost bin. When I got home from work, I found my cooler all washed and cleaned on the kitchen counter. All the kitchen scraps I had saved for three days were gone. I went outside to the front yard and asked my mother what had happened to my kitchen scraps.

"I threw them out," she said. "I thought it was trash, so I dumped them in the trash bin outside."

I was furious at her for taking over my yard, my kitchen, my house. Furious at myself for letting it get this far. "Well, it isn't trash. I was saving them for my compost bin. Now you go and put them back in my cooler!" I slammed the door and went into my bedroom, seething.

When I came out, I could see my mother bending over the bin out back, digging through the trash and gathering the kitchen scraps. *Just tell her to leave it,* I said to myself. *Tomorrow you'll have more scraps. Stop humiliating her like this.* But the frustration I had been bottling up about the yard sale got the better of me, and I stood there and watched my mother digging into the trash with her bare hands, putting banana peels, eggshells, coffee grounds, and vegetable pieces back into my cooler.

She handed me the cooler without looking at me and went back out to her yard sale. I stood there by the window and saw her chatting with the fruit vendor while my son laughed and played with Güero.

Later that night when I spoke with Betty, the first thing she told me was that my mother had called her and told her I made her dig through the trash. "She was crying," Betty said.

"I feel awful about it. It was a shitty thing to do to her," I said. "There are times when I can't help myself. There are times when I want to hurt her the way she hurt me—us."

"I know," she said. "I understand."

But the thought of me making my mother cry filled me with

guilt. Why couldn't I be like her? Why couldn't I forgive the abuse and the lack of love?

The next morning, when she came back to put out her yard sale, I wanted to apologize to her, but I found myself unable to do it. *I'm sorry* were difficult words for me to say. Instead, I made her a meal, and later, I helped her pack up her wares and fold the tarp. How could I tell her that I was just like Güero now? That I could only take so much.

Rey came to get her, and as he loaded up the van, Güero ran into the street and my mother ran after him so that he wouldn't get hit by a car.

"You could've gotten killed, you stupid dog!" She smacked him on the head before squeezing him tight and kissing his head. I realized then how complicated my mother's love was. How she could hurt and love at the same time. As I watched her drive away, I wondered if that was how things between us would always be.

40

Mago and Reyna with their children

Nᴏᴛ ʟᴏɴɢ ᴀꜰᴛᴇʀ my mother's yard sales came to an end, Mago showed up at my house with her belongings in black trash bags. She had called me that morning to ask if she could come stay with me.

"What happened?" I asked.

"I left him," she said. "I can't stand it anymore. I can't continue to make a home with a man who makes me feel so miserable. I've nothing in common with him except our three kids."

It wasn't the first time she had left her common-law husband, but it was the first time she had asked if she could stay with me. "I'll stay here until I find a full-time job and can afford a place of my own."

She brought the kids with her three days a week, and the other days they stayed with their father. I felt bad seeing her drive forty-five miles to Chino to drop off the kids at school, wait for them until they got out, and then drive the forty-five miles back to my house.

Luckily, Mago quickly found a job as an insurance agent but was now faced with the difficult choice to leave the kids with Victor. I did not like the idea.

"Just remember that our stepmother did the same, and it didn't turn out well for her," I reminded her. When she met my father, Mila was married and had three children, and she left her husband for my father and, just like Mago, left her children with her husband until she and my father found a bigger place. But by the time that happened, Mila had already lost legal custody of the children and there was nothing she could do about it. On top of that, she had to pay child support.

"I am not abandoning my children, Nena," Mago replied defensively. "I need to find a place for us to live, and I can't do it without this job. I have to spend more time at work right now since I'm in training, so my time is limited. It's a sacrifice I'm making for them. Soon I'll have an apartment and get my kids back."

I remembered how not long ago I had also made the decision to pursue my goals over sacrificing time to be with my child. Now Mago was doing the same, and I needed to support her in every way I could. "I'm sure everything will turn out okay," I said. "Stay here for as long as you need to."

"Thanks. I'll find a place soon," she said.

Just like my father, she had chosen to stay in the garage. Despite feeling bad about Mago's failed relationship, and the fact that she had temporarily left her children, I was happy to have my sister with me. I never saw enough of her. Thankfully, she wasn't like my father in that she didn't avoid me. When we came home from work, we would hang out together in the dining room and sometimes talk late into the night just like we had when we shared a room in our father's house.

But our conversations were different now. We talked about the demands of being adults, our relationships with our partners, the trials and tribulations of motherhood, our desire to be better mothers. It almost felt like the old days. Some nights Mago just wanted to vent about her conflict with her common-law husband, Victor, and I would listen. When she told him she had made the decision to end their relationship for good, he had refused to move out of the house and had told her that since she wanted to break up the family, then she should be the one to leave. He threw her belongings out of the house, and she had scrambled to put things in trash bags and load whatever she could fit in her car. The rest she had left behind. "I can't believe he treated me like that," she said in tears.

I didn't know Victor well. He wasn't very talkative, and the times I had gone to their house, he had locked himself up in his room and not come out.

Mago would shake her head and say, "I don't know what his problem is. I don't do that to his family."

Before she met Victor, Mago had been very social. She loved dancing and would go out to clubs on the weekend. She was addicted to beautiful clothes and could expertly do her makeup and style her hair. Unlike me and my shy ways, Mago had a great sense of humor and liked making people laugh. Victor was the main reason she had moved out of my father's house. She had wanted to be free to date without my father's curfews getting in the way. She was so in love that she had left our father's house—and me in it—and rented an apartment with her best friend. A few months after she moved out, my father's prophecy came true. She got pregnant at twenty-one years old and moved in with Victor.

But the biggest irony of her life was realizing that she had made a home with a man exactly like my father. Victor was serious, introverted, private. He didn't like to go out, especially to clubs. He kept to himself and, like my father, if he wasn't at work, he was at home. Once they were in a relationship, he didn't want Mago to go out, and he resented her friends. He wanted her home taking care of the kids.

Through their many years together, Mago had struggled with focusing on being a good mother and a wife and had tried to suppress her desire to have friends and a social life. She felt she had lost herself in the relationship. Sometimes, it got to be too much and she would run away, like now.

Mago didn't stay long. One Saturday night she brought her two daughters over to visit; her son didn't want to come. He was very loyal to his father, and my sister could not convince him to come with her. Cory had gone out, so Mago and I were in the dining room talking while Nathan and my nieces played with their toys in the living room. It was 9:00 p.m. and the street was quiet when suddenly someone started banging on the door. The children got scared. I rushed to the door and looked through the peephole but saw nothing. Then the window started to rattle. Whoever was out there was now banging on the glass.

"I'm calling the police!" I yelled.

Suddenly, there was an explosion of glass as the picture window shattered. The children cried out as I pulled them with me back to the dining room away from the shards. Mago called the police.

We huddled in the dining room, terrified. There was no more noise, but it was too dark to see outside. We were afraid to move, to see who was out there. As we waited, Mago and I held on to our kids, trying to remain calm so as to not scare them even more. Miraculously, the police showed up within five minutes. They found a homeless man lying in the front yard, his hand bleeding. They told me the man was high on drugs and probably hadn't realized what he was doing. Cory showed up just as the police and the ambulance were leaving, taking the man away.

"What happened?" he asked as he came in. "Are you okay?"

"Nena, you gotta move," Mago said. "How can you stand living here?"

Her daughters clung to her, asking to go home. "We don't want to be here anymore. We want to go home with Daddy," they said. Mago grabbed her purse and drove them back to their two-story home in the suburbs instead of having them sleep over as planned.

I was used to this neighborhood. I had never thought I would live in South Central, but I'd ended up here and it wasn't easy to get out. Buying a home in a better area would require a lot of money, plus the Teacher Next Door Program required that I live in the house for three full years. Besides, even if I could move, I didn't want to move to the suburbs and spend my life stuck in traffic driving to and from work.

Mago left with her daughters and didn't return until well past midnight. She didn't come into the house even though I had stayed up waiting for her. She entered through the patio door and went straight to the garage without coming in to say good night. I knew something had changed between us.

"Nena, I can't live here anymore," Mago said a few days later. "Now my kids don't want to visit me. Not here, they said. I think I might have to go back."

I didn't want to be in Mago's shoes. I didn't know what choice I would make. Would I leave or would I stay?

"How could she do it?" Mago asked, referring to our mother. "How did she have the guts to walk away from us, her own children? I want to know how she did it, because right now I wish I had the courage to continue walking and not come back."

It was interesting for me to hear the question we had often asked ourselves put in a different way. Before, we had thought our mother had been selfish to leave us and put her own needs first. Now Mago was wondering how our mother had found the strength to do so. Like me, my sister had spent her whole life yearning for a home and had even given up on college to create one. But what happens when your home no longer gives you joy? How do you destroy the home you worked so hard to build when it no longer feels like home?

For the third time, she returned to Victor to try to keep her family together. "I can't do this to my children," she said.

"Take care of yourself," I told her. It was a tough spot to be in, to want to stay and go at the same time. I wanted to tell her that she needed to think of her own happiness, her own dreams. The problem was doing those things without neglecting her children and their needs. I thought of my mother, of how she had pursued her own desires and left us to fend for ourselves. When we were little, all we wanted was to have a mother and a father. We wanted a family. As adults, Mago and I were seeing things from the other side—as parents. For years we had criticized our father and mother for prioritizing their own needs above their children's. I was finally beginning to understand that it takes as much courage to leave as it does to stay, and that being a parent was way more complicated than I had ever imagined.

41

WHEN WINTER BREAK arrived, Cory took Nathan and me to his hometown, Racine, a mid-sized city in Wisconsin an hour and a half north of Chicago. I wasn't prepared for Racine. It was such a contrast to where I had grown up.

His mother, Carol, lived a couple of blocks from Lake Michigan. I had never seen the lake, and when I first saw it, I thought it was an ocean. "That can't be a lake," I said to Cory as we drove by it. There was no end in sight, the blue went on and on until you couldn't tell where water and sky met. And it had waves, too, like the Pacific Ocean on a gentle day.

We turned onto College Avenue and I was blown away—this time by the beautiful street paved with red brick and lined with tall sycamore trees. Victorian houses built in the 1800s stood majestically on either side, and candles glowed from every window of each house.

"Here we are," Carol said as she pulled into the driveway of a two-story Victorian painted a blue-gray and trimmed with purple. We got out of the car, and I shivered as the cold air hit me like a thousand needles. Cory had warned me, and yet I wasn't prepared for twenty-degree weather. I felt as if I had stepped into a freezer!

Carol lit the fireplace and soon the house was deliciously warm. This wasn't my first time meeting Cory's mom—she had come out to visit him for a few days in the spring—but still I felt nervous and tongue-tied. I didn't want to say or do the wrong thing. When he had told his mom he had broken up with his ex-girlfriend, she cried. She had liked her, and although this had happened in February and it was now December, I wondered if she still missed that other girl whom I had displaced. She had spent many Christmases here with them. I couldn't help but wonder if Carol would compare me to Cory's ex the whole time I was here. Would she disapprove of her son having hooked up with a Mexican immigrant and single mother? Would she think less of me that I only had a BA degree whereas his ex had been working on her PhD? I also worried about Nathan. How would Carol and everyone else treat my little boy since he wasn't Cory's child and they didn't "owe" him affection?

I soon learned that my fears were unfounded. Carol turned out to be a very generous woman, not just with me but also with Nathan. She took on the role of "grandma" right away and spoiled my son in every way possible. Prior to our arrival, she had bought his favorite snacks, fleece winter pajamas, books for bedtime stories, toys for playtime—even for the bathtub—and his own bath towel in the shape of a lion. She bought him a snowsuit and Buzz Lightyear snow boots. She had child-proofed her home to make sure he didn't get hurt, and the minute we arrived, she was vigilant of her pets to make sure my little boy was always safe around them. At seeing that Nathan was a big animal lover, Carol spent hours with him, supervising playtime with her two golden retrievers and her three cats. We didn't have pets at home and Nathan was having a fantastic time with Carol's, feeding them, giving them snacks, walking them, tossing balls to them, and even riding those two enormous but docile dogs.

The next day it snowed. At twenty-nine years old, I was watching my very first snowfall. I sat on the couch mesmerized by the dance outside, the flakes fluttering down, twisting and turning like ballerinas. Carol came up to me with a thick blanket and said, "Are you cold?" She put the blanket over me, tucking it around my legs and hips with motherly familiarity, and then went back to the kitchen, where Nathan was watching cartoons with her while she prepared dinner. I sat there on the couch, suddenly overwhelmed with emotion. I tried to remember if my own mother had ever done that for me—tucked a blanket around me, making sure I was warm enough. She must have done it when I was a baby, when I was too young to remember, but I had no memory of her doing that and it saddened me to not be sure. Carol's motherly gesture touched me deeply. When Cory came to sit next to me to watch the snow, I felt my love for him increase a thousandfold because of his mother.

"Want to go get a Christmas tree?" he asked.

"Sure," I said.

Carol lent me her winter gear and I bundled up from head to toe. I went outside and looked up and felt the snow fall on my face. I cringed at the extreme cold, yet was in awe of how beautiful the landscape was.

"Maybe we can make a snowman later," I said. I thought of the movies I had watched. How I had always wanted to make a snowman.

"It's not the right kind of snow," Cory said.

"What does that mean?"

"This is cold, dry snow," he said. He picked up a handful and showed me what he meant. It didn't hold its shape. "We need packing snow. You know, wetter, the kind for snowballs."

I had no idea what he meant, so I just nodded. He, Nathan, and I drove for forty minutes, and I kept looking for Christmas tree vendors but didn't see any. In L.A., vendors would rent out vacant lots where they would set up their cut Christmas trees for sale, but we hadn't passed any.

I was in for a surprise. We pulled into a farm that had acres of pine and fir trees. Cory took out a saw from the trunk of the car and said, "You ready?"

"You serious?" I asked. "We have to cut down our own tree?"

"Yep."

We walked around, looking at trees of all sizes, some even smaller than Nathan, until we found an eight-foot-tall Douglas fir that Cory and I liked. He positioned the saw and began cutting. I held Nathan in my arms, taking in the image of Cory with a saw cutting down our Christmas tree while it snowed all around us. It was a beautiful sight, and my heart felt ready to burst with the love I had for this man. There was nowhere on earth I would have rather been at that moment.

Carol was a high school English teacher. Cory's stepfather, Andrew, was a retired Shakespeare professor, used bookstore owner, and a rare book collector. Carol introduced me to the work of her favorite author, Barbara Kingsolver, and had me read *The Bean Trees* and *The Poisonwood Bible*. Learning that Kahlil Gibran was one of my favorite authors, Andrew gave me an old edition of *The Prophet*. They both loved that I was a writer, and I soon found myself talking about books and literature every day that I was there. Carol and Andrew wanted to know everything about me and my writing. While I waited for the long months ahead as *Across a Hundred Mountains* journeyed through the publication process, I had made progress on my new novel, *Dancing with Butterflies,* and was excited to tell Carol and Andrew about my project, about all the folklórico shows I had been attending in L.A. as part of my research, and the dozens of dancers I had interviewed. They listened attentively and even offered to proofread anything I wrote and give me their feedback.

"I hope you know how lucky you are," I said as I snuggled next to Cory in bed.

"I do know," he said. "But you're lucky, too. Because of your experiences you have perseverance, drive, an unyielding desire to succeed. Those are valuable traits to have."

I wondered if growing up in comfort had some disadvantages.

You don't learn how to struggle, to do without, to suffer. If I hadn't gone through what I went through, I wondered what kind of person I would have been.

Cory's sister, Morgan, arrived from Washington, DC, where she was working for Amnesty International. When she arrived, the games came out. Cory and Morgan taught me to play Apples to Apples, Monopoly, Cribbage, Clue, Charades, and more. Morgan was enamored of Nathan, and soon, he with her. She gave him baths, read him stories, scattered toys all over the floor and played with him for hours. Between Morgan and Carol, I really didn't have a lot of time with Nathan. I was grateful for the free time, a luxury I never had in L.A., and I spent my days reading, writing, and playing Scrabble with Cory.

The pile of presents under the tree grew bigger and bigger, and when Christmas arrived we spent hours opening presents. For me, it was both exciting and overwhelming. Because I had grown up in a house where you were lucky to get one gift for Christmas, this abundance made me uncomfortable, and yet I felt as excited as Nathan every time someone put a present in my lap.

The day after Christmas, Cory took me to visit his grandmothers. One of them lived near Madison, in a beautiful two-story lakefront house that had once been the family's summer home, when they lived in Chicago years ago. His grandmother had attended UW, Madison, and as she entertained us with stories of her time at the university, I tried to imagine my own grandmothers in college, but couldn't. Cory's paternal grandmother lived in the Northwoods of Wisconsin, in a little town called Manitowish Waters, where the infamous Dillinger gang had hidden before having a shoot-out with the FBI.

Everywhere I looked was white—the snow, the birch trees, the frozen lakes, the dormant cranberry marshes. I had my very first snowmobile ride, and Nathan had his first sled ride. I also got my wish when the "right" kind of snow fell and Nathan, Cory, and I spent the rest of the day making a giant snowman in his grandmother's front yard.

This was middle-class, white America and so unfamiliar to me that it felt like being in another country. I participated in their games, family outings, and activities, but no matter how welcoming they were, a part of me still felt like an outsider. My shyness and insecurity were in hyper mode with all these new people and experiences. I soon found myself desperately craving Mexican food, my comfort food. Carol was a good cook, but I missed the spices, the hot peppers, and the saltiness I was used to. I knew that as soon as I took a break from the mashed potatoes and green bean casseroles and ate some of my own food, I would feel much better.

As if reading my thoughts, when we got back to Racine, Carol asked me if I wanted to make dinner for the family.

"Sure," I said.

I decided to make chiles rellenos, and we went to the store to buy the ingredients. In Mexico, in L.A., whenever we made chiles rellenos, we roasted the green chili peppers directly over the flames of the gas stove. I panicked when I realized that Carol's electric stove was not going to allow me to roast my peppers, to cook them the only way I knew how.

"How about you use the oven?" she suggested.

I had never roasted peppers in an oven. I didn't know if it was possible. I was already in an unfamiliar kitchen, in an unfamiliar world, and the last thing I needed was to try to improvise when I was asked to cook dinner for the family, especially when I was already nervous enough about doing it right.

"It has to be over the flame," I insisted. "I need fire. Do you have a barbecue grill?"

"I do," she said. "But you're going to go out there in the cold?"

"Yes, it's the only way," I said.

She sent her husband to pull the grill, which they hadn't used since the summer, out of the garage, while I bundled up from head to toe, preparing to go outside in the freezing cold. I spent half an hour shivering in the snow, roasting the peppers on the grill while Carol watched me from the window. I swore I heard her laughing.

Finally, the peppers were roasted. I peeled them and stuffed them with cheese, made the creamy tomato sauce, cooked the rice, and finally announced that dinner was ready.

"It all looks beautiful," Carol said as she passed the chiles rellenos around on a platter. And to my relief, they ate them all.

When our break was over and it was time to leave, I found myself not wanting to go back to L.A. I could picture us living in one of those beautiful two-story Victorian houses, which cost the same as my tiny two-bedroom house in South Central. We could live near the lake, close to Carol, Andrew, and the adorable grandmas.

Reyna's first snowman

Reyna and Nathan's first sled ride

"Wouldn't you want to live here again?" I asked Cory as we were packing our things.

"Not really," Cory said. "I'm happy where we live. I like our home."

He had always referred to the South Central house as "your house." This time, at hearing him say "our home," I didn't feel so bad about leaving Racine and going back to Los Angeles, to the place that had never quite felt like home to me, but now did.

42

Reyna at her publication party for Across a Hundred Mountains

O N JUNE 20, 2006, my dream finally came true. I became a published author, and by doing so I began a lifelong quest to advocate for the Mexican immigrant community by sharing our stories with the world, and using art to build bridges.

Publishers Weekly gave *Across a Hundred Mountains* a starred review. *People* magazine said it was "elegantly written, a timely and riveting read." The *El Paso Times* called it a "breathtaking debut." The following year, it would win an American Book Award. I couldn't have been more elated—and relieved. The critics loved it, and now I had to go out and find readers who would care to read it.

I swore I would do everything in my power to honor the opportunity I had been given, not just for me, but for all those writers of color out there who hadn't been as fortunate.

At my publication party at Skylight Books in Los Feliz, I gathered with my family and friends, colleagues, and the Emerging Voices community, and it felt like a birth of sorts—we were welcoming my first book into the world.

I thought about what that editor had once said, *No one is going to care . . .* But as I looked at my friends and family in the audience—my mother, my siblings, my nieces and nephews, Diana, Cory, Nathan, Jenoyne, the EV fellows and the program director—I pushed those thoughts away, and with a deep breath I began my reading by saying, "Thank you for being here, for listening, for caring."

And as I held my book in my hands, feeling its comforting weight, its thick cover as sturdy as concrete walls, the words on the page lined up like rows and rows of bricks, my name in capital letters stretched across the cover, I realized what I had done.

I had finally built a home that I could carry.

Reyna with her first book, Across a Hundred Mountains

My publisher scheduled several readings for me in cities across the country, and I experienced the famous book tour I had heard so much about: the airplanes, the hotels, the cities, the literary escorts my publisher hired to pick me up at the airport. When I spotted them holding up a sign with the name "GRANDE" on it, I would rush up to them saying "I'm here! It's me!" feeling that it was all a dream.

The reading that was the most special to me was at UC, Santa Cruz. My creative writing teacher, Micah, gave me the wonderful news that *Across a Hundred Mountains* had been chosen as the Freshman Read for the Kresge and Porter College students. She invited me to do a presentation of my book in the fall of 2006.

Exactly ten years after I had first journeyed to Santa Cruz to pursue my degree, I made my journey north once again.

I brought my mother with me to help with Nathan, and since she and Betty rarely saw each other, I figured it would be good for her to spend time with her youngest daughter. Betty and Omar were now living in Watsonville, working full-time and raising my nephew. Spending the day with Betty and my mother made this trip extra special. To my relief, there was no awkwardness between Betty and me. As my sister had once said, she had nothing to forgive me for, and she had meant it.

We went to campus early so that I could have time to walk among the redwoods and revisit the place that had been my home.

"How do you feel about tonight?" Betty asked as we made our way to the venue.

"Excited and nervous," I said. The presentation at UCSC was special because not only was I presenting for my first time at my alma mater, but this was the first time my book had been assigned as required reading. *Across a Hundred Mountains* had been released three months earlier, but I still didn't feel comfortable onstage.

"You'll be great," Betty said.

When the lights dimmed, I couldn't really see the faces in the audience. Micah called me up to the stage, and I glanced at my mother and Betty sitting off to the side with the boys on their laps. My sister gave me a smile of encouragement. My mother looked just as scared as I was.

As I walked up to the stage, my stomach began to hurt, my jaw tightened. What was I doing there? Who did I think I was to speak to an audience of 350 students? What if they didn't understand my story or didn't care for it? I wanted to run out and hide among the redwood trees. But then I thought of Jeanne Wakatsuki Houston and remembered how much meeting her had meant to me. Once upon a time, I had been a student in the audience. Sitting on those chairs was a student like me needing to be encouraged, wanting to hear my message.

"Thank you," I said. "I'm honored to be with you today here in Santa Cruz, where it all began for me."

When I finished, the students applauded, and I was escorted to the table to sign books. My mother and Betty sat next to me as I signed book after book for the next forty minutes. Some students, especially the handful of Latinos in attendance, thanked me. One young woman said, "Thank you for writing your story. You've inspired me to keep fighting for my dreams."

It was then that I knew my struggle had been worth it.

My mother's lack of English kept her from understanding most of what I had said during my presentation, but she was impressed by the size of the audience. "They all read your book, Reyna?" she asked as I finished signing the very last book of the night.

"Yes," I said. "It was required reading."

As we drove to the hotel, my mother kept talking about all those books I had just signed. I was glad that she got to share that moment with me. I longed to bring her into my world. I wished she would tell me she was proud of me. But neither she nor my father had ever said that to me, just as no one had said it to them.

Then, something magical happened in the car—my mother began to ask me questions like those the students had just asked me. In the car, I did a Q&A session in Spanish just for her.

"Reyna, when did you start writing?"

"Why did you want to be a writer?"

"Why did you write *Across a Hundred Mountains*?"

"How long did it take you to write the book?"

"Where do you get your inspiration?"

I looked out the window and wiped away the tears that were gathering in my eyes. Finally, for the first time in my life, my mother sat next to me and, with undivided attention, listened to my story.

One lazy Sunday morning, not long after my trips came to an end, I said to Cory, "Want to play Scrabble?"

He shrugged and said, "Sure." We sat down with the board between us and grabbed our tiles. I loved the feel of the smooth tiles, the challenge of arranging and rearranging letters to find the right word, and placing the word in just the right place on the board. At the end of each game, I loved looking at the board to see how the words connected to tell a story. Every game we played was different, unique. It was a perfect game for a writer. I especially liked the surprise of seeing what letters I would get every time my hand went into the bag. Scrabble was so similar to what I knew of life—sometimes you get great letters, sometimes you get bad ones, but either way, you have to do your best with what you've been given.

After a few turns, I put my hand in the bag to grab my tiles, and was shocked to find not just letters, but a diamond ring, nestled in my palm. I stared at it, wondering what a ring was doing in the tile bag. Where had it come from? What did it mean?

Cory got up from his chair, knelt down before me, and said, "Will you marry me?"

"Wait. What?" I asked.

Cory took the ring from my palm and held it between his fingers. "Reyna Grande, will you marry me?" he asked again.

I was wearing an old robe, hadn't even showered or brushed my hair yet, but I didn't care how I looked and neither did Cory. This was the moment I had dreamed of the last three years.

"Yes!" I said. I threw myself into his arms and clung to him, unable to believe that soon I would call this man my husband. "You amaze me," I said as he put the ring on my finger. "You really do."

"You amaze me, too," he said.

"How long has that ring been in the bag?" I couldn't remember when we had last played.

"Two weeks."

"What? Why didn't you ask me to play earlier? We could have been engaged two weeks ago!"

He shook his head, smiling. "I needed you to ask for a game," he said. "It had to be you."

"What if I hadn't asked today? It could have been months!" I said.

"Well, good thing it was only two weeks then."

With joy, we continued our game. We took turns putting down a word, and then another, and then another, laying the foundation for our new life together, one word at a time.

Epilogue

Reyna with her family, 2008

WHILE PREPARING FOR our wedding, Cory and I learned that I was pregnant. So when our wedding day arrived in August 2007, I had a baby bump showing under my wedding dress.

Though my dream of being a published author had come true, I was still determined to continue my education and hone my writer's craft. While I was planning my wedding, I was also working on my master of fine arts degree in creative writing. I was four weeks from giving birth when I walked onstage to receive my second university diploma. My father attended the graduation, and this time, I did not give any humiliating speeches about him.

In January 2008, two days before Cory's thirty-second birthday, our daughter, Eva Alana, was born. He said it was the best gift he had ever gotten. My daughter was three weeks old when she began to travel with me for my author presentations. At this point, she's a pro at traveling. By pursuing my career, I hope to teach Eva to be an independent woman and not to let herself be defined by being someone's daughter or sister, mother or wife. I want her to know that it is possible to be those things while still belonging to herself.

My daughter is now the same age I was when I crossed the border and entered the U.S. I look at her and wonder: *Would my own child survive what I survived?* I don't know. What I do know is that if I were put in my father's place, I would do the same thing. I would risk everything for my children. Knowing that Eva and Nathan will be spared what I went through gives me the strength to look to the future with hope. I want for them what I have managed to have— an education, a successful career, a good home, a life lived to the fullest—without the heartache that it took me to get those things.

In 2010, my father was diagnosed with liver cancer. That final year of his life was difficult for us all. But it was that very year when my dream of being together for the holidays came true—my father invited all of us to his house for Thanksgiving. He put a lot of effort into preparing his very first turkey, marinating it for twenty-four hours in orange juice and herbs, and when he served it to us, it was served with love. My siblings and I marveled at how delicious the turkey was. We enjoyed every bite. But it turned out my father had never heard of a meat thermometer, so the next day, we all got diarrhea. My siblings and I would laugh about this for years to come.

When my father died in 2011, I found solace in my writing. Though he is gone, I can bring him back to life again and again in the stories I write about him. The words I put on the page allow me to get to know him in a way I never could while he was alive. In my writing, my father lives on.

In 2016, Cory and I moved our family to Northern California. Leaving Los Angeles after almost thirty years of residing there was bittersweet. We finally bought a dream house, a beautiful two-story Victorian like the house Cory grew up in. *How many words would it take to get my dream house?* I had often wondered. Over half a million words, and more to be written.

My siblings and I grew up dreaming of a loving, stable home. Our journeys to making such a home were long and difficult, but one way or another, despite the obstacles we encountered in life, we have managed to build a good life and a better future for ourselves and our families. We are what my father wanted us to be, hardworking and self-sufficient. Our priority now is teaching our children how to be those things, too.

Though it has taken nineteen years since my college graduation from UCSC, I'm proud that the next generation of college graduates in the Grande family is on its way. My nieces Natalia and Nadia are studying at a four-year university. My niece Alexa and my nephew Randy are both in community college with plans to transfer to a four-year university. My niece Sophia, her brother Carlitos, and my son, Nathan, are now in high school, on their way to college. And of course, there is my little girl, Eva, and Betty's two youngest children, Ryan and Leilani, who are in elementary school, with their futures ahead of them. Maybe one of them will follow in my footsteps and end up in Santa Cruz. I dream that one day my children or grandchildren will come visit me and give me a T-shirt that says UCSC MOM or UCSC GRANDMA. I would wear it with pride.

I continue to write for the same reason I first put pen to paper when I was thirteen years old—to remember, to understand, to give meaning to my experiences as a Mexican immigrant and woman of color. I have been blessed with a successful writing career, have won awards, shared the stage with authors I admire, and published my work internationally. But what I am most proud of is that my books have landed in the hands of thousands of young people, whom I hope to provide with a little inspiration for their own journeys. I wish to tell them: "Yes, the Dream still exists, despite those who have tried to take it away from us. It is worth fighting for."

Now more than ever, I am determined to write, and encourage others to write, stories that celebrate the resilience and tenacity of the millions of immigrants in the U.S. who fight every day for their dreams, for their right to remain, for their stories to matter.

I hope that by telling our stories we will help make the U.S. a place where we value our commonalities and respect our differences, where we celebrate the diversity that makes this country strong and unique, where every one of us—regardless of where we come from—knows that we belong.

And that we are enough.

Acknowledgments

An important lesson I learned as a young woman was to surround myself with people who believe in me. I took that lesson to heart and continue to practice it to this day. Who would I be without the people who have come into my life and, through their love and encouragement, have helped me reach my dreams? This book is my latest dream, a dream that was made into a reality by the people who I now wish to thank.

My lovely editor, Johanna Castillo, and the whole team at Atria Books, and my tenacious literary agent, Adriana Dominguez at Full Circle Literary. Thank you both for believing in this book and helping me bring it into existence.

To Leslie Schwartz, for giving me the tough love I asked for and coaching me through the revision process.

My mentors, Diana Savas, Marta Navarro, and Micah Perks, my professors who to this day continue to guide me and encourage me to reach my full potential.

My writer friends—Daisy Hernandez, Julissa Arce, Ruth Behar, Norma Cantú, Natalia Treviño, Maria del Toro, Melinda Palacio, Ibarionex Perello, Kirin Khan, Corina Martinez-Chaudhry, and Majella Maas—thank you for being an extra set of "eyes" and carefully reading the many versions of this manuscript.

My friends from UCSC: Yaccaira de la Torre, Erica Ocegueda, Alfredo Zuany, and Robin McDuff for reminiscing about the good old days in Santa Cruz.

Magda Bogin and the amazing Under the Volcano Writers Conference, thank you for your insightful feedback and a magical setting in which to write—Tepoztlán, Mexico.

I'm grateful to my mother-in-law, Carol Ruxton, for her proofreading abilities and for the beautiful Christmas celebrations in Wisconsin.

To my sisters—Magloria Grande and Elizabeth Quintero—for giving me your memories and supporting me on this journey. To my brother, Carlos, and my sister-in-law, Norma, for the couch and the encouragement.

Most of all, I want to thank my husband, Cory Rayala, for his wisdom and keen insights. Thank you for the endless hours of brainstorming, editing, proofreading, and problem-solving. Now that the book is finished, we can go back to Scrabble!

Photography Credits

Page 26: Courtesy of Lance Yep

Page 118: Courtesy of Jon Kersey Photography

Page 238: Courtesy of PEN Center USA West

Page 243: Courtesy of Ibarionex Perello

All other photos courtesy of the Grande Family Archive.